About Island Press

Island Press is the only nonprofit organization in the United States whose principal purpose is the publication of books on environmental issues and natural resource management. We provide solutions-oriented information to professionals, public officials, business and community leaders, and concerned citizens who are shaping responses to environmental problems.

In 2000, Island Press celebrates its sixteenth anniversary as the leading provider of timely and practical books that take a multidisciplinary approach to critical environmental concerns. Our growing list of titles reflects our commitment to bringing the best of an expanding body of literature to the environmental community throughout North America and the world.

Support for Island Press is provided by The Jenifer Altman Foundation, The Bullitt Foundation, The Mary Flagler Cary Charitable Trust, The Nathan Cummings Foundation, The Geraldine R. Dodge Foundation, The Charles Engelhard Foundation, The Ford Foundation, The German Marshall Fund of the United States, The George Gund Foundation, The Vira I. Heinz Endowment, The William and Flora Hewlett Foundation, The W. Alton Jones Foundation, The John D. and Catherine T. MacArthur Foundation, The Andrew W. Mellon Foundation, The Charles Stewart Mott Foundation, The Curtis and Edith Munson Foundation, The National Fish and Wildlife Foundation, The New-Land Foundation, The Oak Foundation, The Overbrook Foundation, The David and Lucile Packard Foundation, The Pew Charitable Trusts, The Rockefeller Brothers Fund, Rockefeller Financial Services, The Winslow Foundation, and individual donors.

Sprawl City

Sprawl City

Race, Politics, and Planning in Atlanta

Edited by **Robert D. Bullard,**
Glenn S. Johnson, and **Angel O. Torres**

ISLAND PRESS
Washington, D.C. • Covelo, California

Copyright © 2000 Island Press

All rights reserved under International and Pan-American Copyright Conventions. No part of this book may be reproduced in any form or by any means without permission in writing from the publisher: Island Press, 1718 Connecticut Avenue, N.W., Suite 300, Washington, DC 20009.

ISLAND PRESS is a trademark of The Center for Resource Economics.

Library of Congress Cataloging-in-Publication Data

Sprawl city : race, politics, and planning in Atlanta / Edited by
Robert D. Bullard, Glenn S. Johnson, Angel O. Torres.
        p. cm.
Includes bibliographical references and index.
    ISBN 1-55963-790-0
    1. Urban ecology—Georgia—Atlanta Metropolitan Area. 2.
Cities and towns—Growth—Atlanta Metropolitan Area. 3.
Afro-Americans—Segregation—Georgia—Atlanta Metropolitan Area.
4. Atlanta (Ga.)—Environmental conditions. 5. Atlanta (Ga.)—Race
relations. I. Bullard, Robert D. (Robert Doyle), 1946– II.
Torres, Angel O. III. Johnson, Glenn S. IV. Title

HT243.U62 A757 2000
307.76'09758'231—dc21   00-008241

Printed on recycled, acid-free paper

Manufactured in the United States of America
10 9 8 7 6 5 4 3 2 1

Contents

Preface

Why study urban sprawl? First, sprawl affects every aspect of our lives and daily routine. Sprawl affects the quality of life where people live, work, play, shop, and go to school. Second, sprawl affects our health—both physical and mental. Third, sprawl intensifies economic and racial polarization. American society has never been classless or color blind. Both race and class have always mattered in shaping the complexion of our cities, suburbs, and rural areas.

Government policies, including housing, education, and transportation policies, have aided and in some cases subsidized separate and unequal economic development and segregated neighborhoods and spatial layout of the nation's central cities and suburbs. Sprawl-fueled growth is pushing people further and further apart geographically, politically, economically, and socially. African Americans and other people of color are largely resigned to economically depressed and deteriorating central cities, not by choice or by chance. This is the case even as economic activity centers and jobs move away from cities.

Roads, highways, freeways, mass transit systems, malls, and strip centers do not materialize out of thin air. They are planned and someone makes a conscious decision as to their location. Conversely, someone makes a conscious decision not to invest in or site a development in a specific location. In addition, zoning and other exclusionary practices systematically limit the mobility of poor people and people of color who are concentrated in central cities, where pollution from automobiles is contributing to the asthma epidemic that is occurring in most urban areas.

Grassroots community groups all over the country are now banding together to address urban problems that are worsened by sprawl. Many of these grassroots groups work on a variety of sprawl issues. Some groups define themselves as environmentalists, others do not. This emerging new leadership base is defining urban transportation, air quality, health, economic investments, and sprawl-related concerns as core environmental justice and civil rights issues. They are not just talking, they are also taking action.

Urban sprawl cuts across political jurisdictions and has unintended consequences that are not randomly distributed. It will take a host of city, county, regional, state, and federal government players to arrest sprawl. Sprawl fuels urban disinvestment, depresses property values, stagnates business opportunities in central cities, and exacerbates environmental problems. Public tax dollars subsidize central city infrastructure decline, deterioration of services, limited home and business ownership opportunities, and out-migration of middle-income residents and businesses. Since sprawl cuts across jurisdictional boundaries, everyone has a stake in seeing that this problem is favorably resolved.

This book uses a multidisciplinary approach to analyze and critique the emerging crisis resulting from urban sprawl in the 10-county Atlanta metropolitan region. Our analysis illuminates the rising class and racial divisions underlying the uneven growth and development in the region. Atlanta has now become the sprawl capital of the nation. Local and national media have featured the region's sprawl problem. Even Atlanta business leaders' alarms were sounded when the region was tagged the "new Los Angeles." Hardly a day passes without some reference to this problem. Nevertheless, most of the reports on the topic gloss over or minimize the social equity implications of Atlanta's sprawl problem, which is intricately linked to both race and class. Atlanta's history is steeped in racial politics; every public policy decision made in the region operated under this backdrop. It has been difficult to erase this legacy.

Some decisions in the area of education, housing, lending, transportation, and the environment actually exacerbated racial segregation, economic disinvestment, abandonment, uneven development, infrastructure decline, environmental degradation, and subsidized sprawl. Atlanta's regional growth policies are implicated in unhealthy air and land-use patterns that lower everyone's quality of life. Clearly, addressing urban sprawl must be given top priority.

The contributors included in *Sprawl City* are sociologists, lawyers, urban planners, economists, educators, and health care professionals. All of the authors examined institutional constraint issues that are embedded in urban sprawl. The chapters are written in a nontechnical, readable style that should be useful to policy analysts, government officials, community leaders, and other individuals working on urban and minority issues.

The topics examined include environmental consequences of sprawl, fair housing, residential patterns, racial polarization, economic opportunity, community development, transportation equity, energy consumption, public health, and schools. The book is directed at urban planners, practitioners, public officials, and community leaders who are interested in understanding urban sprawl from a holistic perspective.

Robert D. Bullard

Acknowledgments

There are a number of persons and organizations we wish to thank for making this book possible. We are especially grateful to Peter Bahouth of the Turner Foundation who supported the work of the Environmental Justice Resource Center and this research undertaking. We all are grateful for the support we received from Cynthia Renfro, whose tireless and enthusiastic work kept us on schedule. We offer special thanks to the contributors who endured the constant nagging about deadlines. We are especially grateful to our contributors, who worked long hours researching and preparing chapters, taking time out of their extremely busy schedules to collaborate with us on this project. Their persistence, patience, and good will were key to bringing this book to fruition. Thanks go out to those colleagues in the Center who provided valuable assistance to the research undertaking, including Tuere Bowles, Marie Green, Kim Hoyt, Chad G. Johnson, and Lisa Sutton. It has been almost a year since we began this study. During this period, we have received valuable assistance, comments, and suggestions from numerous individuals, groups, and organizations working on sprawl issues.

Introduction:
Anatomy of Sprawl

Robert D. Bullard

Sprawl is a fact of life in urban America. Whether we like it or not, it is real and must be addressed with the urgency that the problem demands. Ask 10 people to define sprawl, and you will probably get 10 different definitions. Sprawl is random unplanned growth characterized by inadequate accessibility to essential land uses such as housing, jobs, and public services like schools, hospitals, and mass transit. Two decades of studies from all parts of the nation reveal that sprawl raises taxes. Low-density settlement sprawl increases the costs of maintaining roads, streets, sewers, water supplies, storm drains, and schools.[1]

Sprawl is not new. Why should we be alarmed about sprawl? Is sprawl an unavoidable by-product of growth and a booming economy? It is quite clear that growth and sprawl are not synonymous. Nevertheless, suburban sprawl has been the dominant growth pattern for nearly all metropolitan areas in the United States for the past five decades.[2] Historically, the decentralization of employment centers has had a major role in shaping metropolitan growth patterns.

Sprawl has pushed housing, population, and jobs deeper into the suburbs. Today, over 60 percent of Americans live in suburbs. Suburbs are expected to account for 80 percent of future metropolitan growth if current trends hold. Sprawl development (highways, strip centers, giant shopping malls, subdivisions) is threatening the "exurbs," rural areas, and forests. Urban sprawl is consuming land faster than population is growing in many cities across the country. In order to take advantage of new suburban housing and jobs, one must have access to an automobile because public transit is usually inadequate or nonexistent.

Typically, strip malls, low-density residential housing subdivisions, and other isolated, scattered developments dot the landscape without any rhyme or reason. In the end, all Americans pay for sprawl with increased health and safety risks, worsening air and water pollution, urban decline, disappearing farmland and wildlife habitat, racial polarization, city/suburban disparities in public education, lack of affordable housing, and the erosion of community.[3]

The housing boom of the 1990s accelerated sprawl and changed the landscape of the nation's metropolitan areas. Low interest rates fueled this housing boom and offered opportunities for millions of families to realize the American Dream. Home ownership rates increased for all Americans. From 1993 to 1997, the number of home loans made to whites and blacks increased by 62 percent. Home loans jumped 58 percent for Hispanics, 29 percent for Asians, and 25 percent for Native Americans during this same period.[4]

An increasing number of Americans are challenging the wisdom of sprawl-driven development that threatens quality of life. Sprawl has "literally sucked the population, jobs, investment capital, and tax base from the urban core."[5] America's cities have become forgotten places, only to get attention after conditions reach some crisis state or when human frustration spills over into major uprisings or riots.

From North to South and East to West, too many of our central cities are in crisis. Their inhabitants are at risk from deteriorating housing, poverty, economic abandonment, and infrastructure decline. The infrastructure in American cities is crumbling at the seams. The physical infrastructure includes such things as roads and bridges, housing stock, schools, public buildings, parks and recreational facilities, public transit, water supply, wastewater treatment, and waste disposal systems.

Taken as a whole, infrastructure decline has a negative impact on the well-being and quality of life for everyone, not just individuals who live in the city. Poor infrastructure conditions in urban areas are a result of a host of factors including the distribution of wealth, uneven development, racial and economic discrimination, redlining, housing and real estate practices, location decisions of industry, differential enforcement of land-use regulations, and unrestrained suburban growth.

The Role of Government

Decades of federal government policies played a key role in the development of spatially differentiated metropolitan areas where African Americans and other people of color are segregated from whites and the poor from more affluent citizens. Collectively, federal policies amounted to a "national suburban policy" that reshaped urban American in the postwar decades.[6]

Discrimination also played an important role in the spatial sorting of neighborhoods by race and income. Federal mortgage subsidies facilitated white movement out of the cities, at the same time that federal restrictions made lending difficult to African Americans desiring to move to the suburbs. Such policies fueled the white exodus to the suburbs and accelerated the abandonment of central cities.

Government policies buttressed and tax dollars subsidized metropolitan decentralization through new roads and highways at the expense of public transit.[7] Many highway construction projects often cut paths through people of color neighborhoods, physically isolating residents from their institutions and disrupting once stable communities.[8] African Americans and Latino Americans are regularly displaced by highways, convention centers, sports arenas, and a host of downtown development projects. Most of those displaced are forced into other segregated areas with little say in the removal process.

Tax subsidies made it possible for new suburban employment centers to become dominant outside of central cities and to pull middle-income workers and homeowners from the urban core.[9] Tax subsidies underwrite suburban homeowners at the rate of $50 to $90 billion a year, making it the largest and most expensive housing subsidy program in the country.[10] However, not all groups have benefited from these housing subsidies. Discrimination plays a major role in restricting African Americans and other people of color to housing choices and options largely in central cities.

Discrimination costs African Americans and other people of color billions of dollars in lost wealth.[11] Housing discrimination alone costs African Americans and Latinos an estimated $3 billion and $2 billion per year, respectively.[12] Discrimination has become more sophisticated, subtle, and in many cases acceptable in suburban communities.[13] Congress passed the Fair Housing Act in 1968 to address housing discrimination. The act was amended in 1988. Over five decades of federal housing policies, programs, and legislative mandates have not eliminated the institutional barriers to free choice.

Many urban neighborhoods have been strangled by the lack of long-term financing as a direct result of disinvestment and redlining practices by banks, savings and loans, mortgage firms, and insurance companies.[14] The federal government recognized this problem when it passed the Community Reinvestment Act (CRA) in 1977. The CRA requires banks and thrifts to lend within the areas where their depositors live. The CRA has been used in conjunction with the Home Mortgage Disclosure Act, a law that requires banks and thrifts to disclose their mortgage lending by census tracts.

All communities are not created equal. Apartheid-type employment, housing, development, and transportation policies have resulted in limited mobility, reduced neighborhood options, decreased residential choices, and diminished job opportunities for African Americans and other people of color who are concentrated in cities. American cities continue to be racially separate and unequal. Residential apartheid is the dominant housing pattern for most African Americans—the most racially segregated group in America.[15]

Residential apartheid did not result from some impersonal super-structural process. It is part of the national heritage.[16] Some three decades ago, the National Advisory Commission on Civil Disorders implicated white racism in creating and maintaining the black ghetto and the drift toward two "separate and unequal societies."[17] These same conditions exist today.[18] The black ghetto, for example, is kept isolated and contained from the larger white society through well-defined institutional practices, private actions, and government policies.[19]

People of color in the housing market are routinely offered inferior products, charged higher fees, provided less counseling assistance, and treated less favorably than their white counterparts. A national study of some 3,800 test audits in two dozen metropolitan areas found that 53 percent of black testers seeking to rent apartments faced discrimination, while 59 percent of black testers seeking to buy homes faced discrimination by real estate sales people.[20] Discrimination is alive and well in the United States.

The drift toward racially segmented metropolitan areas is most pronounced in public education. Author Myron Orfield contends that "schools are the first victims and the most powerful perpetrator of metropolitan polarization."[21] Most urban public schools are more segregated today than they were in the 1970s. Nationally, over a third of black children attend schools where the enrollment is 90 percent to 100 percent minority.[22] Race played a big part in white middle-class flight from cities and urban school districts.

Huge disparities exist between affluent suburban schools and their poor inner-city counterparts. These disparities are buttressed by the archaic school financing method: namely, property taxes. Our current taxing system encourages speculation, creates artificial land scarcity, rewards infrastructure abandonment, fosters scattered development, and promotes urban sprawl.[23] Sprawl development has now forced many suburban school districts to come face-to-face with overcrowding and inadequate infrastructure problems— problems long associated with cities.

Most of the literature on race and the city focuses on the underclass and the underlying theoretical underpinning akin to a type of market-centered economics.[24] Racial issues are reduced to economic issues. But race must be treated as an independent variable. The modern American city has its roots in racism.[25] For example, insurance companies routinely used race as a factor in appraising and underwriting property. Racial redlining results in homeowners in mostly black urban neighborhoods paying higher insurance premiums than their white suburban counterparts.[26] This scenario holds true even when the property loss ratios are greater in the suburbs.

Uneven Development and Widening Disparities

Racial segregation in housing, as well as in schools and jobs, is fundamental to the geography of the modern American city.[27] Spatial mobility and social mobility are interrelated. Sociologists Douglas Massey and Nancy Denton contend that "segregation constitutes a powerful impediment to black socioeconomic progress."[28] Racial segregation results from continuing discrimination.[29]

In the 1980s and 1990s, jobs moved away from the central city to the suburbs and outlying areas. Few attempts have been made by the government to reverse job flight and subsequent decline of urban centers. Poverty is becoming more concentrated in core inner-city neighborhoods where jobs are scarce.[30] Government-backed urban enterprise zones, special taxing districts, and economic investment incentives have amounted to more talk than action. Nevertheless, government still has an important role to play in rebuilding our cities.

Numerous examples abound where government actors have targeted regions for infrastructure improvements and amenities such as water irrigation systems, ship channels, road and bridge projects, mass transit systems, and even shopping malls. For example, the Georgia Department of

The 1.7 million square foot Mall of Georgia covers 100 acres and has parking spaces for 8,600 cars.

Transportation committed $46 million in taxpayer money to make Gwinnett County's Mall of Georgia possible.[31] The 1.7 million square foot, 100-acre mall, located in Atlanta's northern suburbs, has parking spaces for 8,600 cars. The giant mall opened in the fall of 1999 and is expected to generate nearly $5 million a year in property taxes and $6 million in sales taxes.[32]

Clearly, economic development policies flow from forces of production and are often dominated and subsidized by federal, state, and local government actors. The absence of a coherent urban agenda in the 1990s allowed cities to become "invisible" places. The quality of life for millions of urban Americans is worse today than it was during the turbulent 1960s. A 1999 *USA Today* survey of experts singled out "wealth disparity" as the biggest issue in cities' development for the next 50 years.[33] The growing economic disparity between racial/ethnic groups has a direct correlation to institutional barriers in housing, lending, employment, education, health, and transportation. Even though the United States made significant gains in reducing poverty and wealth disparities during the 1960s, few substantial gains were made in the 1990s.

The chances of poor families escaping poverty have dropped since the 1970s. This fact is particularly distressing because of the alarming number of children now living in poverty. Today, one out of every four children under the age of six in the United States lives beneath the poverty level. Fifty-eight percent of the children in poverty are children of color. Among this group, African American children are 4 times more likely than white children to be poor; Latino children are 3.5 times and other racial/ethnic minority children are 2 times more likely than white children to be poor.

Besides acting to entrap a disproportionate number of people of color in poverty, institutional barriers compound the risks of life. There remain significant inequities for access to proper health care. African Americans, for example, are twice as likely as white Americans to be without a regular source of health care other than a health clinic or hospital emergency room. Hospitals and clinics in many inner-city neighborhoods are typically overcrowded, understaffed, and underfunded.[34]

Changing demographic trends point to a more diverse multiracial and multiethnic society. The U.S. Census Bureau projects that the African American population will increase from 11.7 percent of the U.S. total in 1980 to 15 percent in 2020. By the same year, African Americans will be nearly one of five children of school age and one of six adults of prime working age. At the same time, immigration trends are also increasing the numbers and proportions of Asians and Latinos in the U.S. population. Much of this population is concentrated in the urban core of the nation's large metropolitan regions.

By the year 2020, the racial and ethnic population in the United States will have more than doubled, to 115 million. By the middle of the twenty-first century, whites will no longer constitute the majority population in the United States.[35] Increasingly, the well-being of the American society will be more and more dependent upon the vitality and productivity of people of color in metropolitan areas. Society at large wins when the infrastructure in cities, suburbs, and rural areas is kept healthy, vibrant, and safe.

The "New Capital" of Sprawl

Communities are now questioning the costs and benefits of suburban sprawl. They are beginning to tackle the problems associated with urban decline and unregulated growth in the suburbs, rural areas, farmlands, and "greenfields."[36] Some urban planners, business leaders, and homeowners are now challenging the growth model that created sprawl. The Atlanta metropolitan region has become the "epicenter of the nation's struggle with road congestion, air pollution, and overdevelopment."[37] Atlanta is considered the "capital" of the New South.[38] It is also the "new poster child" for sprawl.

Atlanta is basically flat and landlocked, with no major bodies of water or mountains to constrain outward growth. The city has come a long way since its humble beginning as an Indian village called Standing Peachtree, which was located at the confluence of Peachtree Creek and the Chattahoochee

Atlanta is the epienter of a struggle to arrest traffic congestion, air pollution, and overdevelopment.

River.[39] Atlanta was burned to the ground by Union forces in 1864. By the 1880s, city officials were successful in promoting Atlanta as the "Gateway to the South." By 1895, Atlanta was celebrating its rebirth as the "Capital of the New South."[40]

A century later, Atlanta and its suburban neighbors are still capitalizing on the region's "growth machine" imagery. Atlanta became the "Mecca" of the Southeast.[41] It emerged as the commercial and financial center of the southeastern United States. The Atlanta region is the center for federal operations as well as the center of communications and transportation. From its Atlanta home base, CNN is beamed around the world. It is hard to fly south without passing through Atlanta's Hartsfield International Airport, the busiest airport in the nation.

Metropolitan Atlanta has experienced constant growth since the 1900s. The region has grown in population at an annual rate of 2.9 percent since 1950. The 1960s were considered the boom years in which Atlanta established its regional dominance. The 1970s and 1980s were characterized as a time during which the city became increasingly black. Since 1960, Atlanta has experienced a steady decrease in its share of the metropolitan region's population.

Metropolitan Atlanta continued to experience record growth in the 1990s. An average of 69,100 people moved into the metropolitan area each year during the 1990s, compared to 61,788 in the 1980s.[42] The 10-county metropolitan area (Cherokee, Cobb, Douglas, Clayton, Fayette, Fulton, Henry, Gwinnett, DeKalb, and Rockdale) has a population of over 3 million persons. Atlanta added more people in the 1990s than any other metropolitan region in the country. Metro Atlanta is the least densely populated metropolitan area in the United States—only 1,370 persons per square mile, compared with 5,400 persons per square mile in Los Angeles.

Between 1990 and 1997, the Atlanta region added 475,600 persons. Population growth was slow in the city of Atlanta, increasing by only 2,647, or less than 1 percent of the total population gain. On the other hand, the northern portion of the region gained 325,939 residents, or 68.5 percent of the region's population growth; the southern part of the region gained 147,014 persons, or 30.9 percent of the population gains during 1990–1997.

In just one 12-month period (from April 1998 to April 1999), metro Atlanta grew by 94,300 people—the second-largest increase in the region's history. On the other hand, the city of Atlanta grew by only 900 people during this same period.[43] In 1998, population growth was 100 times greater in Atlanta's suburbs than in Atlanta's urban core. The Atlanta Regional Commission (ARC) predicts some population slowdown in the coming years.[44] However, Gwinnett, Cobb, and Fulton counties added large numbers of people in the later 1990s. Gwinnett County added over 20,300 (6.6%

Population growth in Atlanta's suburbs was 100 times greater than in the city's urban core (courtesy of the *Atlanta Journal-Constitution*).

increase) to its 499,200 population during the 1997–1998 period; Cobb County added 15,100 persons (2.7% increase) to its 550,000 population, and Fulton County added 13,200 (1.7% increase) to its 773,000 population during the 1997–1998 period. Experts forecast the region to grow by a million more people by 2025. Most of this population increase is expected in Atlanta's sprawling suburbs.

The boundaries of the Atlanta metropolitan region doubled in the 1990s. The region measured 65 miles from north to south in 1990. Today, Atlanta's economic dominance reaches well beyond 110 miles from north to south.[45] Much of the region's growth in the 1990s was characterized by suburban sprawl and economic disinvestment in Atlanta's central city.[46] Record numbers of building permits contributed to the region being called "Hotlanta." The Atlanta region led the nation in residential construction during the 1990–1996 period.

In 1996, the Atlanta region issued 48,262 residential building permits—the busiest housing market in the nation. Following Atlanta, the other "hot" housing-construction markets making the top ten list included Phoenix–Mesa (39,354); Chicago (34,254); Las Vegas (32,410); Washington, D.C. (31,076); Dallas (28,522); Houston (20,821); Detroit (19,925); Portland, OR–Vancouver, WA (19,346); and Charlotte–Rock Hill–Gastonia (18,458).[47] Sunbelt cities were favorite places for new housing. Five of the

Low-density sprawl settlement increases the cost of maintaining roads, streets, sewers, water, storm drains, and schools.

seven busiest residential housing markets were located in the Sunbelt region in 1996.

Metro Atlanta's economic engine was in part powered by prosperity: housing and job booms. New subdivisions mushroomed across Atlanta's suburbs, forests, and rural farmland. Over 80 percent of the new housing built in the 10-county region consisted of single-family units. During the period from 1990 to 1998, the Atlanta region added over 228,573 housing units, a 21.7 percent increase.[48]

The Atlanta regional economy boomed in the 1990s. Newcomers chose the Atlanta region for an obvious reason—jobs. Unemployment remained low and job growth remained strong. Between 1990 and 1997, over 348,000 jobs were added to the region. Most new jobs and newcomers settled outside the city. The city of Atlanta lagged far behind its job-rich suburbs. The region's city–suburban jobs gap widened in the 1990s. The city captured about 40 percent of the region's jobs in 1980. By 1990, Atlanta's share had slipped to 28.3 percent and by 1997, to 19.08 percent.[49]

Clearly, Atlanta's northern suburbs reaped the lion's share of jobs and economic development. From 1990 to 1997, Atlanta's northern suburbs added 272,915 jobs. This accounted for 78.4 percent of all jobs added in the region. Another 70,582 jobs, or 20.3 percent, were added in the southern part of the region. Only 4,503 jobs were added in the region's central core of Atlanta, representing just 1.3 percent of all jobs created during the height of the region's booming economy.[50]

Flight of jobs and white, middle-income families to the suburbs has contributed to and exacerbated both economic and racial polarization in metro Atlanta's housing and schools. Central city Atlanta has become increasingly black and poor. The region's middle-income suburbs that encircle the city are largely white. While suburbanization largely meant out-migration of whites, some middle-income and poor black Atlantans also found expanded home ownership opportunities in Atlanta suburbs, while low-income blacks found suburban rental units in the post-1996 Olympic apartment glut period. Black expansion into Atlanta's suburbs quite often reflected the segregated housing pattern typical of central-city neighborhoods. It is not uncommon to find enclaves of mostly black "apartment ghettos" in Atlanta's close-in and older suburbs in Cobb, DeKalb, Fulton, and Gwinnett counties. However, a number of obstacles still keep many blacks out of the suburbs, including low income, housing discrimination, restrictive zoning practices, inadequate public transportation, and fear.

An increasing number of the region's middle-income blacks are choosing black neighborhoods over integrated or all-white areas. These affluent suburban blacks have to grapple with some of the same sprawl-induced traffic congestion, air pollution, and development problems as their white suburban counterparts. For example, southern DeKalb County rivals Prince George County, Maryland, as one of the most affluent African American communities in the nation. Nevertheless, many obstacles still disproportionately and adversely affect affluent and poor black communities; these include housing discrimination, redlining by banks and insurance companies, inadequate public transportation, encroachment from nonresidential activities, and environmental hazards from locally unwanted land uses or LULUs.

Threatened Quality of Life

Sprawl-related problems have caused some businesses to think twice about the Atlanta region. In 1996, the Atlanta region topped the list of 18 metropolitan areas rated for potential business investments. In 1998, the region slipped to 16th place. Some businesses are not willing to make the investment in metro Atlanta because of the region's severe traffic congestion, air pollution, and other environmental problems.

Sprawl-fueled development has scalped the region's landscape of tree cover. Deforestation and loss of vegetation increase the region's "heat island," thereby raising Atlantans' summer electric bills. Loss of vegetation also exacerbates soil erosion and adds to the region's air pollution problem. From

1973 to 1998, the region lost over 341,000 acres of tree cover. The region has lost an average of 50 acres of tree cover per day since 1987.[51] Much of this loss is a direct result of low-density sprawl development encroaching into forests and rural areas.

In 1998, the Sierra Club rated Atlanta as the "most sprawl threatened" large city (over one million population) in the nation.[52] Other sprawl-threatened big cities that made the Sierra Club's "top ten" list included St. Louis, Washington, D.C., Cincinnati, Kansas City, Denver, Seattle, Minneapolis–St. Paul, Fort Lauderdale, and Chicago. The criteria for the ranking included such factors as population trends, land use, traffic congestion, and open space.[53]

From New York to Los Angeles and many smaller cities in between, people are talking about sprawl. If nothing else, anti-sprawl and "smart growth" gatherings are bringing diverse populations and constituents into the same room. People are beginning to talk to each other. However, talk is cheap, and the stakes are high. Atlantans are calling for action, not a debate about sprawl. Numerous articles have been written about sprawl. Nearly all of these stories cite the case of Atlanta as the symbol of what not to do. No city wants to become another "Sprawlanta." Some Atlantans are even complaining about Atlanta—something they would never have done a decade ago.

The Cost of Gridlock

From the ground and from the air, Atlanta looks a lot like many other sprawl-threatened cities. Sprawl has created a car-dependent citizenry. Everyone who drives feels the effects of congestion, longer commutes, and wasted time and energy spent in heavy traffic. The Texas Transportation Institute rated traffic gridlock in the nation's 68 largest metropolitan areas and found that the average driver spent 34 hours a year stuck in traffic. Drivers in the 20 most-congested metropolitan areas spent more than 40 hours in gridlock and wasted four extra tanks of gasoline. Atlanta ranked fourth, behind Los Angeles, Washington, D.C., and Seattle as the metropolitan areas with the worst traffic congestion. Drivers in Los Angeles spent 82 hours annually in gridlock, compared to 76 hours in Washington, D.C., 69 hours in Seattle, 68 hours in Atlanta, and 66 hours in Boston.

Congestion is hitting drivers in their wallets; traffic delays cost Americans $72 billion in 1997. While the nation's biggest urban population grew by 22 percent over the past 15 years, congestion grew by a staggering 235 percent. In addition to more cars on the road, people are driving farther and taking more trips. The number of vehicle miles traveled (VMT) jumped 125 percent over the past 27 years, from 1.1 trillion to 2.5 trillion miles annually.[54] Traffic gridlock costs metro Atlanta drivers $2.27 billion per year in fuel and lost productivity. Nationally, the total vehicle miles driven increased 59 percent from 1980 to 1995. The amount of driving has risen a whopping 139 percent in metro Atlanta since 1982.[55]

Metro Atlantans drive an average of 34 miles per day. This is 50 percent further than drivers in Los Angeles—a region that is synonymous with the automobile. In 1986, metro Atlanta had 1.9 million registered vehicles. In 1995, the region had more than 2.5 million vehicles clogging the streets. The largest increase in motor vehicles occurred in Atlanta's northern suburbs. The Georgia Department of Transportation adopted the "build them and they will come" road-building program as its regional-planning model. Mobility is equated with driving since mass transit has not penetrated much of the Atlanta region.

More highways translate into more cars. More cars mean more congestion and more pollution. Another harmful by-product of air pollution is increased asthma and other respiratory illnesses. Environmental justice leader Carl Anthony, who directs the San Francisco–based Urban Habitat Program, says "suburbs are making us sick."[56] A 1999 report from the Clean Air Task Force linked asthma and respiratory problems with smog.[57] The study tracked hospital and emergency room visits in 37 eastern states between April and October 1997. High smog levels were associated with rising respiratory-related hospital admissions and emergency room visits. Atlanta had 580 hospital admissions and 1,740 emergency room visits linked to bad air. A sampling of the smog-related emergency room visits in other cities included 12,300 in New York, 4,800 in Philadelphia, 4,500 in Chicago, 3,600 in Miami–Fort Lauderdale, 2,700 in Detroit, and 2,400 in Washington, D.C.

A 1994 Centers for Disease Control (CDC) study also linked ground-level ozone to asthma in Atlanta. Atlanta is a nonattainment area for ground-level ozone. The CDC researchers found that visits by children to the emergency room at Atlanta's Grady Memorial Hospital increased by one-third following days with peak ozone levels.[58] Atlanta can take some pride in not being the "number one smog city." On October 7, 1999, Houston earned that unfortunate title, supplanting Los Angeles. Houston experienced 44 days of ozone levels that exceeded national health standards. Los Angeles registered 43 days.[59] However, all is not well in Atlanta—the region had 37 consecutive unhealthy ozone days in the summer of 1999. It also experienced a record 69 smog-alert days in 1999.

Lack of real alternatives to driving is partly to blame for Atlanta's soaring traffic gridlock, smog, and rising asthma problem. Atlanta is not alone in this dilemma. Nationally, nearly 8 of every 10 commuters drive alone to work. Only 9.3 percent of the U.S. population use a nonautomobile mode of travel (public transit, bicycle, walk) to get to work. A little over 11 percent of the nation's commuters car pool to work. Public transit is not a real option in many of the nation's sprawling suburbs.

Nationally, about 5.3 percent of Americans take public transit to work. Over 47.3 percent of workers in New York, 19.5 percent in the San Francisco Bay Area, 17.1 percent in Chicago, and 14.2 percent in Boston commute using public transit. Only 6.5 percent of workers in Los Angeles and 4.7 percent in Atlanta (less than the national average) commute to work via public transit. Poor planning has gotten us in this fix. Regional planning that incorporates "smart growth" principles may get us out of this quagmire. It should be noted that "smart growth is not antigrowth."[60] The U.S. EPA's Smart Growth Network delineated some major elements of smart growth:

> [Smart growth] recognizes that how buildings are built and where development takes place are factors that make development either a community asset or liability. Smart growth advocates seek growth and development where it will build community, protect environmental amenities, promote fiscal health and keep taxes low, maximize return on public and private investment, and encourage economic efficiency.[61]

Transportation and land use are major components in the smart-growth movement. Deciding where transportation investments should go lies at the heart of many smart-growth debates in most metropolitan regions. Automobile-dominated transportation and energy policies have subsidized sprawl. For example, Georgia's low motor-fuels tax encourages driving and road building. The 7.5 cent gasoline tax is one of the lowest in the country. The tax is restricted by state law to be used only for roads.

Each day, environmentalists and new converts and coalitions from the Atlanta area business establishment, inner-city, suburbs, and rural communities are joining the local grassroots anti-sprawl campaigns to make the region healthier and safer. Even some suburban communities are beginning to plan for linked and coordinated regional public transit. Atlantans are demanding bicycle lanes, sidewalks, and safe streets for walking. Sidewalks could greatly improve pedestrian safety and reduce fatalities in high-risk cities such as Fort Lauderdale, Miami, and Atlanta—the nation's three most dangerous large metropolitan areas for walking.[62]

Thoughts on the Future

The 1990s saw the Atlanta region's population grow at record speed. The region's housing starts, job growth, and low unemployment rate were envied by many other cities and metropolitan areas. However, there was a down side to the region's sprawl-dominated growth. Sprawl placed the health of the region and its residents at risk. Polluted rivers and streams, clogged freeways, and fouled air threatened the quality of life and business climate that attracted people and jobs to the area in the first place.

Although Atlanta's share of the metropolitan population, housing, and jobs experienced a steady decline over the years, the health of the city is still important to the region's overall vitality. Atlanta matters. Atlanta is not an island. The city of 400,000 (in a region of 3 million) is still the cultural, educational, sports, and financial core of the region. What happens inside and outside Atlanta's city limits affects everyone in the region. Sprawl development accelerates urban core disinvestment, infrastructure decline, and segregation by race and income. The future of the region is intricately bound to how government, business, and community leaders address sprawl and Atlanta's quality of life issues.

It should not take articles in the *Wall Street Journal, Newsweek,* or the *New York Times* for Atlantans to know and understand that the region is in serious trouble. The problem is not one of "bad press" that can be resolved with a well-financed "media blitz." Sprawl is real. Real problems need real solutions. Nevertheless, when the national press sounds the alarm that the region's traffic congestion and poor air quality may keep new businesses from relocating to the area, even the Atlanta Chamber of Commerce takes the "wake-up call" and becomes an antisprawl advocate. But words do not automatically translate into action. Only time will tell if the region's business and political leaders will heed the call to rein in sprawl-driven development and adopt a "smart-growth" approach.

Will the Atlanta region take a bold stance and address urban reinvestment and redevelopment, fair housing, public schools, public transit, and environmental and public health needs? Transportation and land-use policies are implicated in all of these issues. The 10-county Atlanta region has a regional transit system only in name. The Metropolitan Atlanta Rapid Transit Authority (MARTA) serves just two counties, Fulton and DeKalb. Cobb County created its own transit system with limited links to MARTA. Gwinnett and Clayton recently approved plans for a bus system. While these decisions represent forward movement, the automobile is still king and rules the road in Atlanta. Overdependence on the automobile remains the number one culprit in the region's nonattainment dilemma.

Historically, planning agencies (Atlanta Regional Commission and Georgia Department of Transportation) were unwilling or unable to address the mounting traffic, air quality, and cross-jurisdictional land-use problems associated with the region's needs. In 1999, Georgia's newly elected governor,

Roy Barnes, created the Georgia Regional Transportation Authority (GRTA), a new superagency whose mission is to increase public transportation services in the region, rein in sprawl, and ultimately improve the region's air quality. GRTA has a big challenge. The Sierra Club's 1999 report, *Solving Sprawl*, gives high marks to the governor for forcing the state and local governments to take strong steps to strengthen regional transportation coordination.[63] GRTA is a major player: "While each region will have to devise its own means for building regional cooperation, the public and private leadership that spawned GRTA exemplifies the kind of bold action that will be needed if we are to begin to undo the problems of suburban sprawl."[64] The report concludes that "local governments in Georgia have the smart growth tools to stop sprawl."[65]

Clearly, city, county, state, and federal officials need to work cooperatively to arrest the region's traffic congestion, air quality problem, declining urban infrastructure, and growing social and economic disparities between the "haves" and the "have nots." Having the tools to stop sprawl and using those tools are two different issues. Sprawl was not created overnight. The solution will take time. Public and private interests—working together and across political, geographic, class, and racial boundaries—can solve this problem. Everybody wins when bold steps are taken to address and eliminate suburban sprawl.

Notes

1. Donella Meadows, "The Escalating Costs of Sprawling Growth," *Neighborhood Works* 20 (November/December 1997), p. 7.
2. Myron Orfield, *Metropolitics: A Regional Agenda for Community and Stability.* Washington, DC: Brookings Institution Press, 1997, p. 2.
3. David Bollier, *How Smart Growth Can Stop Sprawl: A Fledgling Citizen Movement Expands.* Washington, DC: Essential Books, 1998, p. 1.
4. Bill Lann Lee, "An Issue of Public Importance: The Justice Department's Enforcement of the Fair Housing Act," *Cityscape: A Journal of Policy Development and Research* 4 (1999), pp. 35–56.
5. Carl Anthony, *Suburbs Are Making Us Sick: Health Implications of Suburban Sprawl and Inner City Abandonment on Communities of Color.* Environmental Justice Health Research Needs Report Series. Atlanta: Environmental Justice Resource Center, 1998.
6. David Rusk, *Inside Game Outside Game: Winning Strategies for Saving Urban America.* Washington, DC: Brookings Institution Press, 1999, p. 86.
7. James J. MacKenzie, Roger C. Dower, and Donald T. Chen, *The Going Rate: What It Really Costs to Drive.* World Resources Institute, June 1992, p. vii; Mark E. Hanson, "Automobile Subsidies and Land Use," *Journal of the American Planning Association* 58 (1992), pp. 60–71; R.D. Bullard and G.S. Johnson, "Just Transportation," in R.D. Bullard and G.S. Johnson, eds., *Just Transportation:*

Dismantling Race and Class Barriers to Mobility (Gabriola Island, BC: New Society Publishers, 1997), pp. 7–21; Conservation Law Foundation, *City Routes, City Rights: Building Livable Neighborhoods and Environmental Justice by Fixing Transportation* (Boston: Conservation Law Foundation, 1998), p. 5.

8. Robert D. Bullard and Glenn S. Johnson, eds., *Just Transportation: Dismantling Race and Class Barriers to Mobility.* Gabriola Island, BC: New Society Publishers, 1997.

9. Charles W. Schmidt, "The Specter of Sprawl," *Environmental Health Perspective* 106 (June 1998), p. 274.

10. Douglas Kelbaugh, *Common Place: Toward Neighborhood and Regional Design.* Seattle: University of Washington Press, 1997, p. 31.

11. Melvin L. Oliver and Thomas M. Shapiro, *Black Wealth/White Wealth: A New Perspective on Racial Inequality.* New York: Routledge, 1996.

12. John Yinger, "Sustaining the Fair Housing Act," *Cityscape: A Journal of Policy Development and Research* 4 (1999), p. 97.

13. See David Rusk, *Cities without Suburbs,* 2nd ed. Washington, DC: Woodrow Wilson Center Press, 1995.

14. D.S. Massey and N.A. Denton, eds. *American Apartheid and the Making of the Underclass.* Cambridge, MA: Harvard University Press, 1993, p. 54.

15. R.D. Bullard, J.E. Grigsby III, and C. Lee, eds., *Residential Apartheid: The American Legacy.* Los Angeles: UCLA Center for African American Studies, 1994, pp. 56–57.

16. Joe R. Feagin and Clairece B. Feagin, *Racial and Ethnic Relations.* Upper Saddle, NJ: Prentice-Hall, 1999.

17. National Advisory Commission on Civil Disorders, *Report of the National Advisory Commission on Civil Disorders.* New York: E.P. Dutton, 1968.

18. Andrew Hacker, *Two Nations: Black and White, Separate, Hostile, and Unequal.* New York: Scribner's, 1992.

19. Joe R. Feagin, *Living with Racism: The Black Middle-Class Experience.* Boston: Beacon Press, 1995, pp. 1–36.

20. Margery Austin Turner, Raymond J. Struyk, and John Yinger, *Housing Discrimination Study: Synthesis.* Washington, DC: U.S. Government Printing Office, 1996.

21. Mryon Orfield, *Metropolitics,* p. 3.

22. James S. Kunen, "The End of Integration," *Time,* April 29, 1996.

23. James Howard Kunstler, *Home from Nowhere: Remaking Our Everyday World for the Twenty-First Century.* New York: Simon & Shuster, 1996, p. 27.

24. William Julius Wilson, *The Truly Disadvantaged: The Inner City, the Underclass and Public Policy.* Chicago: Review Press, 1987.

25. R.D. Bullard and Joe R. Feagin, "Racism and the City," in M. Gottdiener and C.G. Pickvance, eds., *Urban Life in Transition.* Newbury Park, CA: Sage Publications, 1991, pp. 55–76.

26. Shelly Emling, "Black Areas in City Pay Steep Rates," *Atlanta Journal-Constitution,* June 30, 1996, p. A16.

27. R.D. Bullard and Joe R. Feagin, "Racism and the City."

28. Massey and Denton, *American Apartheid,* p. 14.
29. Joe R. Feagin, "Excluding Blacks and Others from Housing: The Foundations of Racism," *Cityscape* 4 (1999), p. 81.
30. William Julius Wilson, *When Work Disappears: The World of the New Urban Poor.* New York: Alfred A. Knopf, 1996.
31. *Atlanta Constitution,* "DOT Needs New Focus," (September 20, 1999), p. A8.
32. David Firestone, "Suburban Comforts Thwart Atlanta's Plans to Limit Sprawl," *The New York Times,* November 21, 1999, p. 30.
33. Haya El Nasser, "Urban Experts Pick Top Factors Influencing Future," *USA Today,* September 27, 1999, p. A4.
34. Ronald Braithwaite and Sandra Taylor, eds., *Health Issues in the Black Community.* San Francisco: Jossey-Bass Publishers, 1992.
35. William A. Henry, "Beyond the Melting Pot," *Time,* April 9, 1990, pp. 28–31.
36. American Farmland Trust, *Living on the Edge: The Costs and Risks of Scatter Development.* Washington, DC: American Farmland Trust, 1998.
37. David Firestone, "Suburban Comforts Thwart Atlanta's Plans to Limit Sprawl."
38. See Robert D. Bullard, *In Search of the New South: The Black Urban Experience in the 1970 and 1980s.* Tuscaloosa: University of Alabama Press, 1991, chap. 1.
39. Metropolitan Planning Commission, *Up Ahead: A Metropolitan Land Use Plan for Metropolitan Atlanta.* Atlanta: Metropolitan Planning Commission, 1952, p. 12.
40. See Bradley R. Rice, "Atlanta: If Dixie Were Atlanta," in R.M. Bernard and B.R. Rice, *Sunbelt Cities: Growth Since World War II.* Austin: University of Texas Press, 1983, p. 31.
41. Robert D. Bullard, *In Search of the New South,* pp. 1–15.
42. The 1998 Atlanta Regional Commission estimates are based on 1990 U.S. census, building permits, and other growth formulas.
43. David Firestone, "Suburban Comforts Thwart Atlanta's Plans to Limit Sprawl."
44. Atlanta Regional Commission, *Atlanta Region Outlook.* Atlanta: ARC, 1998, p. 55.
45. Christopher Leinberger, "The Metropolis Observed," *Urban Land 57* (October 1998), pp. 28–33.
46. David Goldberg, "Regional Growing Pains," *Atlanta Journal-Constitution,* March 10, 1997, p. E05.
47. *Atlanta Journal and Constitution,* "Growing a New Atlanta," June 8, 1997, p. G5.
48. Atlanta Regional Commission, *Atlanta Region Outlook,* p. 55.
49. Ibid.
50. Ibid.
51. Charles Seabrook, "Satellite Data Show Rapid Clear-Cutting," *Atlanta Journal-Constitution,* February 19, 1999, p. A1.
52. Sierra Club, *The Dark Side of the American Dream: The Cost and Consequences of Suburban Sprawl.* College Park, MD: Sierra Club, 1998, p. 3.
53. Ibid.
54. Scott Bowles, "National Gridlock: 167 Worst Bottlenecks," *USA Today,* November 23, 1999, p. 2A.

55. Gita M. Smith, "It's Official: Traffic Worse," *Atlanta Journal-Constitution*, November 17, 1999, p. A1.

56. Carl Anthony, *Suburbs are Making Us Sick,* pp. 3–9.

57. Abt Associates and Clean Air Force Task, *Out of Breath: Health Effects from Ozone in the Eastern United States.* Washington, DC: Author, 1999.

58. Mary C. White, Ruth A. Etzel, Wallace D. Wilcox, and Catherine Lloyd, "Exacerbation of Childhood Asthma and Ozone Pollution in Atlanta," *Environmental Research* 65 (1994), p. 56.

59. David Whitman, "Houston, You've Got a Problem," *U.S. News & World Report,* October 25, 1999, p. 28.

60. David Bollier, *How Smart Growth Can Stop Sprawl: A Fledgling Citizen Movement Expands.* Washington, DC: Essential Books, 1998, p. 3.

61. For more information see Smart Growth Network, U.S. EPA, Urban and Economic Development Division, Web site address at http://www.smart-growth.org.

62. B.A. Cohen, R. Wiles, C. Campbell, D. Chen, J. Kruse, and J. Corless, *Mean Streets: Pedestrian Safety and Reform of the Nation's Transportation Law.* Washington, DC: Environmental Working Group/The Tides Center, April 1997.

63. Sierra Club, *Solving Sprawl: The Sierra Club Rates the States.* San Francisco: Sierra Club, 1999, p. 14.

64. Ibid.

65. Sierra Club News Release, "Sierra Club Report Shows Local Governments in Georgia Have the Smart Growth Tools to Stop Sprawl," October 4, 1999, p. 1. The full report can be viewed at http://www.sierraclub.org/sprawl/report 99.

CHAPTER 1

Environmental Costs and Consequences of Sprawl

Robert D. Bullard, Glenn S. Johnson, and Angel O. Torres

The environmental quality in urban areas results from a host of factors, including the distribution of wealth, patterns of racial and economic discrimination, redlining, housing and real estate practices, location of industry, and differential enforcement of land use and environmental regulations. The imbalance between residential amenities and land uses assigned to central cities and suburbs cannot be explained by class factors alone. The ability of an individual to escape a health-threatening physical environment is usually related to affluence. However, racial barriers complicate this process for many African Americans.[1] It has been difficult for African Americans in segregated neighborhoods to say "not in my backyard" (NIMBY) if they do not have a backyard.[2]

Most African Americans live in neighborhoods where they are in the majority. Residential segregation decreases for most racial and ethnic groups with additional education, income, and occupational status.[3] However, this scenario does not hold true for most African Americans. African Americans, no matter what their educational or occupational achievement or income level, are subjected to more rigid segregation and are exposed to higher crime rates, less effective educational systems, higher mortality risks, more dilapidated surroundings, and greater environmental threats because of their race.[4]

Institutionalized discrimination plays a prominent role in sorting people into residential neighborhoods, land uses, and environmental quality. The development of spatially differentiated metropolitan areas where African Americans are segregated from other Americans have resulted from governmental policies and marketing practices of the housing industry and lending institutions. Millions of Americans are geographically isolated in economically depressed and polluted urban neighborhoods away from the expanding suburban job centers.[5]

Blacks and whites do not have the same opportunities to "vote with their feet" and escape undesirable physical environments.[6] Homeowners are the strongest advocates of the NIMBY positions taken against locally unwanted land uses (LULUs) such as garbage dumps, landfills, incinerators, sewer treatment plants, recycling centers, chemical plants, and other polluting facilities. Overall, white communities have greater access than communities of color when it comes to influencing land use and environmental decision making.

Environmental Disparities

Studies dating back to the 1970s reveal that low-income persons and people of color have borne greater health and environmental risk burdens than society at large.[7] Pollution takes its toll on individual and community health. For example, elevated health risks are found in some populations even when income is held constant, as in the case of childhood lead poisoning.[8] Race has been found to be independent of income in the distribution of municipal landfills, incinerators,[9] abandoned toxic waste dumps,[10] smelters, and other polluting industries.[11] Generally, federal efforts to reduce childhood lead poisoning can be deemed a real success story. In October 1991, the Centers for Disease Control (CDC) issued a statement, *Preventing Lead Poisoning in Young Children,* lowering the acceptable blood level from 25 μg/dl to 10 μg/dl. The average blood lead level has dropped for all children with the phasing out of leaded gasoline.

A 1997 CDC report indicates that the "risk for lead exposure in children is primarily determined by environmental conditions of the child's residence."[12] Lead-based paint (chips and dust) is the most common source of lead exposure for children. Children may also be exposed through soil and dust contamination built up from vehicle exhaust, lead concentration in soils in urban areas, and lead dust brought into the home on parents' work clothes. Too many poor children are still living in older inner-city homes with lead paint that endangers their health. The health (mental and physical) of millions of lead poisoned urban youth has been written off as expendable. Instead of a haven, a home becomes a health threat.

The social, economic, and financial costs associated with pollution are great. However, the costs and benefits associated with growth and industrial development are not borne equally by all residents. Costs are more localized, while benefits are more dispersed. The negative environmental and health impacts of sprawl-driven growth fall heaviest on individuals, groups, and communities at the lower end of the socioeconomic spectrum.

Generally, unplanned urban growth has contributed to more cars, roads, traffic jams, garbage, landfills, incinerators, pollution, and threats to public health. Sprawl is an unwanted, though predictable, consequence of uncontrolled random growth. Who pays for sprawl? We all pay in dollars, decreased mobility, and diminished quality of life.

Zoning and Land Use

For the most part, zoning is considered a local matter. Implementation of zoning ordinances and land-use plans have a political, economic, and racial dimension. Competition often results between special interest groups (e.g., real estate interests, developers, civic clubs, neighborhood associations, environmentalists) for what these groups regard as more advantageous land use. Real estate interests generally have a great deal of influence over zoning boards and local officials who make the decisions.

In their quest for quality neighborhoods, residents often find themselves competing for desirable neighborhood amenities (e.g., good schools, police and fire protection, quality health care, parks, open space, recreational facilities) and resisting outputs that are viewed as having negative consequences (e.g., landfills, incinerators, sewage treatment facilities, polluting industries, chemical plants). The differential residential amenities and land uses assigned in the region cannot be explained by class alone. Generally, government officials have done a miserable job of protecting communities of low-income and working-class people and people of color from pollution assaults, industrial encroachment, and environmental degradation.

Zoning has not been able to protect some communities from environmental assaults. Race underlies and interpenetrates with other factors in explaining the sociospatial layout of the Atlanta metropolitan area, including housing patterns, street and highway configuration, commercial development, and industrial facility siting. Poor whites and poor blacks do not have the same opportunities to "vote with their feet" and escape undesirable physical environments. People of color and low income residential areas are disproportionately and adversely affected by unregulated growth, ineffective regulation of industrial toxins, and public policy decisions authorizing LULUs that favor those with political and economic clout.

Paying for Water Pollution

According to the environmental group American Rivers, the Chattahoochee River is under severe stress from "untreated sewage, tons of sediment, storm water runoff from both city and agricultural areas, and a general lack of enforcement of clean water laws on all levels."[13] All along its 526-mile journey to the Gulf of Mexico, the Chattahoochee River shoulders the burden of new developments, industrial wastes, pollution from poultry and hog farms, and poorly treated or raw human sewage.[14]

In an attempt to comply with clean water regulations, Atlantans have had to pay for the city's infrastructure neglect and burdens caused by overloaded wastewater treatment systems. Water pollution problems are exacerbated by broken city pipes, antiquated sewage treatment plants, and combined sewer overflows (CSOs). CSOs represent sewers that combine storm water with raw sewage and overflow into city creeks or onto streets during heavy rains.[15] CSOs pose health risks since many contain heavy metals, organic compounds and petroleum products as well as viruses and fecal coliform bacteria from humans and animals.[16] People of color communities are at greatest risk from CSOs (see Table 1.1). Atlanta's CSOs are more likely to occur in low-income and mostly African American neighborhoods. Seven of the nine (77.7%) CSOs in Atlanta are located in mostly African American neighborhoods where home values fall well below the median.

The deficiencies in the city's sewer pipes and treatment plants led to a crackdown by the Environmental Protection Agency (EPA) and the Environmental Protection Division (EPD) on Atlanta's discharges into the Chattahoochee River. From October 1990 to March 1994, the city was fined $1.72 million for wastewater violations.[17] Most of the fines were assessed because of CSOs. In 1998, the city signed a consent order to pay a $2.5 million fine for water quality violations. In July 1999, the EPA imposed a $700,000 fine on the city of Atlanta for spills and leaks from its overloaded sewer system. The combined fines represent the largest Clean Water Act

Table 1.1. Combined Sewer Overflows and Demographic Characteristics (Atlanta)

CSO at 1-Mile Radius	Population	% Black	% White	% Other	% Owner	Median $
Clear Creek	9,390	9.1	88.8	3.9	41.3	$54,551
Tanyard Branch	11,053	10.4	86.7	5.2	36.2	$50,899
North Avenue	5,948	80.5	18.4	2.9	33.9	$13,865
Greensferry	17,135	99.3	0.3	0.8	37.2	$15,718
Utoy Creek–North	12,561	98.2	1.6	0.3	68.6	$26,360
Utoy Creek–South	14,280	97.8	2.0	0.4	71.0	$28,256
McDaniel Street	16,077	93.3	6.3	1.1	37.4	$14,045
Custer Avenue	10,864	54.6	33.0	28.0	41.8	$25,098
Intrenchment Creek	5,846	87.5	11.6	36.4	36.4	$22,422

Source: U.S. EPA (1996). All data from Landview III CD-ROM, 1992 census data.

penalty ever assessed against a municipality. In a federally mandated order, the city of Atlanta is required to implement a rigorous program to improve its sewer pipes and treatment plants that will cost local taxpayers more than $1 billion during the next 14 years.[18]

The Right to Breathe Clean Air

Clean air is everyone's dream. This sentiment cuts across race, class, gender, geographic, and political lines. Urban air pollution problems have been with us for some time now. Before the federal government stepped in, issues related to air pollution were handled primarily by states and local governments. Because states and local governments did such a poor job, the federal government set out to establish national clean air standards. Congress enacted the Clean Air Act (CAA) in 1970 and mandated the EPA to carry out this law. Subsequent amendments (1977 and 1990) were made to the CAA that form the current federal program. The CAA was a response to states' unwillingness to protect air quality. Many states used their own lackadaisical enforcement of environmental laws as lures for business and economic development.[19]

African Americans and Latinos are more likely to live in areas with reduced air quality than are whites. For example, Argonne National Laboratory researchers discovered that 437 of the 3,109 counties and independent cities failed to meet at least one of the EPA ambient air quality standards. Specifically, 57 percent of whites, 65 percent of African Americans, and 80 percent of Hispanics live in the 437 counties with substandard air quality. Nationwide, 33 percent of whites, 50 percent of African Americans, and 60 percent of Hispanics live in the 136 counties in which two or more air pollutants exceed standards. Similar patterns were found for the 29 counties designated as nonattainment areas for three or more pollutants. Again, 12 percent of whites, 20 percent of African Americans, and 31 percent of Hispanics resided in the worst nonattainment areas.[20]

The Atlanta metropolitan region is a nonattainment area for ozone, one of the six criteria pollutants listed under the National Ambient Air Quality Standards (NAAQS). There is a price to be paid for nonattainment. Costs include future federal funding assistance (i.e., transportation dollars are often tied to states conforming with requirements of the Clean Air Act) and public health concerns (rising asthma and other respiratory illnesses). In the Atlanta nonattainment area, motor vehicles account for the primary source for both volatile organic compounds (VOCs) and nitrogen oxides (NO_x).[21]

Asthma is an emerging epidemic in the United States. The annual age-adjusted death rate from asthma increased by 40 percent between 1982 and 1991, from 1.34 to 1.88 per 100,000 population,[22] with the highest rates being consistently reported among blacks ages 15 to 24 years during the period 1980–1993.[23] Poverty and minority status are important risk factors for asthma mortality. The age-adjusted prevalence rate of self-reported asthma increased 42 percent between 1982 and 1992, from 3,470 to 4,940 per 100,000.

Children are at special risk from ozone.[24] Children also represent a considerable share of the asthma burden. It is the most common chronic disease of childhood. Asthma affects almost 5 million children under 18 years of age. Although the overall annual age-adjusted hospital discharge rate for asthma among children under 15 years decreased slightly from 184 to 179 per 100,000 between 1982 and 1992, the decrease was slower compared to other childhood diseases,[25] resulting in a 70 percent increase in the proportion of hospital admissions related to asthma during the 1980s. Inner city children have the highest rates for asthma prevalence, hospitalization, and mortality.[26] In the United States, asthma is the fourth leading cause of disability among children under 17.[27]

The public health community has insufficient information to explain the magnitude of some of the air pollution–related health problems. However, it is known that persons suffering from asthma are particularly sensitive to the effects of carbon monoxide, sulfur dioxides, particulate matter, ozone, and nitrogen oxides.[28] Ground-level ozone may exacerbate health problems such as asthma, nasal congestion, throat irritation, respiratory tract inflammation, reduced resistance to infection, changes in cell function, loss of lung elasticity, chest pains, lung scarring, formation of lesions within the lungs, and premature aging of lung tissues.[29]

Although air pollution is not thought to cause asthma and related respiratory illnesses, "bad air hurts,"[30] and is a major trigger. A 1999 study from the Clean Air Task Force, a coalition of environmental and consumer groups, linked asthma and respiratory problems and smog (see Table 1.2).[31] High smog levels are associated with rising respiratory-related hospital admissions and emergency room visits in cities across the eastern United States. Metropolitan Atlanta had 69 days of unhealthy air in the summer of 1999.[32]

A 1996 report from the CDC shows hospitalization and death rates from asthma increasing for persons 25 years old or less.[33] The greatest increases occurred among African Americans. African Americans are two to six times more likely than whites to die from asthma.[34] The hospitalization rate for African Americans is 3.4 times the rate for whites.[35]

Asthma has reached epidemic proportions in the Atlanta region. Atlanta area residents are paying for sprawl with their hard-earned dollars as well as with their health. A 1994 CDC-sponsored study showed that pediatric emergency department visits at Atlanta Grady Memorial Hospital increased by one-third following peak ozone levels. The study also found that the asthma rate among African American children is 26 percent higher than the asthma rate among whites.[36] Since children with asthma in Atlanta may not have visited the emergency department for their care, the true prevalence of asthma in the community is likely to be higher.

Table 1.2. Ozone-Related Adverse Effects by City (April–October 1997)

Metropolitan Area	Respiratory Hospital Admissions	Respiratory Emergency Room Visits	Asthma Attacks
Atlanta	580	1,740	100,000
Baltimore	630	1,890	86,000
Chicago	1,500	4,500	200,000
Cincinnati	390	1,170	57,000
Cleveland	760	2,280	89,000
Detroit	930	2,790	100,000
Hartford	660	1,980	75,000
Miami/Ft. Lauderdale	1,200	3,600	110,000
Minneapolis/St. Paul	470	1,410	66,000
New York	4,100	12,300	520,000
Philadelphia	1,600	4,800	200,000
Pittsburgh	730	2,190	79,000
St. Louis	610	1,830	100,000
Tampa/St. Petersburg	780	2,340	68,000
Washington, D.C.	800	2,400	130,000

Source: Abt Associates, Inc., and Clean Air Task Force, *Adverse Health Effects Associated with Ozone in the Eastern United States* (1999).

The American Lung Association estimates that 73,610 people out of a population of 1.3 million suffer from chronic obstructive pulmonary disease (COPD).[37] Of this total, 44,258 are adults and 23,011 are children suffering from asthma. Four counties in the Atlanta metropolitan region (DeKalb, Douglas, Fulton, and Rockdale counties) exceed national ozone standards. The incidence of childhood asthma by county reveals the following: Fulton (11,234), DeKalb (9,509), Douglas (1,272), and Rockdale (996). It is important to note that a disproportionately large share of the childhood asthma cases (90.1 percent) in the Atlanta region occurs in Fulton and DeKalb counties—two counties with the largest share of people of color.

Given the heavy dependence on the automobile in the region and the limited role of public transit in the region, it is doubtful that emission-control technologies adopted under the 1990 Clean Air Act Amendments (CAAA) are adequate to ensure that transportation fairly contributes to attainment of healthful air quality in the region.

Communities at Risk

As noted earlier, the Atlanta metropolitan region includes ten counties (see Figure 1.1). This study examines environmental quality in the five largest counties: Fulton, Cobb, DeKalb, Clayton, and Gwinnett. These counties were selected because of their population size and their proximity to the city of Atlanta. Geographic information system (GIS) analysis was used to map the

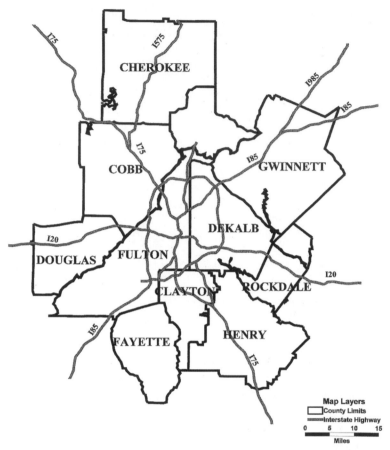

Figure 1.1. The 10-County Atlanta Metropolitan Region. *Source:* Atlanta Regional Commission, *Region Outlook* (1998).

distribution of polluting facilities by county. The concept "people of color" and "minority" are used interchangeably in this study. The category includes blacks/African Americans, Hispanics/Latinos, Asians/Pacific Islanders, and Indians/Native Americans.

Toxic time bombs are not randomly scattered across the urban landscape. These facilities are often located in communities that have high percentages of poor, elderly, young, and people of color residents.[38] Nearly 83 percent of Atlanta's African American population compared to 60 percent of whites live in zip codes that have an uncontrolled hazardous waste site.

African Americans and other people of color are disproportionately represented in metro Atlanta zip codes with highest concentration of Toxic

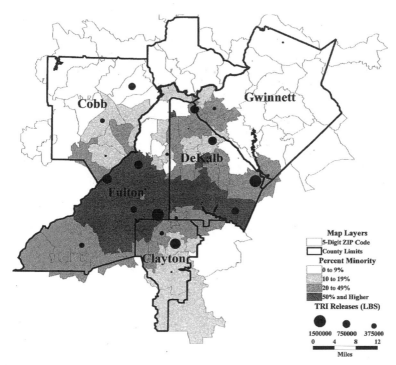

Figure 1.2. TRI Releases in 5-County Area by Minority Status. *Source:* U.S. EPA, Toxic Release Inventory Database (1996).

Release Inventory (TRI) reporting facilities (see Figure 1.2). This concentration of pollution is more striking in Fulton and DeKalb counties (see Figure 1.3). Most of the polluting facilities are located in south Fulton and south DeKalb—areas with heavy minority concentrations.

While people of color constitute 29.8 percent of the population in the five largest counties contiguous to Atlanta (Fulton, DeKalb, Cobb, Gwinnett, and Clayton counties), they represent the majority of residents in five of the ten "dirtiest" zip codes in these large counties (see Figure 1.4). Within these ten "dirtiest" zip codes, residents of the five majority white zip codes are exposed to an average of 32.0 pounds of toxic releases per person annually compared to an average of 38.5 pounds of toxic releases per person in the five majority people of color zip codes.

The nonrandom pattern of polluting facilities is not due to chance or the luck of the draw. Location decisions often involve cooperation between government and industry officials. Clearly, health and environmental risks fall heaviest on people of color neighborhoods and their residents who are least able to escape these environmental and health assaults.

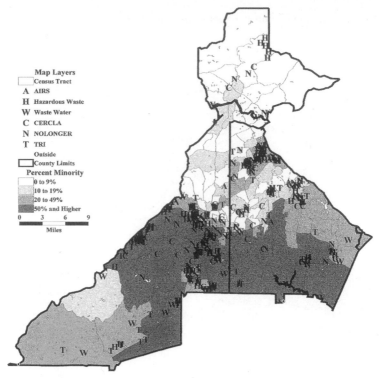

Figure 1.3. Polluting Facilities in Fulton and DeKalb Counties by Race. *Source:* U.S. EPA, Toxic Release Inventory Database (1996).

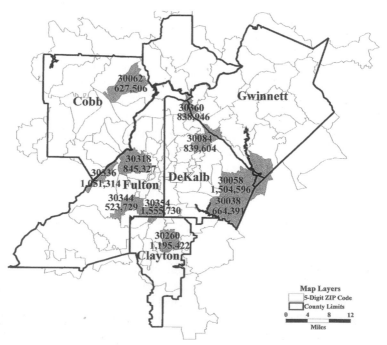

Figure 1.4. Ten "Dirtiest" Zip Codes and TRI Releases in Pounds. *Source:* U.S. EPA, Toxic Release Inventory Database (1996).

Atlanta's African American neighborhoods have more than their fair share of polluting facilities.

Toxics in the Neighborhood

Toxic pollution is not randomly distributed. The federal EPA Office of Prevention, Pesticides, and Toxic Substances maintains the TRI database that contains information submitted from the industries it regulates. One limitation of the TRI data is that it is self-reported by the industry. Similarly, many toxic agents are not regulated by the EPA and, therefore, are not included in this data.

The EPA regulates many large releases, omitting many small-quantity generators that could make up the majority of the releases. Although the data used is imperfect, it is the best information available that can give an indication of the magnitude of toxic releases in the five-county area (Fulton, DeKalb, Clayton, Cobb, and Gwinnett). There are some specifications used to determine which companies must report to TRI. A facility must report if it meets the following criteria: conducts manufacturing operations within Standard Industrial Classification (SIC) codes 20 to 39; has 10 or more full-time employees; and manufactures and processes more than 10,000 pounds of any listed chemical during the calendar year.

The companies that meet the above specifications must submit a report to EPA. The latest TRI information released by EPA in 1996 indicated that

The Atlantic Steel site is an attempt to reclaim an old industrial site under Atlanta's Brownfields Redevelopment initiative.

11.7 million pounds of toxic chemicals were released within the 40 zip codes that are partially or completely inside of the five-county study area (see Table 1.3). Fulton County ranked the highest with 4,689,876 pounds in 12 zip codes, covering an area of 343.67 square miles. Those zip codes recorded an average minority population of 60.54 percent and 20.41 per-

Table 1.3. Total Toxic Releases in the Five-County Area

County	Population	Total Releases (lbs)	Lbs/Person	% Minority	% Below Poverty
Fulton	648,951	4,689,876	7.23	60.5	20.4
DeKalb	545,837	4,141,726	7.59	43.3	9.2
Clayton	182,052	1,528,675	8.40	20.2	9.4
Cobb	447,745	1,019,464	2.28	14.1	6.7
Gwinnett	352,910	290,930	0.82	10.9	5.5
Totals	2,177,495	11,670,671	5.36	29.8	10.2

Note: Percentages of minority and poor population were calculated using zip code boundaries and thus disparities will be present.

Source: U.S. EPA, Toxic Release Inventory Database (1996).

cent poor. The "dirtiest" zip code (i.e., 30354) in the five-county area is located in Fulton County and receives over 1.55 million pounds of toxic releases annually; people of color make up 69.1 percent of the population in zip code 30354. Residents in zip code 30336 are subjected to 873.9 pounds of toxic releases per person annually; zip code 30336 is 98.2 percent black.

DeKalb County recorded the second highest total releases with 4,141,726 pounds, and it averaged 43.33 percent minority and 9.24 percent poor in 14 zip codes covering an area of 221.42 square miles. Clayton County ranked third with 1,528,675 pounds, averaging 20.22 percent minority and 9.36 percent poor in three zip codes covering an area of 74.49 square miles. Cobb County ranked fourth with 1,019,464 pounds, averaging 14.09 percent minority and 6.73 percent poor and covering an area of 126.1 square miles. Gwinnett County ranked last with 290,930 pounds, averaging 10.85 percent minority and 5.46 percent poor and covering an area of 261.83 square miles.

Four zip codes recorded releases larger than 1 million pounds of toxic chemicals; two of these zip codes were found in Fulton County (see Table 1.4). The largest recorded releases and most polluted zip code in the five-county area is zip code 30354 in Fulton County with 1,555,730 pounds. Zip code 30354 is 69.1 percent minority and 26.9 percent poor. The residents of this zip code are faced with 95.10 pounds of toxic chemicals per person, the second-highest toxic output of the top 10 "dirtiest" zip codes. The second

Table 1.4. Ten "Dirtiest" Zip Codes and Their Corresponding Counties

Rank	Zip Code	County	Total Releases (lbs)	Lbs/Person	% Minority	% Below Poverty
1	30354	Fulton	1,555,730	95.10	69.1	26.9
2	30058	DeKalb	1,504,596	39.85	38.0	5.3
3	30260	Clayton	1,195,422	58.08	17.1	8.3
4	30336	Fulton	1,051,314	873.91	98.2	59.0
5	30318	Fulton	845,327	15.72	75.3	32.1
6	30084	DeKalb	839,604	28.50	12.6	4.2
7	30360	DeKalb	838,946	52.45	20.7	5.5
8	30038	DeKalb	664,391	42.44	63.5	3.4
9	30062	Cobb	627,506	11.95	8.0	3.3
10	30344	Fulton	523,729	15.64	68.0	16.9

Note: Percentages of minority and poor population were calculated using zip code boundaries and thus disparities will be present.

Source: U.S. EPA, Toxic Release Inventory Database (1996).

Table 1.5. Distribution of Polluting Facilities in Five Counties by Minority Status and Zip Code

	0 to 9%		10 to 19%		20 to 49%		50% and up		Total	
	Total	%	Total	%	Total	%	Total	%	Total	%
# of TRI[a]	30	20.0	20	13.3	36	24.0	64	42.7	150	100
# of zip codes	33	33.7	17	17.3	23	23.5	25	25.5	98	100
Area (sq. mi.)	1167.4	53.5	306.4	14.1	410.5	18.8	295.9	13.6	2180.2	100

Source: U.S. EPA, Toxic Release Inventory Database (1996).

[a] TRI = Toxic Release Inventory facilities

largest recorded releases are found in zip code 30058 in DeKalb County, with 1,504,596 pounds of toxic chemicals released for a total of 39.85 pounds per person. Zip code 30058 is 38.0 percent minority.

The third-largest release was found in zip code 30260 in Clayton County, with 1,195,422 pounds of toxic chemicals and 58.08 pounds per resident. Zip code 30260 is 17.1 percent minority and 8.3 percent poor. The other zip code with releases over 1 million (1,051,314) is located in Fulton County. Zip code 30336 is 98.2 percent minority and has 59.0 percent poverty rate. This zip code has toxic chemical releases of 873.91 pounds per person.

Overall, the zip codes with the highest percentage minority population also had the highest total outputs of pollution per resident (see Table 1.5). The five-county area has a total of 150 TRI facilities. Over two-fifths (42.7%) of the TRI facilities were located in zip codes where people of color made up the majority of residents. More important, this large concentration of polluting facilities is concentrated in an area that covers only 13.6 percent of the total land area for the five counties. On the other hand, polluting facilities in mostly white areas are more dispersed. For example, one-fifth of the TRI facilities were located in zip codes that had less than a 10 percent minority population. These facilities were spread out over an area that covers 53.5 percent of the total land area in the five counties.

Conclusion

African Americans and other people of color have begun to treat their struggle for a clean environment as an extension of the struggle for basic human rights. Just as social justice activists fought for equal access to education, employment, and housing, they are now defining the opportunity to live in an unpolluted physical environment as a basic right. Moreover, many groups are now convinced that the targeting of their communities with polluting industries, such as waste disposal facilities, contributes to urban infrastructure decline comparable to housing discrimination, redlining practices, and disinvestment decisions of lending institutions.

All communities are not created equal. This is true in the Atlanta region as it is elsewhere. People of color in the Atlanta region are more likely than their white counterparts to be threatened by environmental hazards, including air and water pollution, industrial toxins, and hazardous waste. Overburdened sewage treatment plants, toxic releases from polluting industries, lead paint in housing, or abandoned hazardous waste sites are all real dangers in neighborhoods inhabited largely by people of color.

The region's African American population is especially vulnerable to environmental discrimination because of limited income and institutional barriers in the housing market. As a result, many black Atlantans are trapped in poverty and polluted neighborhoods. Many industrial firms, especially waste disposal companies and industries that have a long history of pollution violations, have come to view the African American community as a pushover, lacking community organization and environmental consciousness. The strong (and sometimes blind) pro-jobs stance—a kind of "don't bite the hand that feeds you" sentiment—has aided in institutionalizing "unacceptable risks" and environmental inequities.

People of color in the Atlanta region and all across the country are beginning to mobilize around quality of life issues, including suburban sprawl and transportation equity. Many activists now view the use of their tax dollars to subsidize uneven growth in the suburbs as unacceptable and unjust. A new form of activism has emerged that, rather than being limited to attacks on well-publicized toxic contamination issues, has begun to seek remedial action on housing, transportation, air quality, and other environmental justice problems that threaten public safety. Grassroots groups are demanding a clean and healthy environment as well as a fair share of the benefits that accrue from public infrastructure investments.

Environmental justice advocates have redefined "environment" to include where we live, work, play, worship, and go to school, as well as the physical and natural world. "Environment" also includes infrastructure, development, and land-use problems that threaten the fabric of our cities and their inhabitants. For example, Atlanta's inadequate sewage treatment plant is viewed as an environmental, health, and economic development problem.

The repair or replacement of decayed sewer lines, reduction of emissions from industrial facilities, cleanup of hazardous waste sites, redevelopment of brownfields sites, elimination of lead threats in housing, and reduction of air pollution from mobile sources (i.e., motor vehicles) are all investments that are needed to improve the quality of life in the Atlanta region. Residents need to feel that they have a say in what happens in their communities. Thus it is important that citizen-involvement plans bring low-income and people of color organizations, grassroots groups, historically black colleges and universities (HBCUs), and other institutions into the decision-making process.

Notes

1. Nancy A. Denton and Douglas S. Massey, "Residential Segregation of Blacks, Hispanics, and Asians by Socioeconomic Status and Generation," *Social Science Quarterly* 69 (1988), pp. 797–817.
2. Robert D. Bullard, *Dumping in Dixie: Race, Class and Environmental Quality.* Boulder, CO: Westview Press, 1994, chap. 1.
3. Denton and Massey, "Residential Segregation of Blacks, Hispanics, and Asians," p. 814.
4. For an in-depth analysis of environmental problems facing communities of color, see Robert D. Bullard, ed., *Unequal Protection: Environmental Justice and Communities of Color.* San Francisco: Sierra Club Books, 1996.
5. Robert D. Bullard, "Ecological Inequities and the New South: Black Communities under Siege," *Journal of Ethnic Studies* 17 (Winter 1990), pp. 101–115; Robert D. Bullard and Beverly H. Wright, "Toxic Waste and the African American Community," *Urban League Review* 13 (Spring 1990), pp. 67–75.
6. Robert D. Bullard, *Unequal Protection,* p. 7.
7. Robert D. Bullard, "Solid Waste Sites and the Black Houston Community." *Sociological Inquiry* 53 (Spring 1983), pp. 273–288; United Church of Christ Commission for Racial Justice, *Toxic Wastes and Race in the United States* (New York: United Church of Christ, 1987); Robert D. Bullard, *Dumping in Dixie,* pp. 1–20; Eric Mann, *L.A.'s Lethal Air: New Strategies for Policy, Organizing, and Action* (Los Angeles: Labor/Community Strategy Center, 1991); D. R. Wernette and L. A. Nieves, "Breathing Polluted Air: Minorities are Disproportionately Exposed." *EPA Journal* 18 (March/April 1992), pp. 16–17; Robert D. Bullard, "In Our Backyards: Minority Communities Get Most of the Dumps." *EPA Journal* 18 (March/April 1992), pp. 11–12; Bunyan Bryant and Paul Mohai, eds., *Race and the Incidence of Environmental Hazards* (Boulder, CO: Westview Press, 1992), pp. 163–176; Robert D. Bullard, ed., *Unequal Protection: Environmental Justice and Communities of Color* (San Francisco: Sierra Club, 1996).
8. Agency for Toxic Substances Disease Registry, *The Nature and Extent of Lead Poisoning in Children in the United States: A Report to Congress.* Atlanta: U.S. Department of Health and Human Services, 1988, pp. 1–12; James L. Pirkle, Debra J. Brody, Elaine W. Gunter, Rachel A. Kramer, Daniel C. Paschal, Katherine M. Flegal, and Thomas D. Matte, "The Decline in Blood Lead Levels in the United States: The National Health and Nutrition Examination Survey (NHANES) III," *Journal of the American Medical Association* 272 (July 27, 1994) pp. 284–291.
9. Robert D. Bullard, "Environmental Racism and Land Use," *Land Use Forum: A Journal of Law, Policy & Practice* 2 (Spring 1993), pp. 6–11.
10. United Church of Christ Commission for Racial Justice, *Toxic Wastes and Race;* Paul Mohai and Bunyan Bryant, "Environmental Racism: Reviewing the Evidence," in Bryant and Mohai, eds., *Race and the Incidence of Environmental Hazards,* pp. 163–176.
11. Bunyan Bryant and Paul Mohai, eds., *Race and the Incidence of Environmental Hazards.*
12. Centers for Disease Control and Prevention, "Update: Blood Lead Levels—

United States, 1991–1994," *Morbidity and Mortality Weekly Report* 46, no. 7 (February 21, 1997), pp. 141–146.

13. Scott Bronstein, "Chattahoochee Cleanup: How Far to Go," *Atlanta Journal-Constitution,* April 20, 1993, p. A3.

14. Charles Seabrook, "A Dirty, Dangerous Journey," *Atlanta Journal-Constitution,* November 23, 1997, p. Q1.

15. Sherrie Russell and Goro Mitchell, "Atlanta's Environment and the Black Community," in Bob Holmes, ed., *The Status of Black Atlanta,* 1994. Atlanta: Southern Center for Studies in Public Policy, Clark Atlanta University, 1994, pp. 98–139.

16. Ibid., pp. 101–102.

17. State of Georgia, Environmental Protection Division, "Listing of Wastewater Enforcement Actions against the City of Atlanta 1990–1994," EPD, 1994.

18. Julie B. Hairston, "Atlanta Will Pay Larger Pollution Fine," *Atlanta Journal-Constitution,* July 30, 1999, p. D1.

19. Arnold W. Reitze, Jr., "A Century of Air Pollution Control Law: What Worked; What Failed; What Might Work," *Environmental Law* 21 (1991), p. 1549.

20. D.R. Wernette and L.A. Nieves, "Breathing Polluted Air: Minorities are Disproportionately Exposed," *EPA Journal* 18 (March 1992), pp. 16–17.

21. Research Atlanta, Inc., *The Costs of Nonattainment: Atlanta's Ozone Imbroglio.* Atlanta: Georgia State University, 1997, p. 20.

22. Centers for Disease Control and Prevention, "Asthma—United States, 1982–1992." *Morbidity and Mortality Weekly Report* 43 (1995), pp. 952–955.

23. Centers for Disease Control and Prevention, "Asthma Mortality and Hospitalization among Children and Young Adults—United States, 1980–1993." *Morbidity and Mortality Weekly Report* 45 (1996), pp. 350–353.

24. Anna E. Pribitkin, "The Need for Revision of Ozone Standards: Why Has the EPA Failed to Respond?" *Temple Environmental Law & Technology Journal* 13 (1994), p. 104.

25. Centers for Disease Control and Prevention/National Center for Health Statistics. *Health United States 1994.* Department of Health and Human Services Publication No. (PHS) 95-1232, Tables 83, 84, 86, and 87.

26. Centers for Disease Control and Prevention, "Asthma—United States, 1982–1992." *Morbidity and Mortality Weekly Report* 43 (1995), pp. 952–955.

27. CDC, "Disabilities among Children Aged Less Than or Equal to 17 years—United States, 1991–1992." *Morbidity and Mortality Weekly Report* 44 (1995), pp. 609–613.

28. See Mann, *L.A.'s Lethal Air.*

29. U.S. EPA, *Review of National Ambient Air Quality Standards for Ozone, Assessment of Scientific and Technical Information, OAQPS Staff Paper.* Research Triangle Park, NC: EPA, 1996; Haluk Ozkaynk, John D. Spengler, Marie O'Neil, Jianping Xue, Hui Zhou, Kathy Gilbert, and Sonja Ramstrom, "Ambient Ozone Exposure and Emergency Hospital Admissions and Emergency Room Visits for Respiratory Problems in Thirteen U.S. Cities," in American Lung Association, *Breathless: Air Pollution and Hospital Admissions/Emergency Room Visits in 13 Cities* (Washington, DC: American Lung Association, 1996); American Lung

Association, *Out of Breath: Populations-at-Risk to Alternative Ozone Levels* (Washington, DC: American Lung Association, 1995).

30. Lucy Soto, "Take it from Kids: Bad Air Hurts," *Atlanta Journal-Constitution,* October 6, 1999, p. B1.

31. Abts Associates, Inc., and Clean Air Task Force, *Out of Breath: Health Effects from Ozone in the Eastern United States.* Washington, DC: Author, 1999.

32. Lucy Soto, "Take it from Kids," p. B4.

33. Centers for Disease Control and Prevention, National Center for Environmental Health, Division of Environmental Hazards and Health Effects, Air Pollution and Respiratory Branch, "Asthma Mortality and Hospitalization among Children and Young Adults—United States, 1980–1993," *Morbidity and Mortality Weekly Report,* 45 (1996), pp. 350–353.

34. Centers for Disease Control, "Asthma: United States, 1980–1990," *Morbidity and Mortality Weekly Report,* 39 (1992), pp. 733–735.

35. H.P. Mak, H. Abbey, and R.C. Talamo, "Prevalence of Asthma and Health Service Utilization of Asthmatic Children in an Inner City," *Journal of Allergy and Clinical Immunology* 70 (1982), pp. 367–372; I.F. Goldstein and A.L. Weinstein, "Air Pollution and Asthma: Effects of Exposure to Short-Term Sulfur Dioxide Peaks," *Environmental Research* 40 (1986), pp. 332–345; J. Schwartz, D. Gold, D.W. Dockey, S.T. Weiss, and F.E. Speizer, "Predictors of Asthma and Persistent Wheeze in a National Sample of Children in the United States," *American Review of Respiratory Disease* 142 (1990), pp. 555–562; F. Crain, K. Weiss, J. Bijur, et al., "An Estimate of the Prevalence of Asthma and Wheezing among Inner-City Children," *Pediatrics* 94 (1994), pp. 356–362.

36. Mary C. White, Ruth A. Etzel, Wallace D. Wilcox, and Christine Lloyd, "Exacerbation of Childhood Asthma and Ozone Pollution in Atlanta," *Environmental Research* 65 (1994), p. 56.

37. American Lung Association, *Out of Breath: Populations-at-Risk to Alternative Ozone Levels,* Table 6.

38. Robert D. Bullard, *Dumping in Dixie;* Robert D. Bullard, ed., *Unequal Protection: Environmental Justice and Communities of Color;* Bunyan Bryant and Paul Mohai, eds., *Race and the Incidence of Environmental Hazards.*

CHAPTER 2

Dismantling Transportation Apartheid: The Quest for Equity

Robert D. Bullard, Glenn S. Johnson, and Angel O. Torres

Transportation touches nearly every aspect of our lives. Most Americans use some form of motorized travel in carrying out their daily routine, whether it involves shopping, visiting friends, attending church, or going to the doctor. While cars have opened up all sorts of new opportunities and freedoms for Americans, they have also exacted an awesome price, not just economically, but socially and personally.[1] The decision to build highways, expressways, and beltways has far-reaching effects on land use, energy policy, and the environment. Transportation also profoundly affects residential and industrial growth as well as physical and social mobility. This chapter examines the social, economic, and environmental consequences of transportation planning in metropolitan Atlanta.

National Trends

The United States is rapidly becoming a suburban nation, spurred on in part by transportation. In 1990, suburbs accounted for 60 percent of the nation's metropolitan population. Over 80 percent of the country's future growth (if current trends hold) is expected to occur in "edge cities" and other suburbs.[2] Sprawl is also pushing development into the "exurbs" and rural communities outside metropolitan areas where public transportation is nonexistent. Nowhere is this pattern more apparent than in the South and Southwest or "Sunbelt" cities of Phoenix, Dallas, and Atlanta. For some urban researchers, these fast-growing metropolitan areas are not cities but "suburban agglomerations" of subdivisions and horizontal developments that have no relation to the original urban cores.[3] In order to navigate these communities, residents almost always need a car.

Other than housing, Americans spend more on transportation than on any other household expense. Americans spend over 2 billion hours a year in their cars. The average American household spends one-fifth of its income—or about $6,000 a year—for each car that it owns and operates.[4] American drivers also waste $72 billion a year from tie-ups in traffic gridlock. Congested roads cost metropolitan Atlantans an estimated $2.27 billion in lost time and gasoline.[5] Davis L. Schrank and Timothy J. Lomax, Texas A&M University researchers, report that Atlanta's highway lane miles grew by an average of 5.8 percent for the period 1992–1996 (see Table 2.1). This compares with 0.08 percent San Diego, 1.3 percent in Phoenix, 2.4 percent in Dallas, 1.9 percent in Miami, 2.6 percent in Houston, and 1.8 in Washington, D.C.[6]

Building more highways has not solved Atlanta's traffic problem. Each metro Atlanta driver spends 68 hours each year in traffic delays. Delays in comparable Sunbelt cities include 37 hours in Phoenix, 38 hours in San Diego, 58 hours in Miami, 63 hours in Dallas, and 66 hours in Houston.

Table 2.1. Comparative Traffic-Related Statistics by Census-Defined Urbanized Area

Statistic or Performance Measure	Atlanta	San Diego	Phoenix	Dallas	Miami	Houston	Washington, D.C.
1996 Estimated population (in thousands)	2,470	2,565	2,340	2,290	2,050	3,050	3,460
Population density (persons/square mile)	1,385	3,420	2,165	1,435	3,795	1,820	3,460
Congestion index	1.24	1.23	1.14	1.11	1.34	1.11	1.43
Annual hours of delay per driver	68	38	37	63	58	66	82
Peak period freeway speeds (MPH)	42	42	42	44	39	40	39
Freeway and major arterial lane miles	4,380	3,595	4,230	3,875	3,090	4,760	4,245
Average annual highway lane mile growth 1992–1996	5.8%	0.08%	1.3%	2.4%	1.9%	2.6%	1.8%

Source: Texas Transportation Institute, *Urban Mobility Study* (November 1998).

Table 2.2. The 20 Worst Bottlenecks in the United States

Metro Area	Intersection
1. Los Angeles	I-405 at I-10
2. Houston	U.S. 59 at I-610
3. Seattle	I-5 at I-90
4. Boston	I-93 at U.S. 1
5. Washington (Md.)	I-495 at I-270
6. Washington (Va.)	I-95 at I-495
7. Los Angeles	U.S. 101 at I-405
8. Los Angeles	State Highway 55 at State Highway 22
9. Los Angeles	I-10 at I-5
10. Albuquerque	I-40 at I-25
11. Atlanta	I-285 at I-85
12. Atlanta	I-75 at I-85
13. Chicago	I-290 at I-88/I-294
14. Denver	I-25 at I-225
15. Houston	I-610 at I-10/U.S. 290
16. Washington (Va.)	I-66 at I-495
17. Washington (Md.)	I-95/I-495 at U.S. 1
18. Atlanta	I-285 at I-75
19. Fort Lauderdale–Hollywood, Fla.	I-95 at I-595
20. San Francisco–Oakland	I-80 east of Bay Bridge

Source: American Highway Users Alliance, Department of Transportation (1999).

Each driver in Washington, D.C., the nation's capital, spends 82 hours in traffic delays each year.[7] A headline-grabbing story in *USA Today* reported that "traffic is worse than ever" and that "congestion on U.S. roads is outpacing population growth."[8] In 1999, the American Highway Users Alliance rated the 167 worst bottlenecks in the country. Metro Atlanta had 3 of the 20 worst bottlenecks in the nation (see Table 2.2). Only Los Angeles and Washington, D.C., were worse with each having 4 intersections to make the top 20 list.

According to the latest figures published in the Federal Highway Administration report, *Highway Statistics,* total vehicle miles traveled (VMT) in the United States increased by 59 percent from 1980 to 1995.[9] Over the past 75 years, automobile production and highway construction have multiplied, while urban mass transit systems have been dismantled or allowed to fall into disrepair. The American automobile culture was spurred on by massive government investments in roads (3 million miles) and interstate highways (45,000 miles). Just 20 percent of the gasoline tax goes to mass transit, while 80 percent goes to highways. The end result has meant more pollution, congestion, wasted energy, residential segregation, and sprawl.[10]

The Role of Government

Federal tax dollars help build and subsidize many of the roads, freeways, and public transit systems in our nation. Building highways to the suburbs and subsidizing the construction of suburban homes were considered two of government's primary responsibilities.[11] Many of these transportation activities had unintended consequences of dividing, isolating, disrupting, and imposing different economic, environmental, and health burdens on some communities. According to longtime civil rights activist and Georgia congressman John Lewis,

> Even in a city like Atlanta, Georgia—a vibrant city with a modern rail and public transit system—thousands of people have been left out and left behind because of discrimination. Like most other major American cities, Atlanta's urban center is worlds apart from its suburbs. The gulf between rich and poor, minorities and whites, the "haves" and "have-nots" continues to widen.[12]

Some communities accrue benefits from transportation development projects, while other communities bear a disproportionate burden and pay the costs in diminished health. Generally, benefits are more dispersed, while costs or burdens are more localized. For example, having a seven-lane freeway next door may not be a benefit to someone who does not even own a car. Low-income and people of color communities are severely impacted by road construction and other transportation projects that result in the incidence of tailpipe pollutants in urban areas. This constitutes evidence that suburban-serving freeways have significant negative impacts on inner-city neighborhoods, yet offer little benefit in return.[13]

Transportation decision making—whether at the federal, regional, state, or local level—often mirrors the power arrangements of the dominant society and its institutions. Some transportation policies distribute the costs in a regressive pattern while providing disproportionate benefits for individuals who fall at the upper end of the education and income scale. All transportation modes are not created equal. Federal transportation policies, taxing structure, and funding schemes have contributed to the inequity between the various transportation modes (e.g., private automobile, rail, buses, air). Most state departments of transportation (DOTs) have become de facto road building programs that buttress the asphalt and construction industries. On the other hand, funding for efficient, clean, regional mass transportation systems has been spotty at best.

The Quest for Environmental Justice

Environmental justice means different things to different people. Environmental justice is defined as the fair treatment and meaningful involvement of all people regardless of race, color, national origin, or income with respect to the development, implementation, and enforcement of environmental laws, regulations, and policies. Fair treatment means that no group of people, including racial, ethnic, or socioeconomic groups, should bear a disproportionate share of the negative environmental consequences resulting from industrial, municipal, and commercial operations or the execution of federal, state, local, and tribal programs and policies.

Environmental justice principles are not meant to shift risks among populations but rather to identify alternatives that may mitigate the impacts of potential disproportionately high and adverse effects. Achieving environmental justice involves identifying where high and adverse impacts occur and ensuring that governmental decisions do not cause or contribute to them. Environmental justice is a public policy objective that has the potential to significantly improve the quality of life for people who often have been left behind as communities grow and change.[14]

On February 11, 1994, President Clinton signed Executive Order 12898, "Federal Actions to Address Environmental Justice in Minority Populations and Low-Income Populations."[15] This executive order reinforces what has been law for at least three decades—the passage of the Civil Rights Act of 1964—which prohibits discriminatory practices in programs receiving federal funds. The Executive Order also focuses on the National Environmental Policy Act (NEPA), a law that set policy goals for the protection, maintenance, and enhancement of the environment. NEPA's goal is "to ensure for all Americans a safe, healthful, productive, and aesthetically and culturally pleasing environment." NEPA requires federal agencies to prepare a detailed statement on the environmental effects of proposed federal actions that significantly affect the quality of human health.

The executive order calls for improved methodologies for assessing and mitigating impacts, health effects from multiple and cumulative exposure, and collection of data on low-income and minority populations who may be disproportionately at risk. It also calls for impacts on subsistence fishers and wildlife consumers. It encourages participation of the impacted populations in the various phases of assessment, including scoping, data gathering, impact identification alternatives, analysis, mitigation, and monitoring.

Some transportation activities have unintentional consequences of dividing, isolating, disrupting, and imposing different economic, environmental, and health burdens on minority and low-income communities. It is important to note that analyzing and addressing environmental justice may assist decision makers in determining the distributional effects of transportation impacts on certain populations. On April 15, 1997, the U.S. DOT issued its Order on Environmental Justice (DOT Order 5610.2) requiring the U.S. DOT to comply with the Federal Order within the framework of existing laws, regulations, and guidance.

Metropolitan planning organizations (MPOs), the bodies of local and state officials responsible for federally supported transportation planning, must seek out and consider the needs of those traditionally underserved by existing transportation systems, including, but not limited to, low-income and minority households.[16] In December 1998, the Federal Highway Administration (FHWA) issued an Order that requires FHWA to implement the principles of the DOT Order 5610.2 and executive order 12898 by incorporating environmental justice in all FHWA programs, policies, and activities. The environmental requirements reinforce a number of regulatory laws and statutes, including Title VI of the Civil Rights Act of 1964, the National Environmental Policy Act of 1969, and the Federal-Aid Highway Act of 1970. Title VI of the Civil Rights Act of 1964 states:

> No person in the United States shall, on the grounds of race, color, or national origin, be excluded from participation in, be denied the benefits of, or be subjected to discrimination under any program or activity receiving Federal financial assistance.[17]

The executive order requires agencies to work to ensure effective public participation and access to information. Thus within its NEPA process and through other appropriate mechanisms, each federal agency shall, "wherever practicable and appropriate, translate crucial public documents, notices and hearings, relating to human health or the environment for limited English speaking populations." In addition, each agency should work to ensure that public documents, notices, and hearings relating to human health or the environment are concise, understandable, and readily accessible to the public.

In addition to the practical reasons for concern about equity impacts in transportation planning, the current environmental justice provisions strengthen federal transportation policy to promote quality of life and eliminate or mitigate adverse and disproportionate health, environmental, social, and economic impacts.

Public involvement is equally important in the interaction of environmental justice, Title VI, and NEPA. The FHWA and the Federal Transit Administration (FTA) and their state and local partners must ensure that the public is involved in transportation decision making and activities, provides input, and has access to public information concerning transportation, health, and environmental impacts. "Knowing the positive and negative impacts of potential changes in transportation systems enables residents of the affected areas to relate these impacts to their own priorities and value premises."[18]

Public involvement can assist transportation analysts in identifying potential environmental justice impacts of concern to minority and low-income communities and determining their severity, extent, and importance. Community leaders can also inform transportation analysts about past projects and similar undertakings in their community and other locations for comparison.

Defining Transportation Equity

For more than a century, people of color have struggled to end transportation discrimination, linking unequal treatment on buses and trains with violation of constitutionally guaranteed civil rights. History has shown that the stakes are high. In 1896, in *Plessy v. Ferguson,* the U.S. Supreme Court upheld Louisiana's segregated "white" and "colored" seating on railroad cars, ushering in the infamous doctrine of "separate but equal." *Plessy* not only codified apartheid on transportation facilities, it also served as the legal basis for racial segregation in education until it was overturned by the 1954 U.S. Supreme Court decision in *Brown v. Board of Education of Topeka.*

The modern civil rights movement has its roots in transportation. From the legendary Rosa Parks to the Montgomery Bus Boycott to the Freedom Riders, all roads pointed to a frontal attack on racist transportation policies and practices. Today, transportation is no less a civil rights and quality of life issue. All communities are still *not* created equal. Some communities accrue benefits from transportation development projects, while other communities bear a disproportionate burden and pay the cost in diminished health. Generally, benefits are more dispersed, while costs or burdens are more localized. Having a seven-lane freeway next door is not a benefit to someone who does not even own a car.

Todd Litman, a researcher with the Canada-based Victoria Transport Policy Institute, contends that transportation is about opportunity and equity.[19] Moreover, how transportation is defined and measured can often determine how equity is evaluated. Litman delineates three general types of transportation equity:

Horizontal Equity. This type focuses on fairness of cost and benefit allocation between individuals and groups who are considered comparable in wealth and ability.

Vertical Equity with Regard to Income and Social Class. This type is concerned with allocation of costs between income and social classes.

Vertical Equity with Regard to Mobility Need and Ability. Here, the focus is on how well an individual's transportation needs are met compared with those of others in the community.[20]

Transportation equity is not a new concept nor is it a new goal. It has long been a goal of the modern civil rights movement. In recent years, social justice advocates (i.e., child care, health providers, housing, educators, environmentalists, organized labor, etc.) have reintroduced transportation equity on the political radar screens. The issues have been couched in social and economic justice contexts. Many poor people and people of color, who are concentrated in central cities, are demanding better transportation that will take them to the job-rich suburbs.[21] Ideally, it would be better if jobs were closer to inner-city residents' homes. However, few urban-core neighborhoods have experienced an economic revitalization that can rival the current jobs in the suburbs.

Transportation equity concerns extend to disparate outcomes in planning, operation and maintenance, and infrastructure development. Transportation is a key component in addressing poverty, unemployment, equal opportunity goals, and ensuring equal access to education, employment, and other public services. In the real world, all transportation decisions do not have the same impact on all groups. Costs and benefits associated with transportation developments are not randomly distributed. Transportation equity is concerned with factors that may create or exacerbate inequities. Environmental justice focuses on measures to prevent or correct disparities in benefits and costs. Disparate transportation outcomes can be subsumed under three broad categories of inequity: procedural, geographic, and social.[22]

> *Procedural Inequity.* Attention is directed to the process by which transportation decisions may or may not be carried out in a uniform, fair, and consistent manner with involvement of diverse public stakeholders. The question here is, do the rules apply equally to everyone?

> *Geographic Inequity.* Transportation decisions may have distributive impacts (positive and negative) that are geographic and spatial, such as rural vs. urban vs. central city. Some communities are physically located on the "wrong side of the tracks" and often receive substandard services. Environmental justice concerns revolve around the extent to which transportation systems address outcomes (diversity and quality of services, resources and investments, facilities and infrastructure, access to primary employment centers, etc.) that disproportionately favor one geographic area or spatial location over another.

> *Social Inequity.* Transportation benefits and burdens are not randomly distributed across population groups. Generally, transportation amenities (benefits) accrue to the wealthier and more educated segment of society, while transportation disamenities (burdens) fall disproportionately on people of color and individuals at the lower end of the socioeconomic spectrum. Intergenerational equity issues are also subsumed under this category. For example, the impacts and consequences of some transportation decisions may reach into several generations.

Such negative impacts or disamenities include transportation infrastructure that physically isolates communities; inequitable distribution of environmental "nuisances" such as maintenance and refueling facilities (air quality), airports (noise); lack of sufficient mitigation measures to correct inequitable distribution of negative impacts such as noise or displacement of homes, parks, and cultural landmarks; diversity of modal choices available to access key economic activity and employment locations; the transit headways and age and condition of the transit fleet; the availability and condition of facilities and services at transit stations such as information kiosks, seating, cleanliness, rest rooms; condition of the roadways that service lower-income and people of color communities; and major transportation investment projects and community economic development "spillover" effect.

Central cities and suburbs are not equal. They often compete for scarce resources. It is not difficult to predict the outcome between affluent suburbs and their less affluent central city competitors. Freeways are the lifeline for suburban commuters, while millions of central-city residents are dependent on public transportation as their primary mode of travel. But recent cuts in mass transit subsidies and fare hikes have reduced access to essential social services and economic activities. Nevertheless, road construction programs are booming—even in areas choked by air pollution.

Clean air appears to be everyone's dream. This sentiment cuts across race, class, gender, and geographic lines. The air quality impacts of transportation are especially significant to low-income persons and people of color who are more likely to live in urban areas with reduced air quality than affluent individuals and whites. No doubt, clean and energy-efficient public transportation could give millions of Americans who live in polluted cities a healthier environment and possibly longer lives. Even after years of government regulations and mandates, people of color and the poor are still exposed to greater health and environmental risk burdens than the society at large.[23] Pollution from multiple sources—smokestacks, incinerators, refineries, hazardous waste dumps, bus barns, freeways, lead in drinking water and paint, runoff and flooding from paved roads—endanger the health and safety of millions of urban residents.

Environmental problems are endangering the health of communities all across this nation. A big contributor to this health threat is pollution from automobiles. Is clean air a right? A growing number of activists are saying no to this question. The question of who pays and who benefits from the current transportation policies is central to any transportation equity analysis. In light of reversals in key civil rights gains of the earlier decades, it is clear that this country needs to revisit the social equity and environmental justice implications of contemporary transportation policies and decisions.

Transportation is basic to many other quality of life indicators such as health, education, employment, economic development, access to municipal services, residential mobility, and environmental quality. Federal commitment to public transportation in urban areas appears to have reached an all-time low. The continued residential segregation of people of color away from emerging suburban job centers (where public transit is inadequate or nonexistent) may signal a new urban crisis and a new form of "residential apartheid."[24] Transportation investments, enhancements, and financial resources have provided advantages for some communities while at the same time other communities have been disadvantaged by transportation decision making.

Researchers at the University of Iowa point to the limited material available on measuring environmental justice impacts of transportation investments.[25] The authors call for increased knowledge in the following areas: development of improved baseline assessments that estimate current levels of inaccessibility and adverse impacts; improved mobility assessment methods; air pollution and noise models that are more capable of microscale (neighborhood) analysis; more effective methods of reaching affected populations and gauging neighborhood-level priorities regarding elements needing preservation or enhancement; better predictive approaches for estimating trip geography and travel desires of low-income populations and minority populations in specific situations; location analysis of public and private facilities that take into account protected populations' abilities to conduct their daily activities; and improved techniques for communicating probable impact, positive and negative, of contemplated transportation system changes.[26]

Confronting Transportation Racism

Historically, transportation development policies did not emerge in a race- and class-neutral society. Institutional racism influences local land use, allocation of funds, enforcement of environmental regulations, facility siting, and where people of color live, work, and play.[27] Discrimination is a manifestation of institutional racism and causes life to be very different for whites and people of color.[28] Transportation racism is not an invention of radical social justice activists. It is just as real as the racism found in the housing industry, educational institutions, the employment arena, and the judicial system.

"Racism" refers to any policy, practice, or directive that differentially affects or disadvantages (whether intended or unintended) individuals, groups, or communities based on race or color. Racism combines with public policies and industry practices to provide benefits for whites while shifting costs to people of color.[29] Racism is reinforced by government, legal, economic, political, and military institutions. In a sense, "every state institution is a racial institution."[30]

In 1953, nearly four decades after the landmark *Plessy v. Ferguson* U.S. Supreme Court decision relegated blacks to the back of the bus, African Americans in Baton Rouge, the capital of Louisiana, staged the nation's first successful bus boycott. Two years later, on December 1, 1955, Rosa Parks refused to give up her seat at the front of a Montgomery, Alabama, city bus to a white man, igniting the modern civil rights movement. By the early 1960s, young "Freedom Riders" were riding Greyhound buses into the Deep South, fighting segregation in interstate travel at risk of death.[31]

Today, transportation is no less a civil rights issue. From New York City to Los Angeles, grassroots activists are demanding an end to unjust, unfair, and unequal transportation policies and practices. They are also demanding an end to transit racism. Transit racism killed 17-year-old Cynthia Wiggins of Buffalo, New York, because some official decided not to build a city bus stop at an upscale suburban shopping mall. The black teenager was crushed by a dump truck while crossing a seven-lane highway because Buffalo's Number Six bus, an inner-city bus used mostly by African Americans, was not allowed to stop at the suburban Walden Galleria Mall (located in Cheektowaga, NY). Cynthia had not been able to find a job in Buffalo but had secured work at a fast-food restaurant in the suburban mall. The Route 6 bus stopped about 300 yards short of the mall. Don Chen, a planner with the Surface Transportation Policy Project, summed up the Cynthia Wiggins tragedy:

> Cynthia's story tells us much about ways in which racism continues to manifest itself in America's metropolitan areas—through geographic separation and concealed discrimination by private institutions. With little public accountability or scrutiny, mall officials found it easy to shut out inner-city bus riders.[32]

The Wiggins family and other members of the African American community charged the Walden Galleria Mall with using the highway as a racial barrier to exclude some city residents. The high-profile trial, argued by attorney Johnnie L. Cochran Jr., began on November 8, 1999. The lawsuit was settled 10 days later with the mall owners, Pyramid Companies of Syracuse, agreeing to pay $2 million of the $2.55 million settlement, over time, to Cynthia Wiggin's four-year-old son. The bus company, Niagara Frontier Transportation Authority, agreed to pay $300,000; and the truck driver, John P. Bunch, agreed to pay $250,000.[33]

Residents in Los Angeles led a successful frontal assault on transit racism.

Residents and their lawyer from the NAACP Legal Defense and Education Fund (NAACP LDF) challenged the inequitable funding and operation of bus transportation used primarily by low-income and people of color residents. A class action lawsuit was filed on behalf of 350,000 low-income, people of color, bus riders represented by the Labor/Community Strategy Center, the Bus Riders Union, Southern Christian Leadership Conference, Korean Immigrant Workers Advocates, and individual bus riders. In *Labor/Community Strategy Center v. Los Angeles Metropolitan Transportation Authority,* the plaintiffs argued that the MTA had used federal funds to pursue a policy of raising costs of bus riders (who are mostly poor and people of color) and reducing quality of service in order to fund rail and other projects in predominately white, suburban areas.

In September 1996, the Labor Community Strategy Center and its lawyers won an historic out-of-court settlement against the MTA.[34] The group was able to win major fare and bus pass concessions from the Los Angeles MTA. They also forced the MTA to spend $89 million on 278 new clean compressed natural gas buses. The struggle, led by the Los Angeles Bus Riders Union, epitomizes grassroots groups challenging transit racism.[35] In the summer of 1998, the Bus Riders Union began a "no seat, no fare" campaign against crowded buses and second-class treatment by the MTA.[36] According to Eric Mann, who directs the Labor Community Strategy Center,

> There is a causal relationship between mobility and a potential escape from poverty. The MTA bus system is a critical link in ameliorating or exacerbating that situation. For many years, the city's previous "two-tiered" transit system was divided between private transportation (cars) and public transportation (buses). . . . Even within the bus system . . . racial discrimination was reflected in policy.[37] Lessons learned from Labor/Community Strategy Center and Bus Riders Union show that Title VI can be a useful tool in attacking transportation polices, at least where legal strategies and grassroots organizing are used together in a unified campaign.[38]

Transit racism is also under siege in Macon, Georgia, a city whose population is evenly divided between blacks and whites.[39] Over 90 percent of the bus riders in Macon are African Americans. African Americans in Macon filed a class action lawsuit challenging Macon and Bibb County's use of federal funds under the Intermodal Surface Transportation Efficiency Act or ISTEA. Over 28 percent of Macon's African Americans are carless compared to only 6 percent of the city's whites.

Mercer University law professor David Oedel reports that a disproportionate share of transportation dollars in Macon and Bibb County go to road construction and maintenance at the expense of the bus system. In 1993, Macon and Bibb County devoted over $33.65 million of federal, state, and local funds for roads, streets, and highways, of which some $10 million came from federal funds. During the same year, local officials accepted no federal funds for the Macon–Bibb County Transit Authority and budgeted only $1.4 million for public transportation. Overall, the bulk of federal transportation monies received by Macon and Bibb County are accepted to support road construction in mostly white suburban areas outside the reach of many African Americans.[40]

Atlanta's Transportation Nightmare

Atlanta's regional transportation policies are implicated in land-use patterns, unhealthy air, and sprawl. Traffic and air pollution have made Atlanta the sprawl poster child. Sprawl has caused the region's ranking as a favored corporate location to be downgraded. The region's economy depends heavily on keeping traffic moving along the three interstate highways (I-20, I-75, and I-85). Atlanta sits at the hub of this sprawling auto-dependent region. The Tom Moreland Interchange or "Spaghetti Junction" (the interchange where I-85 and I-285 come together) typifies the traffic and pollution that poor planning has brought to greater Atlanta. Sprawl represented progress. And the automobile is the undisputed king of the road. Writing in its 1999 Atlanta Region Outlook, the Atlanta Regional Commission sees highways as a mixed blessing and a key factor in the region's success:

> The Atlanta region's highway system has been a primary catalyst of economic growth and development for the past two decades. Suburban development has followed the freeway system as shopping centers, hotels, and office and industrial parks have risen at exits and major intersections. . . . While transportation improvements have served and continue to serve as generators of growth in this region, related problems have emerged. The dependency of the region's population on the automobile to access home and job played a large role in the region's failure to meet federal air quality standards under the Clean Air Act. This failure jeopardizes our ability to continue to secure the federal funding needed to build and maintain infrastructure needed to serve projected growth.[41]

Atlanta's political class considered sprawl a fact of life until confronted with the realities of the federal Clean Air Act.[42] The Atlanta metropolitan area has been in violation of the Clean Air Act for some time now. The region is a nonattainment area for ground-level ozone, with cars, trucks, and buses as the largest source of this pollution. Ozone is formed by the reaction of oxygen radicals with precursors such as volatile organic compounds and nitrogen oxides (NO$_x$), common components of car exhaust.[43]

Transportation and land-use plans have also contributed to and exacerbated social and economic inequities. Freeway congestion tells the story. Building roads to everywhere is the problem—not the solution. Despite decades of transportation investments, residents of the region face severe congestion, drive farther, breathe unhealthy air, and are more automobile dependent than ever before. For many Atlantans, the automobile has become their home away from home.

Sprawl is the reason why Atlanta residents drive long distances to shop and get to work and to school. For the period from 1990 to 2020, Atlantans are expected to travel an average of 15,000 miles per year. On average, people in the region drive 34 miles per day—more than anyone else on the face of the planet (50 percent farther than Los Angeles area residents). Atlantans lead the nation in miles driven per day (over 100 million miles per day).

The Atlanta region has been tagged the "most sprawl-threatened large city" in the United States.[44] Traffic congestion was a major component in the Sierra Club ranking of sprawl-threatened cities. The Atlanta region had more than 2.5 million registered vehicles in 1995, up from 1.9 million registered vehicles in 1986. The largest increase in registered vehicles during this period came in Gwinnett and Cobb counties. The number of Gwinnett County vehicles jumped from 261,674 to 412,885 between 1986 and 1995. Similarly, Cobb County vehicles increased from 366,514 in 1985 to 476,967 in 1996.[45] The two northern suburban counties alone added more than 261,000 vehicles to the region's crowded roads during the 10-year period.

Most Atlantans drive to their jobs. The region's economic activity centers and emerging activity centers are concentrated in the northern suburbs. Fifteen of the eighteen activity centers are located north of the I-20 Freeway, a freeway that historically divided the region racially and geographically. Only one of the five emerging activity centers is located south of the I-20 Freeway (see Figure 2.1).

The region's transportation dilemma is complicated by use and amount of the state's motor fuel tax. Georgia's motor fuel tax is one of the lowest in the nation. At 7.5 cents per gallon, the tax hardly discourages driving. Conversely, the state taxing structure has no built-in incentives to support mass transportation. The Georgia motor fuel tax currently can only be used for roads and bridges. The end result is a state transportation agency that only pays lip service to mass transit. The real money goes to sprawl-driven roads and more roads.

Atlantans are growing weary of traffic gridlock, long commutes, and polluted air. Atlanta's smog is also hurting its image as an attractive business climate. Amid signs that federal highway dollars would be frozen, Georgia's

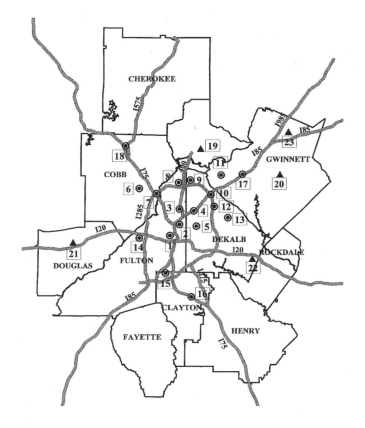

Activity Centers

1. Atlanta Central Business District
2. Midtown/Pershing Point
3. Buckhead
4. N. Druid Hills/I-85
5. Emory/CDC
6. Lockheed/Dobbins
7. Cumberland/Galleria
8. Sandy Springs
9. Perimeter Center
10. Doraville/I-85
11. Peachtree Corners
12. Northlake
13. Mountain Industrial District
14. Fulton Industrial District
15. Hartsfield International Airport
16. Southlake
17. Gwinnett Place
18. Town Center at Cobb

Emerging Activity Centers

19. North Point
20. Lawrenceville
21. Arbor Place
22. Stone Crest
23. Mall of Georgia

Figure 2.1. Atlanta Economic Activity Centers. *Source:* Atlanta Regional Commission, *Outlook Atlanta* (1998).

Environmental Protection Division (EPD) helped to create the Partnership for a Smog-Free Georgia (PSG). The PSG operates from the workplace and is the beginning point for changing Atlantans' commuting habits. Since its birth in 1998, PSG has recruited over 160 "partners" into its program. The program also has a dozen public sector partners and links to 85 state agencies and universities and 25 federal agencies. Some of the large corporate partners include the Coca-Cola Company, Delta Airlines, Turner Broadcasting Systems, BellSouth, and IBM.[46]

After making some progress in reducing NO_x emissions in the early 1990s, as a result of cleaner-running cars and tighter emission inspections, the region is now experiencing reversals in air quality. In the summer of 1999, the Atlanta region experienced 37 consecutive ozone-alert days. The region exceeds the National Ambient Air Quality Standards for ozone by 33 to 50 percent.

The Atlanta Regional Commission (ARC) is the metropolitan planning organization (MPO) responsible for land use and transportation planning in the region. In order to receive federal transportation funds, ARC was required to develop a Transportation Improvement Program (TIP) that would conform to federal standards. ARC developed an Interim Transportation Improvement Program (ITIP).[47] Because of the severe ozone nonattainment, the federal government criticized the ARC's plan for concentrating too heavily on roads and failing to show how it would improve the region's poor air quality. Federal officials have also identified public participation as a major problem in ARC's planning and decision making.[48]

In 1998, two separate coalitions of citizens groups challenged ARC's leadership, planning, and decision making that leans toward new roads. Several environmental organizations and a coalition of mainly African American environmental justice, neighborhood, and civic groups filed a notice to sue (under the Clean Air Act) the ARC, state, and federal government for approving 61 "grandfathered" new road projects funded under the ITIP that they felt would add to and exacerbate the region's already severe air quality problem.[49]

In addition to challenging the illegal exemption of grandfathered road projects, the environmental justice coalition raised equity concerns with the grandfathered roads and the region's $700 million transportation spending plan.[50] The groups charged that highway-dominated plans would disproportionately and adversely affect the health and safety of African Americans and other people of color.

The environmental group followed through with a lawsuit that resulted in a settlement that eliminated 44 of the 61 grandfathered road projects.[51] Seventeen projects were allowed to proceed because Georgia DOT had already awarded contracts to construct the roads. The settlement freed up millions of dollars for transportation alternatives that will improve air quality and mobility in the region.[52] The settlement restricts projects from proceeding until the state includes them in a regional transportation plan that meets federal clean air standards. The settlement has several requirements: that the ARC make its computer traffic modeling public; that Georgia DOT conduct a major study of transportation and congestion in the northern suburbs; and that the U.S. DOT study the social equity impacts of transportation investments in the region.[53]

Shortly after the June 1999 settlement, the environmental justice coalition entered into informal negotiations with the U.S. DOT and state and local agencies, including the ARC, that would begin addressing transportation equity, environmental justice, and Title VI concerns of the groups.[54] Equity concerns revolve around three broad areas: how environmental justice issues are addressed in the planning process; how the benefits are distributed across various populations; and how the burdens of transportation investments are distributed across various populations.

Preliminary negotiations call for a two-phase analysis of transportation equity in the Atlanta region. Phase one consists primarily of addressing the "procedural aspect of the planning process, focusing on how public participation of low income and minority communities can be enhanced and how the concerns of these communities can be better identified and addressed in the planning process."[55] Phase two will focus on the "substantive outcomes of the planning process, examining the distribution of transportation burdens and benefits to low income and minority communities and expanding effective participation by low income and minority communities in the planning process."[56]

Getting There on Public Transit

Nationally, only about 5.3 percent of all Americans use public transit to get to work.[57] Only 11.1 percent of the nation's commuters use car pools. Most American workers opt for the private automobile that provides them speed and convenience. Generally, people who commute using public transit spend twice as much time traveling as those who use their cars. The average commute takes about 20 minutes in a car, 38 minutes on a bus, and 45 minutes on a train. Nationally, 79.6 percent of the commuters drive alone to work.[58] People of color are twice as likely to use nonauto modes of travel (public transit, walk, bicycle) to get to work than their white counterparts (see Table 2.3).

The percentage of Atlantan commuters using public transit to get to work, 4.7 percent, is lower than the national average. The percentage of workers who commute using public transit for comparable U.S. metropolitan areas includes: Boston (14.2%), Chicago (17.1%), San Francisco Bay

Public transit operates in only 3 of the 10 metro Atlanta counties.

Table 2.3. How People Get to Work in the United States

	People of Color in Cities	Whites (Non-Hispanic) in Cities	Entire Population in U.S.
Public transit	20.3	7.3	5.3
Walk	5.8	5.4	3.9
Bicycle	0.5	0.7	0.4
Total nonauto	26.6	13.4	9.6

Source: U.S. Department of Commerce, Bureau of the Census (1993).

Area (19.5%), and New York/Tri State (47.3%). Atlanta did fare better than Detroit, the "Motor City," (2.4%) in getting commuters out of their cars and into public transit. Overall, African American Atlantan commuters are more likely to use public transit than are whites. In Atlanta, 28.2 percent of black males and 35.0 percent of black females take public transit to work. On the other hand, 4.4 percent of white males and 6.7 percent of white females Atlantans ride public transit to work.[59]

Getting There on MARTA

The 10-county Atlanta metropolitan area has a regional public transit system only in name. The Metropolitan Atlanta Rapid Transit Authority (MARTA) serves just two counties, Fulton and DeKalb (see Figure 2.2). In the 1960s,

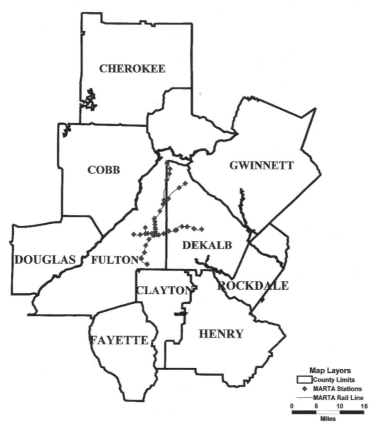

Figure 2.2. MARTA Rail Line

MARTA was hailed as the solution to the region's growing traffic and pollution problems. The first referendum to create a five-county rapid rail system failed in 1968. However, in 1971, the city of Atlanta, Fulton County, and DeKalb County approved a referendum for a 1 percent sales tax to support a rapid rail and feeder bus system. Cobb County and Gwinnett County voters rejected the MARTA system.

MARTA has grown from 13 rail stations in 1979 to 36 rail stations in 1999. Two additional stations (Sandy Springs and North Springs) along the north line are under construction.[60] With its $270.4 million annual budget, MARTA operates 700 buses and 240 rail cars. The system handles over 534,000 passengers on an average weekday. MARTA operates 154 bus routes that cover 1,531 miles and carry 275,000 passengers on an average weekday. MARTA's rail lines cover 100 miles, with cars carrying 259,000 passengers on an average weekday. MARTA's two new northern stations, Sandy Springs and North Springs, are expected to open in December 2000.

Where MARTA builds the next lines is hotly debated among diverse neighborhood constituents in Atlanta, Fulton County, and DeKalb County. Competition between MARTA's service area "haves" and "have-nots" will likely intensify in the future.[61] Just how far MARTA lines extend has proved to be a thorny issue. There is no agreement where MARTA should go next. Several proposals are under consideration to extend MARTA lines: one north up GA 400, one west from the H. E. Holmes station to Fulton Industrial Boulevard, and another southeast from near Hapeville to serve a fifth runway at Hartsfield Atlanta International Airport.[62] Politics may play a role in determining where the next MARTA lines go, since Fulton County has 34 miles of track compared to 15 miles in DeKalb County.

Talk of expanding the MARTA system into the suburbs raises a red flag among many suburbanites. A proposal by MARTA for a 4.5-mile, light-rail line that would extend the Lindbergh station into the Emory University area and on to Northlake Mall angered residents in the neighborhoods north of Decatur.[63] Discussion of rail without using MARTA can generate some agreement among suburban homeowners.[64]

Who Rides MARTA?

A recent rider survey revealed that 78 percent of MARTA's rail and bus riders are African American and other people of color.[65] Whites make up 22 percent of MARTA riders.

Where Do MARTA Riders Live?

Over 45 percent of MARTA riders live in the city of Atlanta, 14 percent live in the remainder of Fulton County, 25 percent live in DeKalb County, and 16 percent of MARTA riders live outside MARTA's service area.

Where Are Weekday MARTA Riders Headed?

The majority (58%) of MARTA's weekday riders are on their way to work. The second-highest use of MARTA was for getting to medical centers and other services (21%). Other MARTA riders use the system for attending special events (8%), shopping (7%), and school.

Who Pays for MARTA?

Even who pays the tab for MARTA is questioned. MARTA's operating budget comes from sales tax (46%), fares (34%), the FTA and other sources (20%). Only Fulton and DeKalb county residents pay for the upkeep and expansion of the system, with a one-cent MARTA sales tax. Revenues from bus fares generated $5 million more than that taken in by rail in 1997.[66] In 1999, the regular one-way fare on MARTA was $1.50, up from $1.00 in 1992.

Who Uses MARTA's Parking Spaces?

MARTA provides nearly 21,000 parking spaces at 23 of its 36 transit stations. Parking at MARTA lots is free except for the overnight lots that cost $3 per day. MARTA provides 1,342 spaces in four overnight lots. All of the overnight lots are on MARTA's North Line. It is becoming increasingly difficult to find a parking space in some MARTA lots. A recent license tag survey, "Who Parks-and-Rides," covering the period 1988–1997, revealed that 44 percent of the cars parked at MARTA lots were from outside the MARTA Fulton/DeKalb county service area.[67] It appears that Fulton and DeKalb county tax payers are subsidizing people who live in outlying counties who park their cars at the park-and-ride lots and ride on MARTA trains into the city and to the airport.

How Has MARTA Impacted Surrounding Development?

Many urban neighborhoods have waited decades for the economic benefits associated with MARTA stations. A 1997 study found MARTA had no significant impact in shaping the region's development pattern. On the other hand, sprawl development and highways were cited as the dominant players. These factors have also hindered transit-oriented development (TOD) around many MARTA stations. Of particular concern is the significant decline in employment in central city neighborhoods.[68] In recent years, MARTA has begun to take a more active role in encouraging development around its stations. MARTA and the Atlanta Development Authority (ADA) have identified some nine sites for mixed-use developments.[69]

TOD got a shot in the arm in 1999 when BellSouth (one of the area's largest employers) announced that it would move 13,000 of its employees to new offices to be built near the MARTA Lindbergh station.[70] BellSouth's plan would also consolidate much of its suburban operations in offices near MARTA's North Springs (under construction), Doraville, and College Park stations.[71]

Getting There on Cobb Community Transit

Cobb County created its own transit system in 1989. Cobb Community Transit (CCT) operates 41 buses that cover 345 miles. The suburban system carries an average of 9,300 passengers on weekdays. The one-way fare inside Cobb County is $1.25. The fare to a MARTA connection is $3 one-way and $4 round-trip (both include MARTA transfers). CCT has limited links to MARTA. However, CCT buses take riders directly into several MARTA stations and stop at the curb in front of major employers. It also operates express routes that run from park-and-ride lots. Transfers are valid between CCT and MARTA. The two systems do not share funds when riders transfer.

Gwinnett and Clayton County Transit Proposals

Gwinnett and Clayton counties voted in 1998 and 1999, respectively, to start bus systems. Clayton County expects its bus system, which links to MARTA, to be operational by June 2000. Clayton County received a $4 million federal grant to help start its bus system. Gwinnett County plans to start its bus system in mid-2001, to become fully operational in 2005. Gwinnett transportation planners project daily ridership will be 1,300 on express buses and 8,000 on local buses. The fully deployed system of 74 buses and vans is expected to cost $80 million.[72]

Creating a Super Transportation Agency

Getting metro Atlantans out of their cars and into some form of coordinated and linked public transit may well be the key to solving a major part of the region's traffic and air quality problems. Widespread support for an integrated transit system exists from ordinary citizens to powerful civic leaders. A June 1998 *Atlanta Constitution* poll showed that 7 of every 10 suburban residents supported some form of a unified rail and bus system.[73] The Atlanta Chamber of Commerce 1998 MATI (Metro Atlanta Transportation Initiative) committee report endorsing the creation of a regional transportation agency even weighed in on the side of public transit.[74]

Realizing the urgent need to address traffic gridlock and metro Atlanta's growth problems, gubernatorial candidate Roy Barnes promised to create a "superagency" to handle transportation. One of the first acts the newly elected Governor Barnes pushed for was the creation of the Georgia Regional Transportation Authority, or GRTA.[75] The GRTA received final approval from the Georgia General Assembly on March 1999.[76] A 15-member GRTA board was appointed by the Governor in June 1999.[77] Governor Barnes cautions Atlantans not to expect GRTA to be a "miracle cure" that brings immediate relief to gridlocked commutes and the thick smog that blankets the skyline. He states: "This is not the end of problems. . . . It's not even the beginning of the end. But its does give us the tools to begin with."[78]

The GRTA board has the authority to coordinate projects in the metro region; fund and operate a new mass transit system and coordinate existing systems; withhold state funding to counties to motivate participation in regional transportation; veto regional development and transportation projects; provide loans or construction agreements to industries that contribute to lowering air emissions; and identify nonregional air pollution sources impacting the region and offer assistance or bring them under authority auspices.[79]

Unsafe Streets and Fear of Traffic

Poor planning affects safety. Potholes and deteriorating highways increase the likelihood of accidents.[80] Unmaintained highways may result in accidents, delays, traffic gridlocks, and pedestrian injuries. Sidewalks could greatly improve the safety of pedestrians. Recent studies reveal that the Atlanta metropolitan area is the third most dangerous large metropolitan area for walking. The region ranked just behind Fort Lauderdale and Miami, Florida, for pedestrian fatalities. Over 300 pedestrians were killed in Cobb, DeKalb, Fulton, and Gwinnett counties during 1994–1998 (see Table 2.4).[81] The Atlanta region pedestrian fatality rate has remained higher than the national rate.

Pedestrian fatality rates were highest for Fulton and DeKalb counties. Rates also varied by ethnicity. Rates for non-Hispanic blacks and Hispanics were two and six times greater, respectively, than for non-Hispanic whites.

Table 2.4. Pedestrian Fatalities in Cobb, DeKalb, Fulton, and Gwinnett Counties—1994–1998

Race/Ethnicity[a]	No. of Deaths	Percentage	Rate
Black, Non-Hispanic	*140*	*45*	*3.85*
White, Non-Hispanic	117	38	1.64
Hispanic	40	13	9.74

Source: Morbidity and Mortality Weekly Report 48 (1999).
[a]Ten persons were of "other" races/ethnicity, and race/ethnicity was unknown for two.

Atlanta, behind Fort Launderdale and Miami, is the third most dangerous place for walking—with blacks and Latinos having the highest pedestrian fatality rate.

People of color account for less than one-third of the region's population and nearly two-thirds of all the pedestrian fatalities in the region. The rate differences by race/ethnicity may be due in part to difference in walking patterns. For example, national studies show that blacks walk 82 percent more than whites, and Hispanics walk 58 percent more than non-Hispanic whites.[82] These statistics clearly point to safety issues related to walking in Atlanta, especially if one happens to be black or Hispanic.

Georgians also register fear about traffic crashes. The roads and highways are real and not imagined threats. According to a 1999 *Georgia Legislative Poll* conducted by Beth Schapiro and Associates, Metro Atlanta residents rated motor vehicle crashes at the top of "their worse fears," higher than fear of cancer, crime, or fire.[83] Over half of the metro Atlantans polled ranked fear of motor vehicle crash as their top fear. Over 68 percent of blacks compared to 48 percent of whites listed motor vehicle crashes as their worst fear.

Conclusion

Transportation is a key component to building economically viable and sustainable communities in the rapidly growing Atlanta metropolitan region. All transportation modes are not created equal. Federal transportation policies, taxing structure, and funding schemes have contributed to the inequity between various transportation modes (i.e., private automobile, rail, bus, and airplane). Georgia DOT and the ARC also have a major responsibility to ensure that their programs, policies, and practices do not discriminate against or adversely impact people of color and the poor in the region.

Transportation is essential to improving economic and physical mobility of Atlanta's poor and people of color who are concentrated in central city neighborhoods and away from suburban economic activity centers. Transportation concerns raised by environmental justice groups revolve around fairness and equity. The regions heavy-handed emphasis on road building has saddled everyone with traffic gridlock and polluted air. Atlantans are paying a high price in traffic delays, wasted energy, and health threats. Sprawl is even making some Atlantans sick, as documented in the region's alarming asthma rate.

Little regional transportation planning has taken place beyond building more and more highways. These policies have worked against developing a unified, coordinated regional transportation system. They have hit African Americans especially hard because of their heavy dependence on public transit. Transportation policies have subsidized, reinforced, and exacerbated residential segregation, economic isolation, and concentration of poverty.

Transportation has had a major role in shaping the far-flung, low-density suburban developments, congested freeways, air quality nonattainment, and loss of greenfields that make Atlanta the most "sprawl-threatened" big city in the nation. Atlantans are no longer sitting back and waiting for planners to "fix" the region's transportation problems. The politics of metro Atlanta's transportation dilemma entered the state house with the election of Governor Roy Barnes.

Barnes created a superagency—GRTA—to rein in the powerful Georgia DOT and the ineffective ARC. All eyes are now focused on GRTA and its charge of creating a unified, coordinated mass transit system in the region. Meshing the transit interests of suburban and central city residents will not be an easy task. Race is still a major factor in planning public transportation in Atlanta. Nevertheless, MARTA, which currently operates in Fulton and DeKalb counties, will need to form the centerpiece of any regionally connected transit plan that extends into the suburban counties.

Some environmental and social justice groups resorted to the courts to force local, state, and federal agencies to address the region's severe nonattainment problem. Building more roads that do nothing for cleaning up the region's dirty air just does not make sense. More roads mean more cars. More cars mean more pollution. The outcome of their efforts resulted in real transportation alternatives to roads.

Citizen-led transportation groups are challenging governmental agencies to open up their planning process and computer modeling, diversify their boards, and begin addressing land use, air quality, and equity issues that disproportionately and adversely impact the region's low-income and people of color communities. Local community leaders are also calling for transportation agencies to identify and address inequitable distribution of transportation benefits and burdens.

Finally, transportation agencies need to work with environmental justice, community-based groups as well as historically black colleges and universities in the design of public involvement and communication plans to reach the most vulnerable populations—urban communities, the poor, the elderly, the disabled, the carless, the young, and people of color.

Notes

1. David Bollier, *How Smart Growth Can Stop Sprawl: A Fledgling Citizen Movement Expands.* Washington, DC: Essential Books, 1998, p. 8.
2. Henry L. Diamond and Patrick F. Noonan, *Land Use in America.* Washington, DC: Island Press, 1996, p. 85.
3. Robert Cervero, *America's Suburban Centers: The Land Use Transportation Link.* Boston: Unwin Hyman, 1989, p. 8.
4. David Bollier, *How Smart Growth Can Stop Sprawl,* p. 8.
5. Joey Ledford, "By the Dollar, Congestion Costly for Drivers Across Atlanta," *Atlanta Journal-Constitution,* November 20, 1998, p. D2.
6. Davis L. Schrank and Timothy J. Lomax, *Urban Roadway Congestion Annual*

Report—1998. College Station: Texas Transportation Institute, Texas A&M University, 1998.

7. Ibid.

8. Scott Bowles, "National Gridlock: 167 Worst Bottlenecks," *USA Today,* November 23, 1999, pp. 1A–2A.

9. Charles W. Schmidt, "The Specter of Sprawl," *Environmental Health Perspectives* 106 (June 1998), p. 275.

10. F. Kaid Benfield, Matthew D. Raimi, and Don Chen, *Once There Were Greenfields: How Urban Sprawl Is Undermining America's Environment, Economy and Social Fabric.* New York: Natural Resource Defense Council and Surface Transportation Policy Project, 1999.

11. Conservation Law Foundation, *City Routes, City Rights: Building Livable Neighborhoods and Environmental Justice by Fixing Transportation.* Boston: Conservation Law Foundation, 1998, p. 18.

12. John Lewis, "Foreword," in Robert D. Bullard and Glenn S. Johnson, eds., *Just Transportation Dismantling Race and Class Barriers to Mobility.* Gabriola Island, BC: New Society Publishers, 1997, pp. xi–xii.

13. Bullard and Johnson, *Just Transportation,* pp. 7–21. See H.P. Hak, H. Abbey, and R.C. Talamo, "Prevalence of Asthma and Health Service Utilization of Asthmatic Children in an Inner City," *Journal of Allergy and Clinical Immunology* 70 (1982), pp. 367–372; I.F. Goldstein and A.L. Weinstein, "Air Pollution and Asthma: Effects of Exposure to Short-Term Sulfur Dioxide Peaks," *Environmental Research* 40 (1986), pp. 332–345; J. Schwartz, D. Gold, D.W. Dockey, et al., "Predictors of Asthma and Persistent Wheeze in a National Sample of Children in the United States," *American Review of Respiratory Disease* 142 (1990), pp. 555–562; as cited in Robert Bullard, "Epilogue," in Bullard and Johnson, *Just Transportation.*

14. David J. Forkenbrock and Lisa A. Schweitzer, *Environmental Justice and Transportation Investment Policy.* Iowa City: University of Iowa Public Policy Center, 1997, p. 69.

15. William Clinton, "Federal Actions Address Environmental Justice Minority Populations and Low-Income Populations." *Federal Register* 59, Section 1–1011, 7630 (1994).

16. Conservation Law Foundation, *City Routes, City Rights: Building Livable Neighborhoods and Environmental Justice by Fixing Transportation.* Boston: Conservation Law Foundation, 1998, p. 24.

17. See "Title VI of the Civil Rights Act of 1964," 42 U.S.C. Pub. 88-352 (July 2, 1964).

18. David J. Forkenbrock and Lisa A. Schweitzer. *Environmental Justice and Transportation Investment Policy,* p. 1.

19. Todd Litman, *Evaluating Transportation Equity.* Victoria, BC: Victoria Transport Policy Institute, December 1997, p. 1.

20. Ibid.

21. Eric Mann, *A New Vision for Urban Transportation.* Los Angeles: Labor Community Strategy Center, 1996.

22. For an in-depth discussion of equity, see R.D. Bullard and G.S. Johnson, eds., *Just Transportation*, pp. 1–6.
23. See Robert D. Bullard, "Solid Waste Sites and the Black Houston Community," *Sociological Inquiry* 53 (Spring, 1983): 273-288; United Church of Christ Commission for Racial Justice, *Toxic Wastes and Race in the United States: A National Study of the Racial and Socioeconomic Characteristics of Communities with Hazardous Waste Sites* (New York: Commission for Racial Justice, 1987); Dick Russell, "Environmental Racism," *The Amicus Journal* 11 (Spring 1989), pp. 22–32; Eric Mann, *L.A.'s Lethal Air: New Strategies for Policy, Organizing, and Action* (Los Angeles: Labor/Community Strategy Center, 1991); Leslie A. Nieves, "Not in Whose Backyard? Minority Population Concentrations and Noxious Facility Sites," paper presented at the Annual Meeting of the American Association for the Advancement of Science, Chicago (February 1991); D.R. Wernette and L.A. Nieves, "Breathing Polluted Air: Minorities are Disproportionately Exposed," *EPA Journal* 18 (March/April 1992), pp. 16–17; Robert D. Bullard, "In Our Backyards: Minority Communities Get Most of the Dumps," *EPA Journal* 18 (March/April 1992), pp. 11–12; Bunyan Bryant and Paul Mohai, eds., *Race and the Incidence of Environmental Hazards* (Boulder, CO: Westview Press, 1992).
24. Robert D. Bullard, J. Eugene Grigsby III, and Charles Lee, eds., *Residential Apartheid: The American Legacy*. Los Angeles: UCLA Center for African American Studies Publication, 1994, chap. 1.
25. David J. Forkenbrock and Lisa A. Schweitzer, *Environmental Justice and Transportation Investment Policy*. Iowa City: Public Policy Center, University of Iowa, 1997, p. 68.
26. Ibid.
27. Joe R. Feagin and Clairece B. Feagin, *Discrimination American Style: Institutional Racism and Sexism* (Malabar, FL: Krieger Publishing, 1986); Robert D. Bullard and Joe R. Feagin, "Racism and the City," in M. Gottdiener and C.V. Pickvance, eds., *Urban Life in Transition* (Newbury Park, CA: Sage, 1991), pp. 55–76.
28. J.M. Jones, "The Concept of Racism and Its Changing Reality." *Impact of Racism on White Americans*. Beverly Hills: Sage, 1981, p. 47.
29. Robert D. Bullard, ed., *Confronting Environmental Racism: Voices from the Grassroots* (Boston: South End, 1993); Robert D. Bullard, "The Threat of Environmental Racism," *Natural Resources and Environment* 7 (Winter 1993), pp. 23–26; Bunyan Bryant and Paul Mohai, eds., *Race and the Incidence of Environmental Hazards;* Regina Austin and Michael Schill, "Black, Brown, Poor and Poisoned: Minority Grassroots Environmentalism and the Quest for Eco-Justice," *Kansas Journal of Law and Public Policy* 1 (1991), pp. 69–82; Kelly C. Colquette and Elizabeth A. Henry Robertson, "Environmental Racism: The Causes, Consequences, and Commendations" *Tulane Environmental Law Journal* 5 (1991), pp. 153–207; Rachel D. Godsil, "Remedying Environmental Racism." *Michigan Law Review* 90 (1991), pp. 394–427.
30. Michael Omi and Howard Winant, *Racial Formation in the United States: From the 1960's to the 1980's*. New York: Routledge and Kegan Paul, 1986, pp. 76–78.
31. Bullard and Johnson, *Just Transportation*, pp. 7–21.

32. Don Chen, "Linking Social Equity with Livable Communities," in Bullard and Johnson, eds., *Just Transportation*, p. 39.

33. David W. Chen, "Suit Charging Racism at Suburban Mall is Settled," *New York Times*, November 18, 1999, p. A25.

34. Robin D.G. Kelly, "Freedom Riders (the Sequel)," *Nation*, February 6, 1996.

35. Eric Mann, "Confronting Transit Racism in Los Angeles," in Bullard and Johnson, eds., *Just Transportation*, pp. 68–83.

36. Steve Lopez, "The Few, the Proud, the Bus Riders," *Time*, August 31, 1998, p. 8.

37. Ibid., p. 69.

38. Conservation Law Foundation, *City Routes, City Rights*, p. 69.

39. David Oedel, "The Legacy of Jim Crow in Macon, Georgia," in Bullard and Johnson, eds., *Just Transportation*, pp. 97–109.

40. Ibid., p. 100.

41. Ibid., pp. 4–5.

42. David Goldberg, "Atlanta Suburbanites Thinking Regionally," *Neighborhood Works*, November/December 1997, p. 13.

43. Charles W. Schmidt, "The Specter of Sprawl," *Environmental Health Perspectives* 106 (June 1998), p. 276.

44. Sierra Club, *The Dark Side of the American Dream: The Cost and Consequences of Suburban Sprawl*. College Park, MD: Sierra Club, 1998, p. 5.

45. "Growing a New Atlanta," *Atlanta Journal-Constitution*, June 8, 1997, p. G5.

46. Gita M. Smith, "Atlanta's 'Working' Solution to Smog," *Atlanta Journal-Constitution*, August 30, 1999, pp. E1, E5.

47. Atlanta Regional Commission, *Proposed 1998 Amendments to the Interim Atlanta Region Transportation Improvement Program FY 1999–FY 2001*. Atlanta: ARC, October 1998.

48. U.S. Department of Transportation, *Federal Highway Administration, Certification Report for the Atlanta Transportation Management Area*, Washington, DC: FHA, September 1998.

49. On November 10, 1998, three environmental groups, Georgians for Transportation Alternatives, Georgia Conservancy, and Sierra Club, filed a 60-day notice to sue local, state, and federal transportation agencies under the Clean Air Act.

50. On December 16, 1998, a coalition of social justice and environmental groups filed a "Notice of Intent to Sue to Remedy Violations of the Clean Air Act," with local, state, and federal transportation agencies. The groups that signed the letter included the Environmental Defense Fund, Southern Organizing Committee for Economic and Social Justice, Rainbow/PUSH Southern Region, Save Atlanta's Fragile Environment, North Georgia African American Environmental Justice Network, Southwest Atlanta Community Roundtable, Center for Democratic Renewal, Rebel Forest Neighborhood Task Force, and Georgia Coalition for People's Agenda.

51. David Goldberg, "17 of 61 Road Projects OK'd," *Atlanta Journal-Constitution*, June 21, 1999, p. A1.

52. Southern Environmental Law Center, "SELC Scores Major Victory in Atlanta Lawsuit," *Southern Resources* (Summer 1999), pp. 1, 5.

53. Ibid.
54. U.S. Department of Transportation, Federal Highway Administration, "Assessment of Environmental Justice Issues in Atlanta Proposed Work Plan Paper," prepared for discussion meeting held on June 28, 1999.
55. Ibid., p. 1.
56. Ibid., p. 2.
57. U.S. Department of Commerce, Bureau of the Census, 1990, Census of Population, *Social and Economic Characteristics,* Washington, DC: Government Printing Office, 1993, Tables 64, 66–68, 125.
58. See Scott Bowles, "Daily Jams Don't Keep Commuters from Cars," *USA Today,* April 4, 1999, p. 17A.
59. Sidney Davis, "Transportation and Black Atlanta," in Bob Holmes, ed., *Status of Black Atlanta 1994.* Atlanta: The Southern Center for Studies in Public Policy, 1994, p. 79.
60. Research Atlanta, Inc., *The Impact of MARTA on Station Area Development.* Atlanta: School of Policy Studies, Georgia State University, 1997, p. 2.
61. Bill Torpy, "Haves, Have-Nots Battle over MARTA Access," *Atlanta Journal Constitution,* May 25, 1998, p. E1.
62. Ibid.; Susan Laccetti Meyer, "Where Should MARTA Go Next?" *Atlanta Journal-Constitution,* December 5, 1998, p. A18.
63. Bill Torpy, "MARTA Proposal Spurs Anger," *Atlanta Journal-Constitution,* October 30, 1998, p. F2.
64. David Goldberg, "Atlanta Suburbanites Thinking Regionally," *Neighborhood Works,* November/December 1997, p. 14.
65. Metropolitan Rapid Transit Authority, based on interviews of more than 3,000 riders in May 1999.
66. Metropolitan Atlanta Rapid Transit Authority, Division of Planning and Policy Development, Transit Research and Analysis, *Chronology,* Atlanta: Author, June, 1996.
67. See Metropolitan Atlanta Rapid Transit Authority, Division of Planning and Policy Development, Department of Research Analysis, "Tag Survey 1988–1997," MARTA, 1999; Goro O. Mitchell, "Transportation, Air Pollution, and Social Equity in Atlanta," in Bob Holmes, ed., *The Status of Black Atlanta* (Atlanta: Southern Center for Studies in Public Policy, Clark Atlanta University, 1999), p. 120.
68. Research Atlanta, Inc., *The Impact of MARTA on Station Area Development.* Atlanta, Georgia: School of Policy Studies Georgia State University, 1997, p. 17.
69. David Pendered, "MARTA Aims to Help Shape Development," *Atlanta Journal-Constitution,* October 19, 1998, p. E1; David Pendered, "MARTA Makes Its Move," *Atlanta Journal-Constitution,* March 29, 1999, p. E1.
70. Joey Ledford, "Beating Traffic Woes by Moving to Town," *Atlanta Journal-Constitution,* February 5, 1999, p. C2.
71. David Pendered, "A Bold New Frontier for MARTA," *Atlanta Journal-Constitution,* February 1, 1999, p. F3.
72. Stacy Shelton, "Gwinnett Knows Buses' Success Hinges on Convenience,"

Atlanta Journal-Constitution, September 20, 1999, p. B6; David Pendered, "Transit Details: Logistics Challenge," *Atlanta Journal-Constitution*, September 20, 1999, p. B6.

73. David Goldberg, "Polls Say Suburbanites Aren't Hostile to MARTA," *Atlanta Journal-Constitution*, June 28, 1998, E7.

74. Atlanta Chamber of Commerce, Metro Atlanta Transportation Initiative, "Addressing Congestion in the Region: Final Report," *MATI* (November 23, 1998).

75. David Goldberg, "A Guiding Hand: Does Metro Atlanta Need a New Agency to Handle Growth Problems? Many Residents Say Yes, But Making it Happen Could Be Tough," *Atlanta Journal-Constitution*, July 20, 1998, p. E1.

76. Kathey Pruitt, "GRTA Clears Final Legislature Hurdles," *Atlanta Journal-Constitution*, March 24, 1999.

77. David Goldberg and Kathey Pruitt, "GRTA Occupies Hot Seat," *Atlanta Journal-Constitution*, June 4, 1999, p. A1.

78. Governor Roy Barnes as quoted in Kathey Pruitt, "Barnes: GRTA No Miracle Cure," *Atlanta Journal-Constitution*, April 7, 1999, p. B1.

79. Ibid.

80. Cameron Y. Yee, *Crash Course in Bay Area Transportation Investment*, San Francisco: The Urban Habitat Program, 1999, p. 28.

81. See B.A. Cohen, R. Wiles, C. Campbell, D. Chen, J. Kruse, and J. Corless, *Mean Streets: Pedestrian Safety and Reform of the Nation's Transportation Law* (Washington, DC: Environmental Working Group/The Tides Center, April 1997); Centers for Disease Control, "Pedestrian Fatalities—Cobb, DeKalb, Fulton, and Gwinnett Counties, Georgia, 1994–1998," *Morbidity and Mortality Weekly Report* 48 (1999), pp. 601–605; U.S. Department of Transportation, National Highway Traffic Safety Administration, *Traffic Safety Facts 1997* (Washington, DC: Author, 1998).

82. U.S. Department of Transportation, FHWA, Office of Highway Policy Information. *Our Nation's Travel: 1995 NPTS Early Results Report, 1997*. Report No. FHWA-PL97-028. Washington, DC: Government Printing Office, 1997.

83. Joey Ledford, "Rating Risks: Georgians Fear Traffic Crashes More Than Cancer." *Atlanta Journal-Constitution*, February 18, 1999, p. C1.

CHAPTER 3

Impact of Building Roads to Everywhere

James Chapman

Despite decades of transportation investment, residents of the Atlanta region face worse traffic congestion, drive farther, and are more automobile-dependent than ever. They also continue to breathe polluted air. The Atlanta Regional Commission estimates that if no transportation or land use changes are made in a timely fashion, transportation conditions will get dramatically worse. These problems create unprecedented opportunities to move the Atlanta region away from roads and sprawl-based development patterns to ones that offer more travel choices, a cleaner environment, and more livable neighborhoods.

The Atlanta Regional Commission (ARC) is the metropolitan planning organization (MPO) for over 3 million people living in the 3,000-square-mile, 10-county Atlanta region (Cherokee, Clayton, Cobb, DeKalb, Douglas, Fayette, Fulton, Gwinnett, Henry, and Rockdale counties). The ARC has a policy board consisting of 39 members—10 county commission chairs, 12 mayors, 1 Atlanta city council member, 1 Georgia Department of Community Affairs representative, and 15 citizens appointed by the elected officials.

The ARC is the lead agency responsible for coordinating the development of the Atlanta Regional Transportation Plan (RTP),[1] the region's 25-year, $35 billion, long-range transportation planning document, and the Transportation Improvement Program (TIP). It is also responsible for the three-year, $2.8 billion, short-range list of specific projects to be funded. The development of the RTP and TIP is done in cooperation with the following implementing agencies: local governments, the Georgia Department of Transportation (GDOT), the Metropolitan Atlanta Rapid Transit Authority

(MARTA), and the newly created Georgia Regional Transportation Authority (GRTA)[2]. The TIP addresses the long-range planning goals by prioritizing projects and allocating to them approximately $900 million annually in federal and local funds. These projects include mass transit, bridges, highways, bicycling, walking facilities, and maintenance.[3]

The ARC is currently updating the region's long-range transportation plan. This plan[4] establishes the region's priorities and goals for the next 25 years. However, the plans must be approved by an ARC board that is functionally dominated by suburban county commission chairs who have been reluctant to support concentrated growth patterns or funding for transportation options.

The 10-county Atlanta metro area, plus Coweta, Forsyth, and Paulding counties, ranks among the worst violators of federal standards for ground-level ozone. Ground-level ozone is a highly reactive gas that forms on hot summer days[5] when car exhaust and pollution from other sources combine with heat and sunlight. When Atlanta's air violates federal standards,[6] residents throughout the region are told to refrain from outdoor activity or run the risk of experiencing breathing difficulties. Those particularly at risk include children, the elderly, those who work or exercise outdoors, and those who suffer from respiratory ailments, such as asthma.[7]

Cars and trucks are responsible for over 50 percent of the region's emissions that combine to form ground-level ozone pollution. To reduce pollution levels, federal law requires transportation policy makers in Atlanta,[8] and other cities suffering from dirty air, to work within an established "pollution budget" or risk losing federal dollars[9] for road construction projects.

Metro Atlanta is arguably facing the biggest transportation and air pollution crisis in the nation.[10] Over 110 million vehicle miles per day are driven on the region's 18,600 miles of roads. At 34 miles per woman, man, and child, Atlantans drive more miles per day than residents of any other metropolitan area in the nation. The average travel time to work was 26 minutes in the Atlanta region in 1995, greater than any other metropolitan area in the United States. ARC estimates that traffic congestion levels by 2020 will result in Atlantans, on a system-wide average, driving 25 percent slower than in 1990. This should come as little surprise given the dearth of transportation options to driving alone. Only 3 of the 13 nonattainment counties (Cobb, DeKalb, Fulton) have public transit.[11] Atlantans' love for their automobile has resulted in the region's failure to comply with the federal standards under the Clean Air Act. The region has an inadequate supply of sidewalks and bicycle-safe roads. The existing high-occupancy vehicle lane system is truncated at I-285, which is the existing beltway.

The region's 2020 population and employment levels are forecasted to be nearly 4.2 million and 2.5 million, respectively, an addition of 1.6 million

Atlantans drive a record 34 miles per day—50 percent further than drivers in Los Angeles.

people since 1990 and 1 million jobs since 2000.[12] Areas north[13] of the Atlanta core are projected to continue a 30-year trend by receiving nearly 60 percent of the region's population growth and more than 72 percent of the region's employment growth.

Litigation over Grandfathered Road Expansions

In 1996, for the first time, the GDOT and the region's local governments found themselves unable to continue their road building plans. An emissions analysis of the proposed three-year list of transportation investments projected that the resulting motor vehicle emissions would violate Clean Air Act requirements for ground-level ozone. These air pollution problems in the region, and the lack of a state plan to reduce pollution, resulted in the federal government constraining the types of transportation projects that can be funded with federal dollars. At the time, the three types of projects allowed to proceed were those with neutral (exempt projects) or beneficial (transportation control measures) impacts on air quality or those that have reached a certain point in the planning process (grandfathered projects.)

Due to metro Atlanta's serious "nonattainment" of air pollution standards, federal law requires transportation policymakers to adopt a long-range plan that stays within an established pollution "budget" to reduce ground-level ozone, or risk losing federal funds[14] for highway projects. Georgia established the budgets at 214 tons per day of oxides of nitrogen (NO_x) and 183 tons per day of volatile organic compounds (VOCs). A plan with projected emissions that comply with these budgets is said to conform to Clean Air Act requirements. A conformity lapse refers to a time during which a region does not comply because of failure to adopt a transportation plan that achieves the necessary budgets. The Atlanta region's conformity lapse began January 17, 1998.

With the January 17 deadline looming, the White House's Council on Environmental Quality (CEQ) mediated disagreements between the Federal Highway Administration (FHWA), Federal Transit Administration (FTA), and the U.S. Environmental Protection Agency (EPA) over the issue of allowing the construction of highway expansions during a time when the region has no transportation plan conforming to air quality standards. The EPA raised concerns about the basis for proceeding with, as well as the actual impact of, additional highway widening projects to FHWA. In a letter received by Larry Dreihaup, Federal Highway Administration, on January 16, 1998, John Hankinson of the EPA wrote, "[T]he 1995 Atlanta Regional Transportation Plan (RTP) update is of limited utility as a basis for National Environmental Policy Act (NEPA) clearance under the Clean Air Act and the Intermodal Surface Transportation Efficiency Act provisions for 'grandfathering' additional single-occupant vehicle (SOV) capacity-increasing highway projects during a conformity lapse. . . . EPA remains concerned that these deficiencies mean that the remaining SOV capacity-increasing highway projects may . . . contribute to new violations, worsen existing violations, or delay attainment of the ozone standard in the 13-county region."[15] The federal agencies grandfathered, or allowed to be built, over 61 capacity-expanding highway projects costing approximately $700 million despite the lack of conformity (see Figure 3.1).

When the GDOT and ARC board first proposed, with the U.S. Department of Transportation's (USDOT) support, allowing road expansion projects to continue despite the lack of a regional plan, Georgians for Transportation Alternatives (GTA) and others objected. GTA and others contend, and ARC staff agreed, these projects would likely make air pollution levels worse. GTA and others were told that funding these projects was legal, because they had reached a stage in their implementation that grandfathered them from the Clean Air Act conformity requirements. This argument ignored the fact that, legal or not, it makes no sense to spend $700 million on 61 road expansion projects[16] which dig us deeper into an air pollution hole.

On November 10, 1998, after exhausting administrative options and other attempts to achieve compliance with the law, GTA, the Georgia Chapter of

Figure 3.1. Metro Atlanta "Grandfathered" Road Projects. *Source:* Atlanta Regional Commission, "Grandfathered Road Projects," ARC handout map (1998).

the Sierra Club, and the Georgia Conservancy, represented by the Southern Environmental Law Center, filed a 60-day notice of intent to sue the USDOT, the Georgia DOT, and the ARC[17] for violations of the Clean Air Act. The notice challenged the approval of funding for the grandfathered road expansion projects that were not part of a conforming long-range plan or transportation improvement program. These grandfathered projects would severely impact the air quality in the Atlanta metropolitan area.[18]

After several unsuccessful attempts to achieve an out-of-court settlement, the groups formally filed a lawsuit on January 20, 1999, in the U.S. District Court for the Northern District of Georgia–*GTA, et al. v. Shackelford et al.*[19] The groups requested the following relief:

- A declaratory judgment that the decisions of defendants to adopt, approve, fund, or assist the allegedly "grandfathered" projects violates the Clean Air Act, the Transportation Equity

Act for the 21st Century, the National Environmental Policy Act, and the Administrative Procedure Act.

• Preliminarily and permanently enjoin all defendants from taking any steps to adopt, approve, fund or assist the allegedly grandfathered projects, including approving any contracts for their funding or construction.

On March 2, 1999, a very favorable decision was handed down by the federal Court of Appeals for the Washington, D.C., Circuit on a previous case brought by the Environmental Defense Fund (EDF) against the EPA. The court's decision greatly restricted federal funding for major road projects in metropolitan areas that have failed to revise their regional transportation plans to meet motor vehicle emission budgets set by states under the Clean Air Act. The decision also requires compliance with requirements enacted in 1990 that hold transportation agencies accountable for air pollution from automobile use across the United States.

The court struck down the EPA rule allowing planned highway projects to be guaranteed funding years in advance of construction, even if the transportation plan for the metropolitan area no longer meets Clean Air Act requirements. The Clean Air Act requires regions with harmful pollution levels to adopt 20-year transportation plans that will achieve regional limits on emissions from motor vehicles adopted in a state's air pollution control plan. This decision insures that federal funds may only be spent on highway projects that do not interfere with a metropolitan area's pollution cleanup plan. As a result of the decision, highway funds may be committed to a project only if the area's transportation plan meets air quality requirements when the project is ready to begin construction, and not only years in advance.[20]

The *GTA et al. v. Shackelford et al.* lawsuit was settled on June 21, 1999. The citizen plaintiffs won a landmark settlement with the USDOT to clean up the dirty air in the Atlanta metropolitan area by revising their transportation planning.[21] Building from the March 2 court decision, this settlement successfully halted funding for 44 of the 61 challenged grandfathered projects. The settlement impacted national guidance established by USDOT regarding the use of federal funds by areas with a conformity lapse. Federal funds are now only available for projects that are exempt from the conformity process; for transportation control measures that are included in an approved state air quality implementation plan; and for projects that have received approval of plans, specifications and estimates (roads), and full funding grant agreements (transit).

Additionally, the defendants agreed to submit modeling for transportation, land use, and air quality for peer review; perform additional modeling of the long-range transportation plan that reveals the air quality impacts of proposed transportation investments; undertake a comprehensive transportation study of the northern Atlanta suburbs, including meaningful consideration of transportation alternatives; and commit in writing to engage in a collaborative undertaking with affected environmental justice groups and community-based organizations to evaluate the planning process in Atlanta in terms of equitable distribution of transportation burdens and benefits.

The on-the-ground local result of the litigation was to reprogram over $250 million from the grandfathered road expansion projects to air quality beneficial projects, such as compressed natural gas buses, bicycle and pedestrian improvements to streets, bus shelters, and educational programs about air pollution and the use of transportation options.

Federal Certification of the Regional Planning Process

Every three years the USDOT reviews the Atlanta region's transportation planning process for compliance with the requirements of several different federal laws—the Federal Transportation Act, Clean Air Act, Americans with Disabilities Act, Civil Rights Act—Title VI, and Executive Order 12898 for environmental justice. According to the 1994 guidance, FHWA and FTA administrators emphasized the following areas for review during the certification process: incorporating the Federal Transportation Act's planning factors in the planning process, creating an effective public involvement plan to reach the traditionally underserved population, studying transportation investment options that offer alternatives for traffic congestion, and developing a regional transportation plan that offers consensus-based policies and projects that address the transportation concerns of the Atlanta metropolitan region.[22]

The first certification of the region's transportation planning process took five days and was conducted in 1995. The second review was completed in three days, May 6 through May 8, 1998. The two and half days of solid meetings were between the nine-member federal review team (FTA, FHWA, and EPA) and dozens of staff from the government agencies responsible for regional planning in Atlanta—ARC, GDOT, EPD, MARTA, and Cobb Community Transit.

As part of the January 1998 compromise between USDOT and EPA, USDOT agreed to perform a regional planning certification review earlier than originally scheduled.[23] The review team's final report on September 23, 1998, conditionally certified the planning process for 18 months, with specific corrective action required in three areas—long-range regional transportation planning, public involvement and its consideration, and the integration of air pollution reduction needs with transportation planning. The

ARC failed to develop a comprehensive and culturally sensitive public involvement plan for the Atlanta metropolitan planning process.[24]

The federal review team expressed some concerns about unfulfilled promises of the Vision 2020 plan (a multiyear, public involvement effort to develop a shared vision for the region) to provide a comprehensive transportation outlook for planned improvement of computer models used to forecast travel demands and emissions. In addition, the plan calls for improved public involvement with the traditionally underserved population in the Atlanta metropolitan area. The federal review team's concerns fell within three major areas: long-range transportation planning, public involvement, and integration of air pollution reduction needs and transportation planning.

Long-Range Transportation Planning

The Vision 2020 plan was a good start, but its promise has gone unfulfilled. There is no present transportation plan that exists that is fiscally constrained, intermodal, or in conformance with air quality requirements. Regional transit planning from a systems level is needed. The ARC must take into consideration the operation and maintenance costs for transportation projects that are necessary for the region. The connection between transportation and land use planning are necessary to protect air quality in the region. The utilization of computer modeling is needed to forecast present and future travel demands and emissions. The team's final report may contain a requirement for ARC to submit a work plan detailing what must be done to complete the long range transportation plan.

Public Involvement

Public involvement is of utmost importance for the Atlanta metropolitan area. The lack of feedback from participants on how their input was used in the transportation planning process is a serious issue between ARC and the public. The lack of an evaluation of the effectiveness of public involvement in the transportation planning process will result in the public feeling as if their concerns are not taken seriously. The lack of a mechanism to reach and consider the needs of the traditionally underserved population in Atlanta must be addressed by collaboration among the ARC, environmental justice groups, and community-based organizations.

Integration of Air Pollution Reduction Needs and
Transportation Planning

Integrating air pollution reduction needs with transportation planning is essential to improving the air quality in the region. Attention should be given to the promotion of a comprehensive plan that simultaneously incorporates healthy air quality and transportation planning. The encouragement of cooperation between the ARC and the EPD in conforming to the State Implementation Plan (SIP) is a step toward cooperation between transportation decisionmakers. There is a push to ensure the cooperation between GDOT and ARC in designing a conformity analysis that is used in the transportation decision process.

Needed Corrective Actions

The regional transportation planning process does not involve a thorough and comprehensive assessment of current and future travel needs. The process focuses almost solely on moving automobiles instead of people. At best, the process considers traffic congestion and then uses limited performance measures focused on vehicle-based level-of-service. There is a lack of needs assessment for such transportation options as transit, walking, and bicycling based on the location and demographics of forecasted population and employment trends.

An example of the type of needs assessment conducted in this region is outlined in *Detailing the Vision: A Development Plan for the Atlanta Region,* a technical report prepared by the ARC staff.[25] The needs identified in this document include meeting federal air quality standards, better transportation and land use relationship planning and implementation, sufficient transportation mode choices, and adequate intermodal connections. The document provides current infrastructure-based analysis of the region's transportation system—miles of roads, number of variable message signs, buses, and vehicle miles traveled. Information on how this infrastructure serves people and goods is missing, except as measured by vehicle-based level of service. For example, while total transit ridership is provided, no information is provided on the level of service, population and jobs accessible by transit, and emerging transit needs. The number of stalls in regional park and ride lots is provided, but not how well they are used and how that may change in the future.

Little interpretation is provided on the impact of traffic patterns in the region. Based on the sparse information provided about forecasted changes in vehicle miles/hours traveled, and average speed, there is no quantification of the various infrastructure changes that may be needed, such as new roads, sidewalks, bicycle lanes, public transit, vanpool service expansion, congestion pricing, and parking management. There is a lack of regional, system-level planning for public transit. What little thought is given to transit is locally based and uncoordinated, especially related to funding needs and sources. Clearly, everyone in the region would benefit from a coordinated, regionwide transit plan.

The Atlanta region's transportation planning process does not provide

Few bicycle lanes are available for Atlanta's 3 million inhabitants.

adequate public demonstration of meeting the federal requirement that federal funds not be programmed for highway projects that increase SOV carrying capacity unless such projects result from a congestion management system (CMS). For example, not all of the grandfathered road project phases are in congested locations as identified by the ARC's congestion-relieving strategy. Also, for those projects that increase SOV capacity in congested locations, it is not clear how all evaluations of reasonable non-SOV strategies were analyzed and judged to be insufficient solutions as required. The lack of before and after studies to evaluate the effectiveness of various congestion relieving strategies is a tremendous weakness in this program.

Public Involvement

The public has expressed tremendous concern about the value of participating in ARC activities and in providing comments on transportation projects in the region.[26] Many people doubt whether their involvement has any affect on the decisions of the ARC board.[27] Board members have routinely characterized ARC citizen involvement as unrepresentative of the region and consisting of narrow special interests. The actual board decisions regarding funding priorities and discussion about managing growth routinely ignore the tremendous public support for transportation options and smart growth. A particularly egregious example of the importance placed on public comment by the ARC board occurred in late 1997. The ARC was forced by the federal agencies to approve the 1998 interim transportation improvement program (ITIP) twice, December 30, 1997, and January 28, 1998, because it failed to develop written responses to public comments received prior to the first approval.

Citizens who submitted written comments on the 1998 ITIP should have been notified of their receipt and told how their comments were used, what the agency response was, and what recourse was available if the person disagreed with the response. The ARC board, prior to any action, should publicly discuss, by category, the comments the ARC staff made, and then vote on whether they support the responses. These changes would provide citizens with a public assurance that their comments were considered and discussed, and would help keep them informed about the board's reaction to public comments. Public comment at the meetings of both the ARC Transportation Air Quality Committee and the full Board is stifled. The agendas for both groups should always provide time for the public to make comments, ask questions, and raise issues.

The ARC should quickly move to formally create a citizen advisory group to provide feedback, guidance, recommendations, and outreach to the public on current and future issues related to transportation, air quality, and growth in the region. The citizen advisory group should have formal membership that is representative of the population, user, and interest groups in the region. The citizen advisory group should have a formal structure that consists of a chair that is charged by the board and bylaws. It should report directly and routinely to relevant committees and the board itself. The citizen advisory group should also have access to the ARC staff and resources to address items of interest and concern.

The timing of meetings is a major concern. Public hearings for draft programs and plans are typically not scheduled early enough to allow notification of the public through monthly publications, which severely limits the ability of citizen organizations to notify their membership in a timely, cost-effective manner. This delay limits opportunities to notify the public of the opportunity to comment on transportation problems or projects in the region. Hearings should be scheduled and published at least three months in advance.

A recent move by the ARC board to consider modifying their bylaws to exclude citizen board members from the possibility of appointment to the Transportation Air Quality Committee is particularly troubling. Such a proposal demonstrates a desire to further prevent citizens and user-group representatives from providing input into transportation decision making. Involving citizens is more common in other ARC activity areas. For example, the voting membership of the Environment and Land Use Committee, another ARC board-level committee, currently includes both citizen board members and selected citizens from the region. A similar structure could be used for the Transportation and Air Quality Committee.

One priority initiative of the ARC Vision 2020 Transportation Collaborative, which completed its work in 1995, is that each local jurisdiction will develop and formalize a process for public input to project nomination and selection prior to presentation to the ARC planning process. Ideally, the process would afford equal access from the entire community and other affected jurisdictions. However, the ARC board, composed of the region's county commission chairs and mayors, has not acted on this initiative. Establishing minimum public involvement and project prioritization requirements for local processes would ensure that projects brought to ARC were selected through a similar process.

With a few exceptions, the local governments have no formal process for involving the public in decisions about those transportation projects that will be funded in the region. A few communities, such as Cobb County, use an iterative process to seek public concerns and develop responses about these concerns to get input on the proposed programs in their county. Others, like Gwinnett County, do not seek comments until late in the process and then only in a limited form with limited information provided for the public to respond and react to reasonably. Most counties do not have a process, other than the annual budget, for considering which transportation projects should be built. This lack of standardization has encouraged uncoordinated transportation planning across the region's counties.

Performance Measures and Public Information

In order to meet basic federal requirements, the regional transportation plans must provide the public with the basic information necessary to develop an understanding and opinion of what the proposed investment will accomplish. It is critical that local and regional changes, relative to both a trend analysis and to current conditions, in travel behavior and land use are clearly documented. It is also important that alternative investment and growth scenarios be analyzed in order to give people a sense of the costs and benefits of various futures.

The ARC scores badly on getting information to the public. A review of the ARC's draft Interim Transportation Improvement Program/Interim Regional Transportation Plan (ITIP/IRTP) (released June 8, 1998) confirms this point. The document failed to provide the public with sufficient information to assess the value and effects of the multiyear transportation investment.[28] While some of the more system-level performance measures (vehicle miles traveled, vehicle hours traveled, speed, pollution levels, etc.) have been developed and released publicly as part of the ARC/RTP process, this very basic information is not provided publicly when TIPs are created.

One method of packaging this information in an accessible way is to create a "day in the life" series that describes the changes of citizens of various population groups in the Atlanta region, the location of employment and residence, and what can be expected from the proposed investments. For each category the following general types of questions could be answered: Will I pay more or less for transportation? Will I spend more or less time traveling? How much gasoline will I use? What travel choices will I have? Will cut-through traffic in my neighborhood increase or decrease? Will my child/grandchild be able to walk to school? Will I be safer walking or bicycling? Will truck traffic increase? What kinds of development will happen in my neighborhood—more apartments, more commercial development, status quo, parking lots instead of farmland, and so forth?

This list represents the kind of questions the public needs answered by the ARC. Atlantans want to know "What does the TIP/RTP accomplish?" Providing information like this enables and promotes consideration of transportation in a regional context, instead of the more common project-level basis.

Evaluating Regional Transportation Needs

The primary criteria used in the Atlanta region to recommend whether a project should move forward is whether it has received local approval and GDOT commitments for funds and has completed the environmental review process. The ARC rarely discusses whether the project is the best one to achieve regional goals with limited funds. The project evaluation process (PEP) developed by ARC in 1994 is one of many important tools available for prioritizing and programming projects that have the greatest benefit to the region.

From the beginning, the full potential of the PEP was not realized. Use of the PEP was limited to new proposed projects. The GDOT and the ARC failed to support using the process to insure projects proposed years ago were still in the best interest of the region, given the new planning context provided by the Intermodal Surface Transportation Efficiency Act (ISTEA) and the Clean Air Act. MARTA and a few local governments faithfully filled out the forms for new projects. The Georgia DOT gave the forms only cursory attention. The ARC dropped the process for a couple of years and suddenly picked it up again the week before the certification review team convened its meetings in May 1998. The ARC staff evaluated new projects submitted for consideration in the update of the 1998 ITIP.[29]

By 1995, local governments and citizen groups identified some areas for improvement to make the process even more useful. However, despite the multiple submission of recommendations and the assurance from the ARC staff that improvements would be made, none of the improvements have been made. Some of the problems with the existing process include acceptance of incomplete forms, inadequate supporting information, and standard answers to questions regardless of the project.

The GDOT uses standard, short, cryptic phrases that provide inadequate information. For example, the GDOT has written that its Advanced Traffic Management System project protects and improves the environment "by reducing vehicle emissions," and interstate interchange projects "support/ promote a more efficient land use pattern by removing the congestion around the interchange." Many of the answers to how projects improve safety and security, mitigate congestion, support economic activity, and improve the mobility of people and goods lack quantification of the assumptions made and have no explanation of the reasoning behind the assumptions.

To reflect the letter and intent of ISTEA and the Clean Air Act, the Atlanta region needs to evaluate transportation plans, programs, and projects to measure their impact on new goals of reducing per capita vehicle miles traveled, vehicle trips, and motor vehicle emissions. The evaluation of transportation plans, programs, and projects must increase the average vehicle occupancy, increase the modal share of nonmotorized vehicles and transit, and improve the transportation system's economic and energy efficiency while reducing its environmental impact. This evaluation requires the collection and development of nontraditional data such as person-trip and dynamic-trip generation rates, walk/bike trips, composite index of transit serviceability and pedestrian friendliness, and actual parking costs.

Travel Behavior and Accessibility

There are five specific questions in this area that should be addressed. How will this investment affect both the corridor level and the regional system in terms of travel speeds, vehicle miles traveled, and number of trips by different modes? How will this investment affect at the individual level, based on being disaggregated by various demographics (race and ethnicity, gender, age, disability, income) and locations (inner city, inner ring suburbs, suburbs, exurbs), miles traveled, travel time, accessibility to transit, and car ownership? What percentage of trips, by type, are less than 1, 2, 3, 5, 10, 15, 20, 30 miles? When do these trips occur? And for each road capacity expansion, what are the impacts on conditions for transit users, bicyclists, and pedestrians?

Environment

Some environmental problems, due to pollution from the automobile, are impacting the quality of life for Atlantans. The major question raised about the environment is: How will this investment affect, at the project level and the regional system level, air and water pollution?

Equity

Equity is of importance because it provides a broader understanding of the distribution of transportation services and projects. The questions about transportation projects are: Where does the money go? How are the benefits of federal transportation investments distributed among different population groups? How do expenditures for the road system compare to expenditures for transit? What percentage of road and transit funding is going to areas with high proportions of communities of color and low-income communities? Is adequate funding being invested to maintain older areas with high populations of communities of color or low-income communities? What percentage of transportation investments are devoted to new projects in newly developing areas? And how do travel patterns differ by population groups?

The questions that address transportation services can be summed up in the following questions: How is the transportation system used by different population groups? What is the accessibility of the transportation system to different population groups? Are communities of color and low-income communities likely to be transit dependent? What does the transportation system look like and how does it function? What are the levels of car ownership among the different population groups? Do transportation services for all population groups link housing with jobs, schools, doctors, churches, parks, and other basic needs of life? Where do the bus lines run? How often does the bus come? How crowded are buses? Where are the highways located? And how congested are the highways?

Safety

Safety is a very important priority for the U.S. DOT and FHWA. Safety should be taken into consideration at both the metropolitan and the statewide levels. The questions that surround safety issues include: What is the change in the number of people injured and killed by each mode of transportation? Does the risk of people using one transportation mode being killed by people using another mode change? For example, do pedestrians face an increased risk of death by motor vehicles? What are the safety funding priorities? What is the money being spent on in relation to who is injured?

Land Use

Land use patterns are changing rapidly in the Atlanta area. This suggests that answers are provided for these questions. Where will future population and employment locate? What effect will this have on densities, amount of newly developed land, use of brownfield sites and other infill opportunities? What is the change in the amount of land paved for roads? How does this relate to new parking space? What is the change in the amount of parking (acres and stalls) and its cost to users and providers? What is the change in the rate of land developed compared to population growth?

Funding and Costs

Transportation projects and services are allocated funding based on their needs in the region. In this case, several questions are put on the drawing board. What is the total amount proposed to be programmed through the TIP/RTP? How is the funding divided between modes and jurisdictions? How is it divided between improvement to or near major activity centers and residential areas? How will this investment affect, both at the project level and for the regional system, future maintenance costs? Of expected city and county level transportation funding, how much is restricted for use only on roads and bridges? How much is available for all types of transportation? What are the average costs of the various facilities types (4, 8, etc. lane road, sidewalk, bicycle lane, bus and train service, and so forth), in the TIP/RTP by mile, additional passenger, etc.? What is the change in personal and household transportation costs—an average for the region as well as by different community types (inner-city, inner suburb, suburb, exurb)? What is the change in auto ownership—regionwide, by household, by community type?

Infrastructure

Transportation infrastructure can provide a bridge or barrier for the community. This raises a question and some concerns. How many new lane-miles of road (by functional classification), and bicycle and pedestrian facilities will be built? At the project level, and for the regional system, it is best to provide the current level of service and the forecasted changes both before and after any investment.

The transportation problems facing the region are demanding attention. Political leaders are now being forced to think regionally and across the political spectrum. The ARC and the GDOT have failed to plan a balanced regional transportation approach that integrates alternatives to roads and private automobiles. In 1999, Governor Roy Barnes created the GRTA to oversee and control transportation projects in the 13-county region.[30] The governor appointed 15 people to this agency to act as the referee between the ARC and DOT.

The GRTA has the responsibility of managing the growth and development of the 13 counties in the Atlanta metropolitan area. A major task of the superagency is to provide a cure for traffic gridlocks and air quality problems and provide alternatives to urban sprawl.[31] The agency is in its infancy stage, which makes it difficult for us to determine if it will convert concrete and asphalt to viable transportation alternatives.

Conclusions

The Atlanta regional transportation planning process is flawed. No RTP exists that is fiscally constrained, intermodal, or conforming with air quality requirements. The ARC's current schedule is to adopt a new RTP in March 2000. Unless corrected, the planning process is highly likely to further the growth of dependence on single-occupant vehicles, delay attainment of improved air quality, and make it more difficult for the region to actually complete a new conforming RTP update. The momentum of the region's historic focus on road building and project-based planning continues to delay achieving air quality standards, investments in transportation options, and linking of land use and transportation planning.

Public understanding and support for transportation options that benefit people and communities have grown in recent years. Atlantans are demanding cleaner air, transportation options, and an improved neighborhood quality of life. The Atlanta region's current transportation planning process endangers the health of the region's residents, reduces accessibility, increases segregation and social stratification, and threatens the economic viability of the region.

If this region is to have healthy air, transportation options, and livable communities, significant changes in the planning process for the Atlanta region are desperately needed. Corrective actions are required in such areas as needs assessment, system planning, public involvement and information, equity issues, use of performance measures, and project evaluation and selection.

The issues of air pollution, traffic congestion, and the disadvantages of unplanned, sprawled development have never had the public visibility and discussion they have now. The time is ripe for positive change. But accomplishing these changes will take the concentrated and sustained effort of all stakeholders involved in transportation planning and decision making. The stakeholders include all levels of government, the general public, businesses, and citizens' groups. All these sectors came together to support the recent creation of Governor Barnes's GRTA. This region has demonstrated its ability to accomplish great, "impossible" things if it has the will. Developing this will require state leadership, regional cooperation, local innovation, long-term planning, and creative thinking. Most importantly, the equal distribution of transportation benefits and burdens among all Atlantans is vital for the political, economic, social, and environmental growth of the metropolitan area.

Notes

1. Atlanta Regional Commission, *Regional Transportation Plan: Needs Assessment Report.* Atlanta: ARC, May 1999.
2. David Goldberg, "Superagency Would Coordinate Area Needs," *Atlanta Journal-Constitution,* November 24, 1998.
3. Atlanta Regional Commission, *Regional Transportation Plan;* David Goldberg, "Deadline Is Looming for a Regional Metro Plan," *Atlanta Journal-Constitution,* December 29, 1996, p. D6.
4. David Goldberg, "Deadline is Looming."
5. American Lung Association of Georgia, "We All Share the Same Air," *Legislative Update* (August/September 1999).
6. Sierra Club, *The Dark Side of the American Dream: The Cost and Consequences of Suburban Sprawl.* College Park, MD: Sierra Club, 1998, p. 5.
7. Charles W. Schmidt, "The Specter of Sprawl," *Environmental Health Perspectives* 106 (June 1998), p. 276.
8. David Pendered, "Transportation Chief Scolds Atlanta Transit," *Atlanta Journal-Constitution,* April 9, 1998, p. E6.
9. Lucy Soto, "Growth Quickly Junked 1950s Atlanta Plan," *Atlanta Journal-Constitution,* August 18, 1997.
10. Sierra Club, *The Dark Side of the American Dream,* p. 5; Julie K. Miller, "Too Much of a Good Thing: Many Question Growth's Price," *Atlanta Journal-Constitution,* July 6, 1997; Julie K. Miller, "Greater Atlanta's Wish List," *Atlanta Journal-Constitution,* July 6, 1997.
11. David Goldberg, "Regional Transit Gets Lift," *Atlanta Journal-Constitution,* November 24, 1998, p. A1; David Goldberg, "Deadline Is Looming."
12. See Atlanta Regional Commission, *Draft Interim Regional Transportation Plan: 2020 and Draft Interim Atlanta Region Transportation Improvement Program FY 1999–FY 2001,* June 5, 1998.
13. Christopher B. Leinberger, "The Favored Quarter," *Atlanta Journal-Constitution,* June 8, 1997, p. G4.
14. David Goldberg, "Gwinnett County's Got a Friend in the Highway Business," *Atlanta Journal-Constitution,* May 5, 1997.
15. Letter received by Larry Dreihaup, Georgia Division administrator, Federal Highway Administration, on January 16, 1998, from John Hankinson, regional administrator, U.S. Environmental Protection Agency.
16. See David Goldberg, "61 Road Projects Opposed by Groups," *Atlanta Journal-Constitution,* November 10, 1998.
17. Ibid.
18. Goro O. Mitchell, "Transportation Air Pollution, and Social Equity in Atlanta," *The Status of Black Atlanta, 1999,* Atlanta: Southern Center for Studies in Public Policy, Clark Atlanta University, 1999.

19. See U.S. District Court for the Northern District of Georgia, "*Georgians for Transportation Alternatives, The Georgia Conservancy, and the Sierra Club* (Plaintiffs), *v. Wayne Shackelford, Commissioner, Georgia Department of Transportation, Georgia Department of Transportation, Rodney Slater, Secretary, U.S. Department of Transportation (USDOT), Kenneth R. Wykle, Administrator, Federal Highway Administration (FHWA), Gordon J. Linton, Administrator, Federal Transit Administration (FTA), Larry Dreihaup, Division Administrator, Georgia Division, FHWA, USDOT, Susan Schruth, Regional Administrator, FTA, USDOT, and Atlanta Regional Commission* (Defendants)." 99-CV-0160. January 20, 1999.

20. See David Goldberg, "Deal Kills Money for 44 Roads but 17 Others Go-ahead as Environmentalists Drop Suit," *Atlanta Journal-Constitution*, June 21, 1999, p. A1.

21. "SELC Scores Major Victory in Atlanta Lawsuit," *Southern Resources: A Newsletter of the Southern Environmental Law Center*, Summer 1999, p. 1.

22. See "Publication of Guidance on Certification of Metropolitan Planning Process; Notification of FY 94 Reviews, FHWA/FTA Docket No. 94-19." *Federal Register* 59, no. 160 (August 18, 1994), pp. 42873–42876.

23. James Chapman, telephone interview by author regarding "Notes from Federal Certification Review Team's Review of the Atlanta Region's Transportation Planning Process," May 6–8, 1998.

24. U.S. Department of Transportation, *Federal Highway Administration, Certification Report for the Atlanta Transportation Management Area*. Washington, DC: Government Printing Office, 1998.

25. See transportation section, *Detailing the Vision: A Development Plan for the Atlanta Region*. Technical Staff Report, Atlanta Regional Commission, May 1977.

26. David Goldberg, "ARC's Planning Efforts Criticized in DOT Review," *Atlanta Journal-Constitution*, September 24, 1998, p. C2. See also Lucy Soto, "Discussing the Nitty-Gritty of Growth," *Atlanta Journal-Constitution*, August 18, 1997, p. E6.

27. Lucy Soto, "Growth Quickly Junked 1950s Atlanta Plan," *Atlanta Journal-Constitution*, August 18, 1997, p. E6.

28. Atlanta Regional Commission, *Draft Interim Atlanta Regional Transportation Plan: 2020 and Draft Interim Atlanta Region Transportation Improvement Program, FY 1999–FY 2001*, June 5, 1998.

29. Atlanta Regional Commission, *Proposed 1998 Amendments to the Interim Atlanta Region Transportation Improvement Program FY 1999–FY 2001*. October 1998.

30. Kathey Pruitt, "Barnes: GRTA No Miracle Cure," *Atlanta Journal-Constitution*, April 7, 1999, p. B1; Kathey Pruitt, "Powerful GRTA Clears Final Hurdle," *Atlanta Journal-Constitution*, March 24, 1999, p. B8; Kathey Pruitt, "Transportation Plan Faces Major Tweaking," *Atlanta Journal-Constitution*, January 26, 1999, p. C1; David Goldberg, "Barnes Superagency Solves Conflict," *Atlanta Journal-Constitution*, January 26, 1999, p. C2; David Goldberg, "A Guiding

Hand: Does Metro Atlanta Need a New Agency to Handle Growth Problems? Many Residents Say Yes, but Making it Happen Could be Tough," *Atlanta Journal-Constitution*, July 20, 1998, p. E1; "Give Barnes a Chance, ARC Chairman Says," *Atlanta Journal-Constitution*, January 28, 1999, p. C6; David Goldberg, "Cleland Vows to Seek Funds for GRTA Aid," *Atlanta Journal-Constitution*, April 10, 1999, p. C1; David Goldberg and Kathey Pruitt, "GRTA Members Face Great Expectations," *Atlanta Journal-Constitution*, June 4, 1999, p. A1.
31. David Goldberg, "Regional Transit Gets Lift," *Atlanta Journal-Constitution*, November 24, 1998, p. A1.

CHAPTER 4

Closed Doors: Persistent Barriers to Fair Housing

Angel O. Torres, Robert D. Bullard, and Chad G. Johnson

Race still matters in the United States. Too many of the inhabitants of our major cities continue to be geographically confined to segregated housing, poverty, economic abandonment, and urban core neighborhoods experiencing infrastructure decline.[1] Racial patterns of cities and metropolitan areas were "caused" by individuals and institutional factors. Residential apartheid is part of our national heritage.[2] Some three decades ago, the National Advisory Commission on Civil Disorders implicated racism in creating and maintaining the black ghetto and the drift toward two "separate and unequal societies."[3] Today, white racism operates much the same for poor and middle-class blacks.[4] The black ghetto is kept isolated and contained from the larger white society through well-defined institutional practices, private actions, and government policies.[5]

Housing discrimination is still rampant in America.[6] Fair housing testing is the most widely used tool for gathering evidence of housing discrimination.[7] Test audits conducted in two dozen large metropolitan areas found that black testers seeking to rent apartments faced discrimination by landlords 53 percent of the time, while black testers seeking to buy a home faced discriminatory treatment by real estate persons 59 percent of the time.[8]

Few whites are willing to accept even minimal black presence, and statistics show that nationally only 13 percent of whites would be willing to do so.[9] According to a survey conducted by Research Atlanta, 90 percent of whites surveyed in metropolitan Atlanta expressed a willingness to move into an area with one black household. As the number of black households increased to eight, however, the percentage of whites willing to move into such a neighborhood decreased to 26 percent.[10] Many whites see nothing wrong with these attitudes and most deny their existence. Moreover, most whites do not believe that housing discrimination exists.[11]

Many real estate and insurance agents respond to the fears and biases of whites. The result is a "discrimination tax." Syracuse University professor John Yinger describes the consequences of this "tax" on black and Latino households:

> The base-case results reveal that when an event, such as a new child or an increase in income, induces a Black or Hispanic household to search for a house or to buy, it must pay, on average, a discrimination "tax" of roughly $3,700. A cost of this magnitude implies that a total cost of current discrimination amounts to about $3 billion per year for all Black households, owners and renters, and to almost $2 billion per year for Hispanic households.[12]

Discrimination lowers the nation's gross national product by almost 2 percent a year.[13] A large share of this loss is a result of housing discrimination. Sociologists Melvin O. Oliver and Thomas M. Shapiro estimate that the current generation of blacks have lost $82 billion due to discrimination. Of this total, $58 billion was lost from lack of housing appreciation, $10.5 billion from paying higher mortgage rates, and $13.5 billion from the denial of mortgages. Real estate agents, brokers, and mortgage lenders cater to the racist attitudes of some of their clients—and in effect determine the racial neighborhoods, cities, suburbs, and metropolitan regions.

Housing discrimination has changed over the past three decades. No overt signs are posted indicating "white only" or "blacks need not apply." Nevertheless, discrimination is just as real. In 1999, former senator Charles McC. Mathias and housing consultant Marion Morris summarized this point:

> Discrimination has become more subtle—a fine art some would say. The terms and conditions of the mortgage one applies for may be a point or two higher, with a greater down-payment requirement than if one were white. The security deposit on a rental may be for two months, where everyone else's is for one month. Available apartments may only be at the back of the building with a view of the parking lot, rather than the front view of the nature preserve.[14]

Ownership of property, land, and business is still a central part of the American dream of success—a dream that has eluded millions of Americans. Discrimination denies a substantial segment of the African American community a basic form of wealth accumulation and investment through home ownership.[15] Only about 59 percent of the nation's middle-class African Americans own their homes, compared with 74 percent of whites. On the other hand, some $50 to $90 billion a year in tax subsidies underwrite suburban homeowners. This middle-class entitlement is by far "the broadest and most expensive welfare program in the U.S.A."[16]

Fair Housing Laws and Mandates

Despite improvements over the years, African American, Latino American, and Native American home buyers face tremendous hurdles in the housing market. The federal government routinely reports that these groups are denied home mortgages at rates twice that of their white counterparts.

During the last five years, many lenders have shifted from using underwriting standards that leave a good deal of discretion to individual loan officers or underwriters to using approaches, including credit scoring, that leave little, if any, discretion to loan officers or underwriters. At the same time that lenders have moved to using standardized lending policies, minority denial rates have increased substantially. These alarming loan rejection statistics still leave some government and industry officials in doubt as to whether the culprit is a function of discrimination or neutral "market forces." Loan officers can help applicants resolve any deficiency in their record by either asking for an explanation or by advising them what steps to follow. But these discretionary extra steps by loan officers are not provided at the same rate to minority applicants as to white applicants.[17]

Federal Fair Housing Act

The federal government passed the Fair Housing Act in 1968. It was later amended and strengthened in 1988 because of the persisting problem of discrimination. The Fair Housing Act makes it illegal to deny a dwelling to anyone based on race, color, religion, or national origin. It also provides protection from impediments to fair housing choice, to include any actions, omissions, or decisions that restrict or have the effect of restricting housing choices or the availability of housing choices taken because of race, sex, color, religion, disability, national origin, or family status.[18]

The 1988 amendments raised limits on punitive damages in civil suits; allowed fees to be awarded to attorneys outside of the U.S. Department of Justice; lengthened the statute of limitations from six months to two years on private suits; granted the U.S. Department of Justice the power to initiate "pattern and practice" cases; allowed HUD to initiate fair housing cases; and established administrative law judges to hear fair housing cases. The act exempts owner-occupied buildings with no more than four units, single-family housing rented or sold without the use of a real estate broker, and housing operated by organizations that limit occupancy to members.[19]

State of Georgia

In 1978, the State of Georgia passed Article 4 of the Georgia Housing Code, which prohibits housing discrimination. The statute was amended effective July 1990 to be consistent with the 1988 amendments to the Fair Housing Act. The Georgia Fair Housing statute generally parallels the federal statute. The principal differences between the statutes are procedural, particularly with regard to the choice of forum for a legal action.

The State Fair Housing statute provides that local municipalities may adopt such provisions. The statute allows the adoption of the state's statute against discriminatory housing practices and restricts the expansion or reduction of rights granted by state law. The state attorney general has interpreted the ordinance to mean that the scope of coverage of municipal fair housing ordinances exceeding that of the Georgia Fair Housing statute is in conflict with the state constitution and hence void.[20]

Fulton County

Fulton County has an ordinance banning housing discrimination. The county's ordinance applies to those unlawful discriminatory practices within unincorporated Fulton County. The county ordinance is implemented and enforced by a fair housing director appointed by the director of contract and compliance, with the approval of the county manager. The fair housing director is responsible for investigating complaints of discrimination, making probable cause determinations, and seeking conciliation among parties to a complaint.

The ordinance also provides for a hearing board, which consists of seven citizens of Fulton County. Each member is appointed by the Board of Commissioners and serves a two-year term. The board hears complaints where the director has found probable cause. The respondent may also initiate a hearing at any time during the conciliation process. Upon a determination of the complaint, the board is required to issue a written order that shall be delivered to the parties and such other public officials as the board deems proper. If the board determines that the respondent has engaged in discrimination, the board usually negotiates a remedy.

Georgia Urban County Consortium

The Georgia Urban County Consortium (composed of Fulton, Cobb, and Gwinnett counties, and the city of Marietta) adopted affirmative marketing procedures for federally assisted housing of five or more units. The affirmative marketing strategy includes: informing tenants, owners, and the public about fair housing laws; using the equal housing opportunity slogan in written communications; securing a contractual commitment from federally assisted project owners on affirmative marketing requirements; monitoring compliance of owners with affirmative marketing requirements; and maintaining a solicitation list of potential participants in federal programs.

Atlanta Mortgage Consortium

The Atlanta Mortgage Consortium (AMC) was started in 1988 in response to the *Atlanta Journal-Constitution*'s Pulitzer Prize–winning series "The Color of Money."[21] The consortium is the first of its kind nationally and provides home loans at below market rates to Atlanta's lower income households. Lending institutions pool their mortgages and share risks, so no mortgage insurance is required. The program allows individuals to obtain 30-year, fixed, below market rate home purchase financing of up to 95 percent of the purchase price.

Neighborhood Assistance Corporation of America

Neighborhood Assistance Corporation of America (NACA), an outgrowth of the Union Neighborhood Assistance Corporation (UNAC), is a nonprofit community advocacy organization that fights discriminatory and predatory lending practices and provides comprehensive housing services. UNAC has been very prominent in research, advocacy, and exposure around the second mortgage scam in which financial institutions targeted long-time homeowners who were predominately elderly, poor, and minority.

Atlanta Metro Fair Housing

Atlanta Metro Fair Housing is one of the oldest private fair housing organizations in the United States. The agency was founded by white homeowners in south DeKalb County who were opposed to blockbusting. Metro Fair Housing receives funds from Fulton County, the city of Atlanta, DeKalb County, and the U.S. Department of Housing and Urban Development. Metro Fair Housing's annual budget is typically around $200,000 but has been as high as $500,000. Grants from local government bodies to Metro Fair Housing have generally ranged between $20,000 and $40,000. Metro Fair Housing currently receives $40,000 a year from the Fulton County government. The agency has never received funds from the counties surrounding DeKalb and Fulton counties.

Discrimination Complaint Activity

Atlanta Metro Fair Housing is the primary group that receives housing discrimination complaints in the region. From 1991 to 1997, a total of 1,355 housing discrimination complaints were filed with the agency. The vast majority (94.5 percent) of the complaints involved rental property. The greatest complaint activity occurred in the years preceding the 1996 Atlanta

Figure 4.1. Atlanta Metro Fair Housing Complaints for 1991–1997. *Source:* Atlanta Metro Fair Housing, "Housing Discrimination Complaint Activity, 1991–1997" (1998).

Olympic Games. For example, 285 housing discrimination complaints were registered with Metro Fair Housing in 1995, accounting for 21 percent of all complaints filed during the seven-year period (see Figure 4.1). Complaint activity leveled off in 1996 and 1997. This may be an effect of the overbuilding and apartment "glut" in the post-Olympic years.

Consistent with national trends, black Atlantans face the stiffest barriers in housing of all racial and ethnic groups. Seventy percent of the complaints filed came from blacks, with whites only accounting for 23 percent of the complaints; Hispanics filed nearly 5 percent of the complaints; Asians and American Indians accounted for less than 1 percent each (see Figure 4.2). Although a complaint does not necessarily translate into a proven case of discrimination, complaint activity is a good indicator of trends and general practices in the housing market.

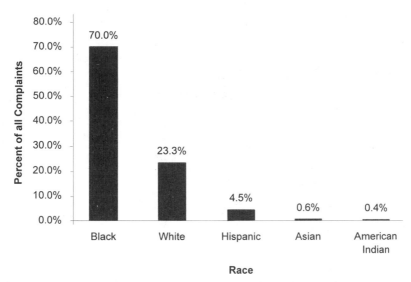

Figure 4.2. Atlanta Housing Discrimination Complaints by Race for 1991–1997.
Source: Atlanta Metro Fair Housing, "Housing Discrimination Complaint Activity,
1991–1997" (1998).

Females, by far, made up the largest group filing housing discrimination
complaints in the region. Over 73 percent of the complaints were filed by
females. Black women appear to have the most problems securing rental
housing in metropolitan Atlanta. Over 57 percent of all complaints were
filed by black females. White females accounted for 17.5 percent of the complaints, compared to 18.3 percent of the complaints filed by black males.

The 1,355 complaints fell into four distinct categories: (1) refusal to sell,
lease, or rent; (2) terms and conditions; (3) differential treatment; and (4)
dispute in pricing and financing. The most frequently cited allegation was
refusal to sell, lease, or rent (34.1 percent), followed closely by differential
treatment (33.3 percent). Nearly one-fourth (23.5 percent) of the complaints
involved terms and conditions. Less than 10 percent (9.1 percent) of the
complaints involved a dispute in pricing and financing (see Figure 4.3).

Complaint activity varied by geographic location. Most complaint properties were located north of Interstate 20 (70.6 percent) and outside of the
city of Atlanta (76.2 percent). A closer examination of the fair housing data
shows that the complaints were clustered in ten "problem" zip codes. These
ten zip codes account for 30 percent of all complaints filed during the
1991–1997 period (see Table 4.1). The two zip codes registering the most
complaints were both located in Cobb County. On the other hand, DeKalb
County and Fulton County accounted for seven of the top ten problem zip
codes on the list. Gwinnett County had one zip code to make the top ten list.

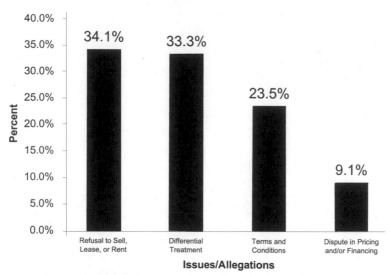

Figure 4.3. Type of Housing discrimination Allegation for 1991–1997. *Source:* Atlanta Metro Fair Housing, "Housing Discrimination Complaint Activity, 1991–1997" (1998).

Clearly, enough housing discrimination complaints continue to be filed to justify targeted fair housing enforcement, especially in the "problem" zip codes. The Atlanta Metro Fair Housing program cannot solve this problem alone. It will take cooperation across multiple county jurisdictions to make fair housing a reality for all metropolitan Atlanta residents.

Table 4.1. The Top Ten Zip Codes Registering Housing Discrimination Complaints

Zip Code	County	Percent Minority	Number of Complaints	Most Common Issue
30060	Cobb	19.9	53	Differential treatment
30080	Cobb	22.7	51	Differential treatment
30083	DeKalb	34.9	49	Refusal to sell, lease, or rent
30032	DeKalb	85.9	42	Differential treatment
30307	DeKalb/Fulton	29.8	41	Refusal to sell, lease, or rent
30311	Fulton	97.3	40	Refusal to sell, lease, or rent
30092	Gwinnett	15.5	39	Differential treatment
30331	Fulton	96.7	39	Differential treatment
30021	DeKalb	58.0	32	Differential treatment
30350	Fulton	11.9	31	Differential treatment

Source: Atlanta Metro Fair Housing, "Housing Discrimination Complaint Activity, 1991–1997" (1998).

Locked Out of the American Dream

Home ownership is still central to the American dream. Much of the nation is currently enjoying a period of economic expansion unseen in earlier generations. Interest rates were recently at an all time low, new residential developments are changing the landscape, and many cities are seeing growth at an alarming rate. For example, a 1996 *Wall Street Journal* article reported a "sharp" rise in mortgage lending to minorities in recent years. This improvement was a result of "tough fair-lending enforcement by the Justice Department."[22]

Over the last 30 years, Congress has passed important legislation to address housing discrimination. The federal Fair Housing Act of 1968 and the Equal Credit Opportunity Act of 1974 prohibited racial discrimination in mortgage lending and credit transactions; the 1975 Home Mortgage Disclosure Act (HMDA) required mortgage lenders to report the race, gender, income, and census tract location of the applicant, as well as whether the loan was accepted or denied. Also, the 1977 Community Reinvestment Act (CRA) required commercial banks and savings and loan institutions to be responsive to the credit needs of their entire service area.[23]

The racial gap in lending has been closing in recent years. Data from the Federal Financial Institutions Examination Council (FFIEC) point to increased mortgage lending to all groups. During the five-year period from 1993 through 1997, the number of home purchase loans increased 62 percent for blacks, 58 percent for Hispanics, 29 percent for Asians, 25 percent for Native Americans, and 62 percent for whites.[24] It appears that when antidiscrimination laws are rigorously enforced, people of color make gains.[25]

The latest housing boom has not touched everyone. Nowhere is this more apparent than in the nation's large urban centers where people of color, the poor, and stable working class persons are concentrated.[26] Fifty years of government subsidized roads have pushed jobs and housing away from central cities. Low-interest Federal Housing Administration (FHA) loans helped subsidize the flight of white, middle class households to the suburbs. Today, suburban homeowners make up the dominant economic and political force in the nation.

Recent data from the 1996 HMDA show that black mortgage loan applicants are denied twice as often as whites. There is some debate as to the extent that outright discrimination accounts for these persisting disparities. However, paired-testing procedures using equally qualified testers revealed that black and Hispanic borrowers are consistently treated differently from their white counterparts. Black and Hispanic borrowers are routinely offered inferior products, charged higher fees, provided less counseling or assistance, or treated less favorably than white borrowers.[27]

Table 4.2. Home Loan Denial Rates in the Ten Most Sprawl-Threatened Large Cities—1996

Metropolitan Area	Black %	Hispanic %	Asian %	White %
Atlanta, GA	23.0	19.6	4.3	13.4
Chicago, IL	23.5	16.3	12.2	10.0
Cincinnati, OH–KY–IN	29.0	21.5	16.0	15.9
Denver, CO	22.1	20.9	16.0	13.2
Fort Lauderdale, FL	24.3	17.9	15.7	15.6
Kansas City, MO–KS	27.8	20.2	12.6	11.9
Minneapolis–St. Paul, MN–WI	27.8	27.7	14.5	13.0
Seattle–Bellevue–Everett, WA	23.8	24.5	16.2	14.3
St. Louis, MO–IL	29.9	23.3	12.0	16.5
Washington, DC–MD–VA–WV	20.5	17.7	13.0	10.9

Source: Loan denial rates are taken from the Home Mortgage Disclosure Act database for the year 1996. The metropolitan areas are from the Sierra Club, *The Dark Side of the American Dream* (1998).

Blacks continue to have the highest loan rejection rate of any group. One out of every four black mortgage applicants is rejected for a loan in the "most sprawl-threatened"[28] big cities, except in the St. Louis and Washington, D.C., metropolitan areas (see Table 4.2). The 1996 HMDA data show that 23 percent of black and 19.6 percent of Hispanic loan applicants in metropolitan Atlanta were rejected, compared to 13.4 percent of white loan applicants. The loan denial rate for Asians in the Atlanta metropolitan area was only 4.3 percent.

During the 1990s, new housing subdivisions mushroomed in Atlanta's suburbs, forests, and rural farmland. Eight of every ten new units built during the 1990–1998 period were single family.[29] The 10-county Atlanta metropolitan region added 228,573 housing units between 1990 and 1998, a whopping 21.7 percent increase. The bulk of the housing was concentrated in northern Atlanta's suburbs, north of I-285. One of every four housing units built in the region in the 1990s was in Gwinnett County. Together, Gwinnett, Fulton, and Cobb counties accounted for nearly two-thirds of the region's net increase in housing during the 1990s.[30] The housing inventory in northern Fulton County more than doubled between 1990 and 1998.

Much of the housing boom passed over the city of Atlanta. The city added only 3,552 new housing units between 1990 and 1998, or a 1.9 percent increase, compared to 58,995 units in Gwinnett County (42.9 percent increase), 43,216 units in Fulton County outside Atlanta (30.5 percent increase), and 40,917 units in Cobb County (21.5 percent increase).[31] These growth trends point to clear disparities between the mostly black city of Atlanta and the mostly white suburbs.

Table 4.3. Mortgage Rejection Rate by Race/Ethnic Group

Jurisdiction	White %	Black %	Hispanic %	Asian %
Fulton County	7.1	17.2	13.4	7.0
DeKalb County	7.3	15.9	15.6	11.2
Cobb County	8.1	15.7	14.7	8.5
Gwinnett County	7.0	13.2	9.3	7.1
Clayton County	13.7	14.5	14.0	13.0
City of Atlanta	7.8	17.2	14.0	10.1
Average[a]	7.7	15.8	12.8	8.6

Source: Federal Reserve Bank Board, *Home Mortgage Disclosure Act* (1996).
[a]The city of Atlanta is not included in the averages shown since it is geographically located inside of Fulton and DeKalb counties and these averages were calculated from the total number of loan applications for the area of study.

In 1996, over 134,459 home mortgage applications were filed in the five counties that surround Atlanta (Fulton, DeKalb, Cobb, Gwinnett, and Clayton). Of this total, 15,237 or 11.3 percent were rejected. A breakdown of the mortgage rejection rate by race for the five counties and the city of Atlanta is presented in Table 4.3. Overall, the mortgage rejection rate for blacks was double that for whites in the city of Atlanta and four of the five counties surrounding Atlanta. The mortgage denial rate in Clayton County was roughly the same for all four racial and ethnic groups. Mortgage denial increased with minority concentration.

The loan rejection rate was highest in census tracts where minorities made up 50 percent or more of the population (Table 4.4). One-fourth or

Table 4.4. Mortgage Rejection Rate by Minority Concentration[a]

Jurisdiction	<10%	10–19%	20–49%	50% and up	Average (%)
Fulton County	7.4	8.6	13.6	17.0	11.4
DeKalb County	6.4	7.4	13.8	16.8	13.4
Cobb County	8.9	12.5	11.9	25.4	10.1
Gwinnett County	8.5	10.0	10.3	NA[b]	8.8
Clayton County	13.0	15.1	16.8	18.4	15.7
City of Atlanta	9.6	7.4	10.7	16.4	13.0
Average[c]	8.8	10.7	13.3	19.4	11.3

Source: Federal Reserve Bank Board, *Home Mortgage Disclosure Act* (1996).
[a]Minority concentration represents percentage minority population in census tracts.
[b]Gwinnett County is the only county in the study area without census tracts with a minority population larger than 50 percent.
[c]The city of Atlanta is not included in the averages shown since it is geographically located inside of Fulton and DeKalb counties and these averages were calculated from the total number of loan applications for the area of study.

Table 4.5. Loan Rejection Rate by Type of Loan and Race/Ethnic Group

Type of Loan	White %	Black %	Hispanic %	Asian %	Average %
Conventional	8.2	19.7	15.8	9.0	12.3
FHA Insured	4.1	8.6	5.3	4.8	7.1
VA Guaranteed	3.9	7.5	4.8	0.0	5.9
FmHA Insured	4.5	12.5	0.0	NA[a]	5.7
Average	7.7	15.8	12.8	8.6	11.3

Source: Federal Reserve Bank Board, *Home Mortgage Disclosure Act* (1996).
[a]There were no loans of this type applied for by this ethnic group.

25.4 percent of the mortgage applications that originated in Cobb County's heavily minority census tracts were rejected, compared with an 8.8 percent rejection rate in nearly all-white census tracts. Similar loan rejection disparities exist throughout the five-county area.

Mortgage rejection rate varied between conventional and government-backed home loans (i.e., Federal Housing Administration Insured, Veterans Administration Guaranteed, Farmers Home Administration Insured). All metropolitan Atlanta groups have fared better with government-backed home loans when compared with conventional loans (Table 4.5). One-fifth or 19.7 percent of the black conventional loan applicants were turned down, compared to 15.8 percent of the Hispanic conventional loan applicants and 8.2 percent of the white conventional loan applicants.

Sprawl pulls needed investments and other resources away from the urban core.

Ethnic minorities in the Atlanta region also face barriers getting loans to fix up their homes. When they try to refinance their homes—and save money by taking advantage of lower interest rates—they are met with stiff rejection. Nearly one-third of the black home improvement loan applicants were turned down. Similarly, nearly 30 percent of Hispanics who applied for similar loans were rejected, compared to 15.4 percent of whites. Home improvement loan rejection increases with minority population concentration. The poor housing conditions in many of Atlanta's minority neighborhoods is exacerbated by the failure of their residents to secure home loans.

Paying More for Less: The Price of Redlining

Studies over the past three decades have clearly documented the relationship between redlining and disinvestment decisions and neighborhood decline.[32] Redlining exists when a mortgage application with a given set of applicant, property, and loan characteristics is more likely to be denied in a minority neighborhood than in a white neighborhood.[33] Redlining "hits the poor where they live."[34] It accelerates the flight of full-service banks, food stores, restaurants, and other shopping centers in inner-city neighborhoods.[35]

Many inner-city homeowners and business owners are hurt by redlining practices by banks, savings and loans, mortgage firms, and insurance companies.[36] The federal government recognized this problem when it passed the CRA in 1977, a law designed to combat discriminatory practices in poor and minority neighborhoods. The CRA requires banks and thrifts to lend within the areas where their depositors live. The CRA establishes that "regulated financial institutions have continuing and affirmative obligation to help meet the credit needs of the local communities in which they are chartered."[37]

Race does matter in urban credit and insurance markets.[38] The insurance industry, like its housing industry counterpart, "has long used race as a factor in appraising and underwriting property."[39] Urban sociologist Gregory Squires asserts that "communities without insurance are communities without hope." In their place, inner-city neighborhoods are left with check-cashing stations, pawn shops, storefront grocery stores, liquor stores, and fast-food operations—all well buttoned-up with wire mesh and bullet-proof glass.[40]

Many white insurance companies routinely redline black neighborhoods. A 1997 Urban Institute insurance study found widespread racial barriers for people of color. The study used black, Latino, and white testers who presented themselves as homeowners seeking insurance. The black and Latino testers were discriminated against 53 percent of the time in such areas as coverage and premium rates.[41] Four major insurance companies (American Family, Allstate, State Farm, and Nationwide) have launched initiatives to

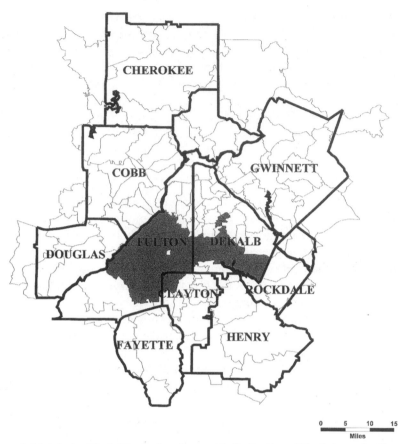

Figure 4.4. Majority Black Zip Codes. *Source:* Shelly Emling, "Black Areas in City Pay Steep Rates," *Atlanta Journal-Constitution* (1996).

end the longstanding tradition of redlining. However, many other companies only change their practices if they are caught.

A 1996 *Atlanta Journal-Constitution* survey discovered stark disparities in property insurance rates between black and white Atlanta neighborhoods.[42] The redlining issue prompted newspaper reporter Shelly Emling to title her story: "Insurance: Is It Still a White Man's Game?"[43] Emling answered her question as follows: "Insurance companies create pricing zones that are mostly white or mostly black, and homeowners in the black zones are paying top dollar."[44]

Insurance redlining is not isolated to an individual insurance agent. The practice is widespread among big and small companies. The largest insurance companies in Georgia (i.e., State Farm, Allstate, Cotton States, Cincinnati Insurance, and USAA) routinely charge consumers 40 to 90 percent

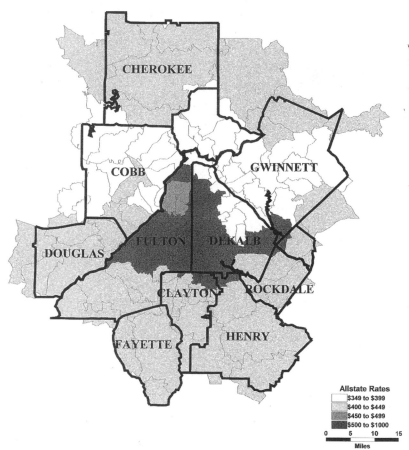

Figure 4.5. Allstate Home Insurance Rates. *Source:* Shelly Emling, "Black Areas in City Pay Steep Rates," *Atlanta Journal-Constitution* (1996).

more to insure homes in Atlanta's predominately black neighborhoods than for similar or identical houses in mostly white suburbs.[45] Affluent blacks as well as poor blacks are levied a "discrimination tax" by the insurance industry. The premium disparity holds true whether blacks live in the low-income Vine City neighborhood or the wealthy Cascade neighborhood that houses Atlanta's black elite.

Atlanta's black population is highly segregated (see Figure 4.4). As the racial composition of a neighborhood becomes mostly black, the price of homeowner insurance rises dramatically.[46] This is the case for both Allstate and State Farm homeowner insurance rates—the two largest home insurers in the state (see Figures 4.5 and 4.6). Homeowners in Atlanta's predominately black neighborhoods are paying higher premiums than their white suburban counterparts. High premiums collected from black residents help

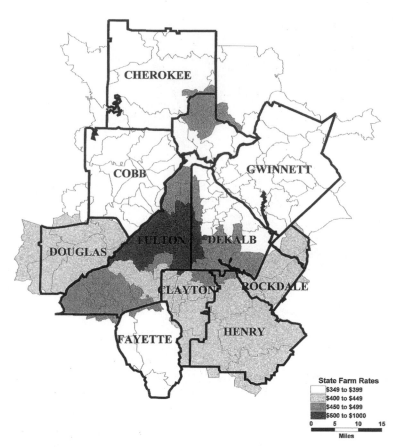

State Farm Rates
- $349 to $399
- $400 to $449
- $450 to $499
- $500 to $1000

Figure 4.6. State Farm Home Insurance Rates. *Source:* Shelly Emling, "Black Areas in City Pay Steep Rates," *Atlanta Journal-Constitution* (1996).

subsidize the low insurance rates in the sprawling, mostly white suburban subdivisions.

Using the state rates for a hypothetical $125,000 brick house (with $250 deductible), the *Atlanta Journal-Constitution* study concluded that "State Farm and Allstate, Georgia's largest insurers, tend to charge their highest rates in zip codes that also contain the highest proportion of black residents."[47] The premium differentials become apparent when one compares the hypothetical $125,000 brick house in different locations in metropolitan Atlanta. Shelley Emling writes:

> To insure that house with State Farm in black sections of the city of Atlanta would cost about $612 a year; in Buckhead, the rate falls to $459. In Cobb, Gwinnett and north Fulton, all more than 80 percent white, the price falls to $363 a year."[48]

Table 4.6. Insurance Premiums of Allstate and State Farm Zones[a]

Insurance Zone	Average Premium[b]	Black Population (%)	1990 Total Premiums[c]	Loss Ratio[d] (%)
ALLSTATE ZONE 2 Central Atlanta	$705	81	$2,509,290	79
ALLSTATE ZONE 6 N.E. Atlanta, Decatur	$518	29	$2,819,330	76
ALLSTATE ZONE 17 Western DeKalb	$573	38	$1,025,407	112
ALLSTATE ZONE 18 N. Fulton, N.W. DeKalb	$349	9	$12,166,975	92
STATE FARM ZONE 7 Central Atlanta	$612	62	N/A	68
STATE FARM ZONE 35 N. Fulton, N.W. DeKalb	$453	11	N/A	92
STATE FARM ZONE 37 Gwinnett, N. Fulton, N. DeKalb, Cent. and E. Cobb, portion of Cherokee	$363	10	N/A	73

Source: Shelly Emling, "Black Areas in City Pay Steep Rates," *Atlanta Journal-Constitution* (1996).
[a]This table examines selected metro Atlanta zones covered by State Farm and Allstate, the leading homeowner's insurance companies in Georgia.
[b]Average premium: Shows what a homeowner would pay on a $125,000 brick home given these conditions: The area has a fire protection rating of 1 to 3 (based on a scale of 1–10, with lower being better; the city of Atlanta, for example, has a 2 rating, and suburban areas tend to have higher ones). The policy is "HO-3," standard in the industry, and carries a $250 deductible.
[c]Total premium (for Allstate only): From a 1993 filing by Allstate. These figures show how much business the company wrote in a given zone in 1990.
[d]Loss ratio: A loss ratio of 79 percent means the company paid out 79 cents in claims for each $1 it collected in premiums. State Farm data are from 1991; Allstate data are from 1990.

The premium differentials between black and white neighborhoods can not be explained solely by loss data (i.e., theft, vandalism, fire, and larceny crimes). In reality, the highest loss ratios are not in black areas. A loss ratio is the sum an insurance company pays in claims versus the amount it collects in premiums. For example, a ratio of 68 percent means that a company paid out 68 cents for each $1 it collected. In general, a company that has a loss ratio of 65 percent turns a healthy profit.

The loss ratio in mostly black Allstate Zone 2 (Central Atlanta) is 79 percent, yet they pay a whopping $705 in annual premiums (Table 4.6). On the other hand, the loss ratio in mostly white Atlanta Zone 18 (North Fulton, Northwest DeKalb) is 92 percent, and the homeowners pay $349—less than half what is paid by residents in Zone 2. There is little doubt that the mostly white suburban communities with the highest loss ratios are not paying their fair share. These premium disparities further illustrate the benefits suburban whites derive from discrimination.

Conclusion

The dream of home ownership continues to elude millions of Americans because of their race, color, national origin, and familial status. Housing discrimination was legally outlawed by the federal government more than three decades ago. Nevertheless, old and new forms of denial operate to create separate and unequal housing and neighborhoods for people of color and whites.

Atlanta experienced a housing boom in the 1990s. New suburban subdivisions sprang up outside Atlanta's central core. The Atlanta region led the nation in housing starts. This boom meant more people, more jobs, more businesses, and more housing construction. It also meant more opportunities for home loans. Low interest rates made it possible for more Atlantans to become homeowners.

Blacks and other ethnic minorities were able to secure more home loans than before as a direct result of tough fair housing enforcement efforts undertaken by the U.S. Justice Department. Still, the loan rejection rate for blacks was twice that for whites seeking home loans. This same trend held true for Atlanta. Black and Hispanic home buyers favored government-backed loans over conventional loans.

Racial barriers play a major role in limiting home ownership options. These options are often limited to central Atlanta areas and older suburbs that are undergoing physical and economic decline. Many metropolitan Atlanta real estate agents, mortgage lenders, and insurance companies respond to the racist attitudes of their white clients. These practices result in black Atlantans paying a "discrimination tax" as the price of becoming homeowners in mostly black neighborhoods. This "tax" takes millions of dollars out of the pockets of black Atlantans who could otherwise use the money to invest in their families, homes, businesses, and communities.

Insurance redlining exacts a heavy toll on residents who live in Atlanta's mostly black neighborhoods. Insurance companies make hefty profits by overcharging their customers in black neighborhoods, while undercharging their customers in the mostly white suburbs. These practices translate into a huge transfer of wealth from black homeowners to white homeowners. It also means that high-profit premiums charged in mostly black Atlanta neighborhoods subsidize the low-profit premiums charged in mostly white suburban areas in metropolitan Atlanta. White suburbanites are not paying the "true" cost of their insurance.

The health of the metropolitan region is tied to the city 's overall health. New challenges are being raised to address urban infrastructure decline, disinvestment, inner-city decay, concentration of poverty, and housing imbalances resulting from sprawl. The city of Atlanta needs a healthy housing stock. The city received few housing and employment gains during the 1990s. Atlanta is still the cultural, sports, and entertainment center of the metropolitan region.

Housing discrimination and residential apartheid can no longer be swept under the rug. These problems are not likely to go away without some renewed attention and government intervention. Working together, government, private fair housing agencies, community-based organizations, and academic institutions can make a difference in the quality of life for all metropolitan Atlanta residents. The future of the region is intricately bound to how well fair housing and equity issues are addressed.

Notes

1. R.D. Bullard, J.E. Grisby III, and C. Lee, eds., *Residential Apartheid: The American Legacy.* Los Angeles: University of California, 1994, p. 1.
2. Christopher Bates Doob, *Racism: An American Cauldron.* New York: Harper-Collins, 1993.
3. National Advisory Commission on Civil Disorders, *Report of the National Advisory Commission on Civil Disorders.* New York: E.P. Dutton, 1968.
4. Joe R. Feagin, "A House Is Not a Home: White Racism and U.S. Housing Practices," in R.D. Bullard, J.E. Grigsby, and C. Lee, eds., *Residential Apartheid: The American Legacy,* 1994; Joe R. Feagin and Melvin P. Sikes, *Living with Racism: The Black Middle-Class Experience* (Boston: Beacon Books, 1995); Joe R. Feagin and Clairece B. Feagin, *Racial and Ethnic Relations* (Upper Saddle, NJ: Prentice-Hall, 1999).
5. D.S. Massey and N.A. Denton, *American Apartheid and the Making of the Underclass.* Cambridge, MA: Harvard University Press, 1993.
6. Joe R. Feagin, "Excluding Blacks and Others from Housing: The Foundations of White Racism," *Cityscape: A Journal of Policy Development and Research* 4 (1999), pp. 79–91.
7. Bill Lann Lee, "An Issue of Public Importance: The Justice Department's Enforcement of the Fair Housing Act," *Cityscape: A Journal of Policy Development and Research* 4 (1999), pp. 35–56.
8. Margery Austin Turner, Raymond J. Struyk, and Jon Yinger, *Housing Discrimination Study: Synthesis.* Washington, DC: U.S. Government Printing Office, 1996.
9. Andrew Hacker. *Two Nations: Black and White, Separate, Hostile, and Unequal.* New York: Scribner's, 1992.
10. Research Atlanta, *Atlanta in Black and White: Racial Attitudes and Perspectives.* Atlanta: Research Atlanta, 1995, p. 13.
11. Jennifer Hochschild, *Facing Up to the American Dream: Race, Class and the Soul of the Nation.* Princeton: Princeton University Press, 1995.

12. John Yinger, "Sustaining the Fair Housing Act," *Cityscape: A Journal of Policy Development and Research* 4 (1999), p. 97.
13. W.L. Updegrade. "Race and Money." *Money* 18 (1989), pp. 152–72.
14. Charles McC. Mathias Jr. and Marion Morris, "Fair Housing Legislation: Not an Easy Row to Hoe," *Cityscape: A Journal of Policy Development and Research* 4 (1999), pp. 21–32.
15. R.D. Bullard, *Invisible Houston: The Black Experience in Boom and Bust* (College Station: Texas A&M University Press, 1987); J.T. Darden. "The Status of Urban Blacks Twenty-five Years after the Civil Rights Act of 1964." *Sociology and Social Research* 73 (1989), pp. 160–173.
16. Douglas Kelbaugh, *Common Place: Toward Neighborhood and Regional Design.* Seattle: University of Washington Press, 1997, p. 31.
17. John Yinger, *Closed Doors, Opportunity Lost: The Continuing Cost of Housing Discrimination.* New York: Russell Sage Foundation, 1995, p. 66.
18. Charles McC. Mathias Jr. and Marion Morris, "Fair Housing Legislation: Not an Easy Row to Hoe."
19. D.J. Miller and Associates, *Fulton County Analysis of Impediments to Fair Housing.* Atlanta: Author, 1996.
20. Ibid., p. 8-8.
21. Bill Dedman, "The Color of Money," *Atlanta Journal-Constitution,* May 1–16, 1988.
22. John Wilke, "Mortgage Lending to Minorities Shows a Sharp 1994 Increase," *Wall Street Journal,* February 13, 1996, pp. A1, A8.
23. Gregory Squires, "The Indelible Color Line," *American Prospect* 42 (January 1999), p. 2.
24. Federal Financial Institutions Examination Council, press release, August 6, 1998. (Available on the Internet at http://www.FFIECG.OVv/pr080698.htm)
25. Christine Robitscher Ladd, "Federal Fair Housing Enforcement: The Clinton Record at the End of the First Term," in *The Continuing Struggle: Civil Rights and the Clinton Administration—Report of the Citizens' Commission on Civil Rights.* Washington, DC: Citizens' Commission on Civil Rights, 1997.
26. William J. Wilson, *When Work Disappears: The World of the New Urban Poor.* New York: Vintage Books, 1996.
27. Gregory Squires, "The Indelible Color Line."
28. Sierra Club, *The Dark Side of the American Dream: The Cost and Consequences of Suburban Sprawl.* College Park, MD: Sierra Club, 1998.
29. Atlanta Regional Commission, *Atlanta Region Outlook.* Atlanta: ARC, 1998, p. 55.
30. Ibid., p. 54.
31. Ibid.
32. J.D. Feins and R.G. Bratt. "Barred in Boston: Racial Discrimination in Housing." *Journal of the American Planning Association* 49 (1983), pp. 344–355.
33. John Yinger. *Closed Doors, Opportunity Lost,* p. 68.
34. Mark Feldstein, "Hitting the Poor Where They Live," *Nation* 58, April 4, 1994, p. 450.

35. Gregory Squires, "Forgoing a Tradition of Redlining for a Future of Reinvestment," *Business Journal Serving Greater Milwaukee* 15 (July 24, 1998), p. 50.
36. Ibid, p. 4.
37. Community Reinvestment Act. Pub. L. No. 95-128, tit. VIII, 91 Stat. 1111, 1147 (1977).
38. Gary Arthur Dymski, "The Theory of Bank Redlining and Discrimination: An Exploration," *Review of Black Political Economy* 23 (Winter 1995), pp. 37–74; Gregory Squires, "Race and Risk: The Reality of Redlining," *National Underwriter (Property & Casualty/Risk & Benefits Management)* 100 (September 16, 1996), pp. 63, 70.
39. Gregory Squires, "Policies of Prejudice: Risky Encounters with the Property Insurance Business," *Challenge* 39 (July 1996), pp. 45–50.
40. R.D. Bullard, J.E. Grisby III, and C. Lee. *Residential Apartheid: The American Legacy,* p. 3.
41. Shanna L. Smith and Cathy Clous, "Documenting Discrimination by Homeowners Insurance Companies through Testing," in *Insurance Redlining: Disinvestment, Reinvestment, and the Evolving Role of Financial Institutions.* Washington, DC: Urban Institute, 1997.
42. Shelly Emling, "Black Areas in City Pay Steep Rates," *Atlanta Journal-Constitution,* June 30, 1996, p. A16.
43. Shelly Emling, "Insurance: Is It Still a White Man's Game?" *Atlanta Journal-Constitution,* June 30, 1996, p. A17.
44. Shelly Emling, "Black Areas in City Pay Steep Rates," p. A16.
45. Ibid.
46. Ibid.
47. Ibid.
48. Ibid.

CHAPTER 5

The Legacy of Residential Segregation

Charles Jaret, Elizabeth P. Ruddiman, and Kurt Phillips

Even Atlanta residents accustomed to hearing their community described with superlatives and hyperbole must have raised an eyebrow when they read urban expert Christopher Leinberger's strong assertion: "Atlanta is probably the fastest-growing of any metropolitan area in the history of the world."[1] Whether we react to this claim with pride, optimism, skepticism, embarrassment, or worry depends on our value system and level of awareness regarding local growth patterns. What is certain, though, is that this large growth in Atlanta's population and land area presents us with challenges, problems, and opportunities. The purpose of this chapter is to analyze recent Atlanta growth trends, often characterized as "suburban sprawl," to see the impact and outcomes they have on the residential distribution of racial groups and people in different income levels. Before looking specifically at these patterns and results in Atlanta, we provide a context for our findings by reviewing what urban sociology has discovered about the challenges, problems, and opportunities associated with suburban sprawl. Then we present findings on growth in Atlanta and conclude with policy recommendations.

Suburban Sprawl in Historical and Sociological Perspective

Although the popular image of Americans' move to suburbia is quite positive, replete with images of cleaner, safer communities, better schools, and ownership of larger, more luxurious homes fulfilling the "American Dream," the phrase "suburban sprawl" is not a positive or even a neutral term; from its inception it had, and still retains, a negative connotation. It implies that the extension of modern suburbia promotes wasteful, often ugly, expansion into the open countryside, creates an over-reliance on the automobile and highway, saps the vitality out of city communities, and does serious damage to the natural environment. Critics of modern massive suburbanization also claim that it "has contributed to the difficulties of large cities of the United States" by weakening the sense of community in metropolitan areas and reducing the "degree of concern and responsibility which suburbanites feel for the plight of core areas."[2] One of the reasons for this outcome is that suburbanization occurred in ways that increased the residential polarization of city and suburban neighborhoods by race and income.[3] We will examine this claim closely, by analyzing recent data on residential distribution of racial groups and income categories in metropolitan Atlanta. We want to see whether or not recent suburbanization here in Atlanta is producing the outcome that the Kerner Commission warned about: the creation of "two societies, one black, one white—separate and unequal."[4]

Despite the reservations of scholars like Jackson or earlier critics of suburbanization,[5] the outward sprawl of suburban communities, accompanied by a general decline of the inner city (except for selective renewal of certain parts of it), was seen by many researchers as part of the natural growth process metropolitan areas undergo. Few experts thought that much could or should be done to stop or tinker with suburban growth. For their part, people who moved to the suburbs generally saw their own settlement there as "progress" and felt they had a basic right to seek and enjoy the "better quality of life" provided them by the opening rounds of suburban home building, commercial development, and land use changes. However, when people or developments that they believe (rightly or wrongly) may threaten their quality of life and/or property values seek to join them in the suburbs, many civic associations and suburban homeowners resist and, with varying degrees of success, try to prevent such incursions in their vicinity. This frequently generates conflicts that are fought out before zoning boards and county commissions or in court rooms, where it becomes rather obvious that deciding what gets built where is not a "natural process" that "just happens." Rather, it is an intensely political process in which groups with conflicting interests (not to mention unequal resources and degrees of power), holding different social values and opposing views about which set of rights have the most legal or moral weight, try to get their way (or failing that, get the best possible compromise). The outcomes of these conflicts usually favor the side with the best organization, connections, resources, and legal acumen; this means that poor people and racial minorities are less likely to obtain the result they seek in disputes over housing or related conflicts.

For a close look at how this occurs in Atlanta, see Roughton's[6] articles on Snellville.

Recently, urban sociologists John Logan and Harvey Molotch have drawn more attention to these problems of unequal and uneven development. One result of their research is wider recognition that suburban sprawl is literally a constructed outcome, and that in most communities a specific set of people work at producing it; many of them profit handsomely from it, while other parties either miss out on the benefits of growth or are actually disadvantaged as a result of it.[7] Their research demonstrates that city and suburban growth does not unfold under the direction of a "master plan" drawn up by planners and citizens for the good of the public in general, nor does it emerge from a scheme created by a small, unified cabal of powerful people. Rather, urban expansion and sprawl are advocated and sponsored by what Logan and Molotch call a "growth coalition"—a network of active developers and other well-placed people linked across the public and private sectors and across local, municipal, county, regional, state, and federal levels, who share a common attitude (that growth is vital to a community) and give greatest priority to the idea that people who own and/or develop real estate have the right to use it in the way that brings them the most financial profit. With this as a starting point, urban sociologists trace out a number of community problems, such as disinvestment from certain neighborhoods (redlining), road and land-use decisions that favor some people and hurt others, racial and income segregation, high concentrations of homeless people in certain areas, spatially unequal educational opportunities, and overexposure in certain neighborhoods to pollution (e.g., waste dumps) or stigmatized activities (e.g., strip clubs, "porno shops"). We will briefly mention some examples of these that have arisen in Atlanta.

Signs of the Problem in Atlanta

Atlantans recently have seen warning signs about community social problems that stem wholly or partly from rapid and extensive suburban growth. Perhaps most obvious is the air pollution caused mainly by automobile emissions. Air quality in 13 metro counties seriously violates federal standards for ground-level ozone, and this causes lung-related health hazards. The U.S. Environmental Protection Agency (EPA) and other federal agencies are requiring the Atlanta Regional Commission (ARC) and the Georgia Environmental Protection Division (EPD) to create a 25-year plan that will significantly reduce ozone levels. In mid-February 1998 they announced that they could not create a plan that meets the required ozone level standards. As a result of this failure, Atlanta will be unable to use federal funds for many road widening and new road projects (which limits growth) and may face restrictions on business and industrial expansion until a satisfactory plan is adopted.[8] Other sprawl-related environmental problems include water shortages in some suburbs during the summer months, and, during heavy rains, flooding from runoff water that is not absorbed into the earth because so much of the ground has been paved over. Sudden population growth in new areas and declining enrollments in other locales cause great burdens to county school systems and taxpayers. Most obvious are the overcrowded classes and trailers (in north Fulton, DeKalb, and Gwinnett counties) and the need to spend millions of dollars to enlarge schools or build new ones in areas where large numbers of new residents are settling. Overcrowding in western Cobb County is now so serious that school administrators may have to shift ninth graders into a middle school. This violates a state regulation on middle schools and jeopardizes $600,000 that Cobb County receives as a middle school grant, unless the state legislature passes a law exempting school districts with "extraordinary growth" from the regulation.[9] Both Cobb and Gwinnett counties are facing a financial squeeze because current tax revenues are not enough to pay for new schools being built. They are planning to take out loans to pay for school construction.[10]

Another sprawl-related problem is the ongoing battle between suburban neighborhood residents and developers of malls, apartments, and office complexes. A good example is the one brewing in north Gwinnett County, where in early 1998 M. D. Hodges Enterprises, an Atlanta developer, proposed a 417-acre mixed-use development that includes five hotels, two apartment complexes, two shopping centers, and several mid-rise office buildings near I-85 and Old Peachtree Road. On February 3, 1998, hundreds of affluent suburban residents protested against this development, claiming it would cause increased traffic congestion, pollution, over-crowded schools, poorer quality of life, and other undesirable results. This project received a negative recommendation from the ARC, which said it would create too much traffic and pollution. However, ARC's position is advisory, not binding, and in March 1998 the Gwinnett County Commission voted unanimously to approve the project, with one important change—the two apartment complexes were deleted.[11] Had this change (which lowers population density and keeps out less affluent residents) not been made, local neighbors would have lobbied political leaders and used the courts to try to prevent or minimize the growth that they do not want.

A different problem faces less affluent residents of Cherokee County. A small headline in the *Atlanta Journal-Constitution* (February 2, 1998:E-5) declares "Mobile homes make way for the wealthy." Two mobile home parks on Bells Ferry Road in southern Cherokee are for sale, with one owner about "to sell his property for $1.5 million to developers of upscale shopping centers or offices catering to wealthy homeowners in the nearby Towne Lake community." The article does not mention where the current residents will find housing nor the disruption that closing the mobile home park will bring them, but nevertheless it is a real problem for them and other low-income people living in areas undergoing rapid development that caters to the more affluent.

Most areas on Atlanta's north side are experiencing so much explosive residential and commercial development that some residents are protesting that there are too many new stores, malls, offices, and subdivisions being built. But in many parts of Atlanta's south side, the opposite problem exists—too little investment and a lack of "desirable" types of development, and either residential and commercial stagnation, loss, or the arrival of "undesirable" businesses (e.g., liquor stores; the controversy in 1997 over the opening of a "9 1/2 Weeks" store in a southwest Atlanta neighborhood). An example of the costs imposed by this uneven development is the problem facing shoppers in south Fulton and south DeKalb counties as many large retailers close stores there and then reinvest on the north side (or elsewhere) by expanding or refurbishing existing stores or opening new ones. This past year Macy's in Shannon Southpark Mall, Target on Old National Highway, Service Merchandise near South DeKalb Mall, and most recently, Service Merchandise on Old National Highway in College Park announced they were closing because their parent companies wanted to "streamline" operations by eliminating "underperforming" stores.[12] While closure of these less profitable stores makes sense to corporate leaders responsible to

Atlanta's northern suburbs captured over three-fourths of all jobs created in the region between 1990 and 1997.

stockholders who want to maximize the return on their investment, lack of good quality retail choices in the area may have a devastating effect on neighborhood residents' satisfaction and desire to remain in the area, not to mention the negative economic impact it has on local employment, property values, and tax revenue.

Another symptom of problems created by sprawl are the bans and moratoria on new building (usually of apartments) in areas where suburban residents feel enough growth has already occurred. By asserting that apartments will bring more children than the local schools can handle, and also more crime and traffic into the area, and by claiming apartment dwellers "use a disproportionate amount of resources . . . and pay less in their taxes," opponents of new construction have succeeded in preventing apartment buildings from being built in many parts of the suburbs.[13] Instead, more expensive homes and developments taking up even more space are built, which contributes to more sprawl and the exclusion of the less affluent and the poor from the new communities. An interview with a real estate agent and our own observations indicate this is happening in the Duluth–Suwanee–Buford corridor of central Gwinnett County.

Finally, suburban sprawl might be exacerbating the problem of white flight and the development of "separate societies" in Atlanta. This could promote racial prejudices, feed inequality of opportunity (schools, health services, job/employment prospects, shopping, and quality of life), create unequal local tax bases, and affect the appreciation of property values and accumulation of wealth. As shown in Research Atlanta's (1997) report, the middle class has left the city of Atlanta in much greater numbers than has been the case in most other U.S. cities. Middle class suburbanization, however, is not simply a racial matter (i.e., it is not just white flight), since much of Atlanta's black middle class has also moved to the suburbs, and the newest emerging area popular among affluent blacks is along Cascade Road beyond I-285.[14] Left behind in the city and old metropolitan core, with no place else to go, are low-income blacks.

We face the prospect of a fragmented metropolitan area composed of defensive, exclusive, gated-communities for the better off, whose prime common interest lies in zoning out residential opportunities for less affluent people, who then must find homes in areas that are less prestigious and less well served by schools, health facilities, stores, and other necessities. But we should not deceive ourselves. Before extensive suburban sprawl and the massive movement out by the middle class, Atlanta was highly segregated by race and income level. The argument regarding racial and income segregation is not that recent suburbanization has created a new problem but that it may continue an already existing problem.

Opportunities

Several events in Atlanta since the late 1980s have created some momentum for change in housing opportunities. Whether these are actually promoting new and better options for the less affluent and formerly excluded racial groups or are reinforcing earlier tendencies toward separation is an open question, though very recent data suggest a little movement in the direction of change. Events setting up the potential for change began with Bill Dedman's Pulitzer Prize–winning "The Color of Money." [15] This series, published in the *Atlanta Journal-Constitution* in 1988, brought to the fore the issue of home mortgage "redlining" by the major Atlanta banks. Dedman's conclusions that Atlanta banks were not actively seeking to make mortgage loans in black neighborhoods and that their percentage of loans to blacks was much lower than to white mortgage seekers (even when their prospective homes were located in areas of equal socioeconomic level) brought protest and bad publicity to the banks. In response, some new practices for serving potential black mortgage customers were arranged along with a bank consortium pool of $65 million for minority home loans. A few years later (1992), Atlanta banks were again under scrutiny, and attention focused on allegations that Decatur Federal Savings & Loan was not adequately providing mortgage loans to blacks. The bank reached a $1 million settlement with 48 plaintiffs and agreed to change its underwriting practices, increase advertising and marketing in minority media, and make other changes to encourage more inner-city lending. [16]

Depending on how these home loan opportunities are implemented and administered, these programs could result in expansion of the range of residential choices available to blacks, including greater access to less segregated neighborhoods, or they could mean more capital made available to purchase or improve housing in existing black neighborhoods (by blacks or by people of other races). In either case, chances for increased residential integration in Atlanta are a little higher as a result of these developments.

Another development in the mid-1990s came with Atlanta's build-up for the 1996 Olympics, which displaced residents of several large predominately black public housing projects. High-level leadership changes were made at the Atlanta Housing Authority (AHA) in 1994, and the new executive director, Renee Lewis Glover, began a policy of downsizing many public housing complexes. The AHA plans to eliminate nearly one-third of its public housing units by the year 2000. [17] It hopes that a continued supply of Section 8 housing subsidy money will enable low-income households to find housing in the private rental market and that more housing for low and very low income Atlantans will be created by other organizations (e.g., nonprofit agencies like Habitat for Humanity). But there is already a long waiting list

The city of Atlanta contains 12 percent of the region's population and 65 percent of the area's public housing.

of people who have applied for Section 8 housing subsidies. Moreover, a survey by the Community Housing Resource Center shows that in 1997 other affordable housing developers added a total of 2,637 housing units to the metro area's stock of housing for low-income households. This does not represent a large increase after you subtract the number of low-income units boarded up or torn down by the AHA.

In the most notable case, Techwood Homes was given to other authorities who totally rehabbed it to house Olympic athletes and subsequently to become Centennial Place, designed to be a mixed-income community and to house university students. The ideal of this new policy is to reduce the concentration of poor families and increase their prospects of living in mixed-race, mixed-income settings. Although some families were given housing vouchers to enable them to rent apartments in "better" areas, and a few others (just 65 out of 635 families[18]) returned to the Techwood area after its conversion to mixed-income, multiracial status, the residential fate of many people forced out of public housing has not been tracked. Since it is possible that many of them moved to other poor black areas or became homeless, we cannot be certain that this development has achieved its goal of reducing racial and income segregation. Similarly, East Lake Meadows public housing project is being redeveloped as the Villages of East Lake, a mixed-income community. In the process, what was 650 units of public housing will be replaced with 540 mixed-income units, of which 249 units (46%) will be on-site public housing.[19] The effort to move the poor out of "poverty ghettos" and integrate them with other income categories is commendable, but doubts still remain as to whether there will be enough housing available for them.

Regardless of the practices of lending institutions, the AHA, and other low-income housing developers, reducing residential segregation and improving the housing options for poor people in Atlanta ultimately depends to a large degree on housing/neighborhood preferences of the general public. If there is little or no desire for or acceptance of more integrated living, then there is little hope for improvement. However, recent public opinion research on white and black Atlantans' attitudes allows some optimism about the potential for more racial integration. A study by Research Atlanta (1995) found that (a) most blacks would be willing to move into an integrated neighborhood; (b) most whites would be comfortable living in a neighborhood that was one-third black, and one-quarter would be willing to move into a majority black area; (c) just over half the blacks thought they would be accepted in such suburban areas as Marietta, Smyrna, and Norcross. [20] Even if some respondents gave socially desirable answers rather than their real attitudes, and recognizing the usual gap between words and actions, these findings still suggest that more racial residential integration is now attainable than currently exists. However, an unstated premise underlying the attitudes of those favorable to racial integration seems to be that it involves mixing people of similar economic status. We are quite sure that less support exists among whites for residential integration if it involves living with many black or other racial minorities that are poor or near poor.

Another factor relating to potentially better housing options for blacks in Atlanta is that for the last few years black average household income has increased (at a higher rate than that of whites) and poverty has declined slightly. This improved financial situation could mean more ability to qualify for home loans or pay for better quality housing in either the city or the suburbs.

In general, Atlanta is faced with the challenge and the opportunity of cultivating a progressive and balanced response to its problem of sprawl, perhaps out of a coalition of several interest groups. Ideally it can begin with people and groups from the environmental movement and with those dedicated to improving the housing options for racial minorities, be it through more residential integration or improved housing and quality of life in predominately minority communities. It should also link and work with socially responsible developers and any suburban political leaders and neighborhood associations that recognize the problem signs described above and want to do more than just remain isolated from them.

Recent Growth in Atlanta

It is widely known that Atlanta is one of the nation's fastest growing metropolitan areas. From 1990 to 1996 Atlanta's population added 581,730 people; Los Angeles was the only metropolitan area that grew by a larger number. Atlantans, more than residents of other metro areas, are buying new housing—in 1997, some 41 percent of all homes sold in Atlanta were brand new, which is more than any other major market area.[21] As a result, Atlanta is rapidly spreading out over more land, since most of the new housing is built in suburban areas. A check of single-family home-building permits for the first 11 months of 1997 found that over 40 percent were located in Gwinnett (25.8%) and Cobb (16.7%) counties. Another large amount of the new single-family home permits were for Fulton (16.6%) and DeKalb (10.9%) counties, with Clayton County having just 4.3 percent. The five remaining metro counties combined for 25.7 percent—Henry (10.4%), Cherokee (6.4%), Fayette (4.3%), Douglas (3.0%), and Rockdale (1.6%).

Atlanta's high growth rate and consumption of new housing are not new phenomena; in the 1970s and 1980s Atlanta was among the metro areas with the highest rates of population increase. This population growth, however, was not concentrated in the densely settled urban sections of Atlanta but instead occurred unevenly, mainly in the northern suburban counties, especially Cobb and Gwinnett. Since 1980 over 70 percent of the population

Atlanta led the nation in residential construction with a record 48,262 residential building permits issued in 1996.

growth was to the areas north and northeast of the downtown core, while about 30 percent or less took place in areas south of I-20.[22]

A clear sign of how this residential and commercial development has sprawled out is the number of counties that have been added to "Metropolitan Atlanta" by two important agencies, the ARC and the U.S. Bureau of the Census. Back in 1970 both defined metropolitan Atlanta as five counties (Fulton, DeKalb, Clayton, Cobb, and Gwinnett). Now ARC uses a 10-county area and the Census Bureau includes 20 counties in its Atlanta metropolitan statistical area.[23] This chapter uses the 10-county ARC definition of metro Atlanta.

Of course, residential and commercial growth in Atlanta is not simply a story of an expanding suburban periphery. Businesses and residential high-rise condominiums and apartments in Midtown and Buckhead have sprung up, and in the 1990s much undeveloped land and many farms and horse stables sandwiched between old suburban subdivisions in DeKalb County have been turned into new, expensive "in-fill" housing. In the city, a few poor neighborhoods have had a modest amount of low- and moderate-income housing built or rehabbed, while a select few neighborhoods have been gentrified extensively. Spurred by the Olympics, apartment construction in the city increased in 1995 and 1996, adding over 5,000 new apartments and lofts to downtown and Midtown. Although occupancy rates declined after the Olympics, they rose sharply after mid-1997.[24]

Table 5.1 shows the population size and growth for the 10 metro Atlanta counties from 1970 to 1997, as well as each county's net migration for the period 1980 to 1990 (the most recent period for which data are available). It shows that in the 1970s and 1980s, Cobb and Gwinnett counties accounted for about half of all the population growth in the 10-county area, and about 43 percent in the 1990s. So large was this population increase that for much of this time Cobb County and/or Gwinnett County were among the 10 fastest-growing counties in the entire nation. Fulton County shows a tremendous turnaround, shifting from a declining population in the 1970s and becoming the third-highest growing metro county in the 1990s. Cherokee and Fayette counties grew steadily if not spectacularly. While DeKalb, Clayton, Douglas, and Rockdale counties have seen their rate of growth decrease, Henry County's has increased markedly each decade.

The last column in Table 5.1 shows how much of each county's 1980s population growth is due directly to residential in-movement (i.e., the component of growth above and beyond having more births than deaths). These numbers, which reflect where people chose to live, vividly show the great popularity of Gwinnett and Cobb counties. Together these two counties attracted almost 65 percent of the metro area's net migration gains in the

Table 5.1. Population of Metropolitan Atlanta Counties (ARC definitions), 1970–1997

County	Population				Change in Population			Net Migration
	1970	1980	1990	1997	1970–80	1980–90	1990–97	1980–1990
Fulton	605,210	589,904	670,800	760,100	−15,306	80,896	89,300	12,347
DeKalb	415,387	483,024	553,800	594,400	67,637	70,776	40,600	17,532
Cobb	196,793	297,718	453,400	535,000	100,925	155,682	81,600	109,152
Clayton	98,126	150,357	184,100	209,500	52,231	33,743	25,400	12,332
Gwinnett	72,349	166,808	356,500	478,900	94,459	189,692	122,400	150,617
Rockdale	18,152	36,747	54,500	64,800	18,595	17,753	10,300	13,613
Henry	23,724	36,309	59,200	95,900	12,585	22,891	36,700	18,311
Douglas	28,659	54,573	71,700	88,400	25,914	17,127	16,700	10,048
Cherokee	31,059	51,699	91,000	122,300	20,640	39,301	31,300	29,289
Fayette	11,364	29,043	62,800	84,100	17,679	33,757	21,300	29,895
Total org (5)	1,387,865	1,687,811	2,218,600	2,577,900	299,946	530,789	359,300	301,980
Total (10)	1,500,823	1,896,182	2,557,800	3,033,400	395,359	661,618	475,600	403,136

Source: Atlanta Regional Commission, *1997 Population and Housing.*

1980s. The least popular counties for people who moved in the 1980s were Douglas, Clayton, Fulton, and Rockdale.

Changing Racial Patterns: County and Superdistrict Analysis

Despite this great population growth and relocation over a 27-year period, the residential distributions of the black/other[25] and white populations have become only slightly more similar. Blacks in Atlanta have moved to the suburbs in large numbers. In fact, of all the metro areas in the United States, only Washington, D.C., has a larger black suburban population than Atlanta.[26] Atlanta's white suburban population is also very large, and in general, the two groups do not live in the same parts of the suburbs. An overview of the patterns by decade, at the county level, is given first, then a closer examination, using ARC's "Superdistricts" will be provided.

Table 5.2 shows the racial distributions and growth trends for the metro counties in 1980 and 1997 and reveals important information. Earlier, in 1970, whites and blacks were concentrated in just two metro counties, Fulton and DeKalb, though they lived in different neighborhoods. Just over 60 percent of the whites in the 10-county area lived in those 2 counties, but for blacks the concentration was much more extreme, as about 90 percent of the metro area's blacks resided in Fulton and DeKalb counties. During the 1970s

Table 5.2. Racial Composition of Metropolitan Atlanta Counties, 1980 to 1997

County	No. of Whites	No. of Blacks	County Racial Composition		Portion of Metro Area's Population	
			% White	% Black	% of All Whites	% of All Blacks
1980						
Fulton	280,334	309,570	47.5	52.5	20.1	62.1
DeKalb	344,254	138,770	71.3	28.7	24.6	27.9
Clayton	137,950	12,407	91.7	8.3	9.9	2.5
Cobb	281,625	16,093	94.6	5.4	20.1	3.2
Gwinnett	161,171	5,637	96.6	3.4	11.5	1.1
Rockdale	33,220	3,527	90.4	9.6	2.4	0.7
Henry	29,646	6,663	81.6	18.4	2.1	1.3
Fayette	27,591	1,452	95.0	5.0	2.0	0.3
Douglas	51,444	3,129	94.3	5.7	3.7	0.6
Cherokee	50,324	1,375	97.3	2.7	3.6	0.3
Total	1,397,559	498,623	73.7	26.3	100.0	100.0
1997						
Fulton	383,530	376,570	50.5	49.5	17.8	42.8
DeKalb	303,979	290,421	51.1	48.9	14.1	32.9
Clayton	150,397	59,103	71.8	28.2	7.0	6.7
Cobb	463,623	71,377	86.7	13.3	21.6	8.1
Gwinnett	433,105	45,795	90.4	9.6	20.1	5.2
Rockdale	57,716	7,084	89.1	10.9	2.7	0.8
Henry	84,467	11,433	88.1	11.9	3.9	1.3
Fayette	76,679	7,421	91.2	8.8	3.6	0.8
Douglas	79,711	8,689	90.2	9.8	3.7	0.9
Cherokee	117,517	4,783	96.1	3.9	5.5	0.5
Total	2,150,724	882,676	70.9	29.1	100.0	100.0

Source: 1980 data are from U.S. Bureau of the Census; 1997 data are from Atlanta Regional Commission, *1997 Population and Housing.*

the different impact of suburbanization on blacks and whites became clear. For whites, the balance tipped during the 1970s so that by 1980 less than half (44.7%) of all whites still lived in Fulton and DeKalb counties. During this period Cobb and Gwinnett counties dramatically gained population at the expense of Fulton and DeKalb. For blacks the suburbanization of the 1970s had a much different meaning. It was relatively smaller in volume and was marked by shifts within Fulton County (e.g., from parts of the city of Atlanta to southwest Fulton County) and from the city of Atlanta to DeKalb County, with negligible black population growth in any of the other metro counties. Thus, by 1980, blacks were still as concentrated in Fulton and DeKalb counties as they had been in 1970 (about 90% of them resided there), and the only difference was a small drop in the percentage living in Fulton County and a small gain in the percentage living in DeKalb County. As a result of these different patterns of residential movement and natural increase, the index of dissimilarity (measured at the county level) between whites and blacks/others increased from 1970 to 1980 (going from 41.6 to 45.2). Simply put, this means that by the end of the 1970s whites and blacks were less likely (rather than more likely) to cohabit a county than they were in 1970, thus residential segregation had increased.

During the 1980s a different racial pattern of population growth and settlement emerged. One important change was that Fulton County experienced a substantial drop in its share of the black population (from 62% in 1980 down to 45% in 1990), and other counties besides DeKalb began to see increases in their share of the black population. In particular, Cobb, Clayton, and Gwinnett counties (along with DeKalb) all had substantial growth in black populations (in fact, by 1990 more blacks lived in those four counties than in Fulton, something that was far from being true in 1980). While DeKalb County was the site of the largest portion of the black population growth during the 1980s (garnering 42% of it), that is not the whole story. Of all the 1980–1990 black population growth (from net migration and natural increase) taking place in the 10-county metro area, 41 percent occurred outside Fulton and DeKalb counties (and almost 60% of the black growth outside of Fulton and DeKalb took place in Cobb and Gwinnett counties). These suburbanization trends for blacks in the 1980s represent significant changes from their pattern in the 1970s.

For whites, suburban growth in the 1980s saw continued shrinkage in Fulton's and DeKalb's share of the white population (in fact, DeKalb County had a net population loss of over 50,000 whites in the 1980s). New developments in the 1980s were a decline in Clayton County's share of the white population and a switch in the county with the fastest-growing white population from Cobb to Gwinnett. Of the 1980–1990 white population growth (from net migration and natural increase) taking place in the 10-county metro area, all of it occurred outside Fulton and DeKalb counties (and just over 70% of all the white growth outside Fulton and DeKalb took place in Cobb and Gwinnett counties). These suburbanization trends for whites in the 1980s represent a continuation of their 1970s patterns.

On balance these developments in the 1980s maintained the drift toward racial residential separation at the county level, or at best slightly reduced it. The index of dissimilarity between blacks/others and whites only declined from 45.2 in 1980 to 44.4 in 1990, indicating that large percentages of the two groups were living in different counties from each other, but slightly fewer people did so in 1990 than had a decade earlier.

Atlanta's high growth in the 1990s brought both continuity and change in housing trends. From 1990 to 1997, the pattern established in the 1980s by blacks continued—slower growth in Fulton and DeKalb counties and more movement to and increase in other suburbs, mainly Cobb and Gwinnett counties. Among whites, the 1990s saw even more extensive movement and growth in Gwinnett and Cobb counties, as well as significant growth in Henry and Cherokee counties. The main change, however, from the previous decade was in Fulton County—instead of continuing to lose whites, it became very attractive to them, especially in north Fulton. In the 1990s, Fulton County added about as many whites as did Cobb County. The index of dissimilarity (over the 10-county area) between whites and blacks/others in 1997 was 43.6, a slight drop from its 1990 level of 44.4. This indicates a continuation of the previous decade's pattern of whites and blacks taking small steps toward a more similar spread across metro Atlanta's counties.

A Closer Look: Superdistricts from 1980 to 1997

Looking at racial patterns at the county level does not tell the full story, since even if many people from different groups reside in the same county, they may still live far apart (e.g., DeKalb County, where whites predominate in the north and blacks in the south). The ARC divides the 10 metro counties into 48 subareas called "superdistricts" to show social conditions at a local level. We use these to see the extent to which racial groups in Atlanta cohabit the same parts of their respective counties.

One important finding at the superdistrict level is that index of dissimilarity has declined. In 1980 it was 69.5; in 1990 it was 58.3; and in 1997 it was 55.2. This means that within counties the black and white populations did become distributed somewhat more equally—they did not become more isolated nor did they remain as isolated in different sections of their counties of residence as they had been in 1980. However, most suburban superdistricts show, for the 1990s, only small increases in the percentage of their residents that are black (e.g., from 1990 to 1997, Sandy Springs went from 10.6% to 12.9% black; Northeast Cobb from 6.4% to 7.5%; Central Gwinnett from 7.3% to 8.7%; West Fayette from 6.5% to 8.5%).

In 1980 only two superdistricts (Northwest Atlanta and Southwest Atlanta) were 80 percent or more black. They were both in the city of Atlanta and these two superdistricts accounted for just over one-third of the black population. This changed in the 1980s, a decade of heavy black suburbanization. By 1990 six superdistricts became 80 percent or more black (Northwest Atlanta, Southwest Atlanta, the Central Business District, Southeast Atlanta, South DeKalb, and Southeast DeKalb). The percentage of the black population living in these overwhelmingly black areas rose to just under half (46.4%) in 1990. This was the high-water mark of black concentration in overwhelmingly black areas. During the 1990s no new superdistricts became more than 80 percent black, and by 1997 the overall percentage of blacks living in the six existing highly black superdistricts dropped a little (to 42.7%), as more black population growth took place in some of the same areas that the white population was growing.

We can see this important change in location of 1990s black population growth by comparing the superdistricts that gained the most black and white population in the 1990s with those in the preceding decade. Table 5.3 shows the 20 superdistricts that gained the most whites and blacks in the 1980s. For whites the top 11 were all in the northern suburbs, led by Central Gwinnett and Northeast Cobb, and only 6 of the 20 superdistricts with large white increases are in the southern suburban rim (East and West Fayette, North and South Henry, South Rockdale, and South Clayton). Note that of the 12

Table 5.3. The Twenty Atlanta Superdistricts with the Largest Increases in White and Black Population, 1980 to 1990

	Areas Ranked by Size of White Population Increase			Areas Ranked by Size of Black Population Increase	
Superdistrict	1980–1990 White Population Growth	1980–1990 Black Population Growth	Superdistrict	1980–1990 Black Population Growth	1980–1990 White Population Growth
Central Gwinnett	53,604	5,702	SE DeKalb	32,253	2,915
NE Cobb	49,253	5,875	NE DeKalb	26,883	−7,549
Norcross	39,266	16,909	South DeKalb	23,619	−12,171
NW Cobb	33,721	2,820	SW DeKalb	18,343	−15,209
Roswell	32,689	4,358	Shannon	18,250	−8,033
Snellville	29,878	1,078	Chamblee	18,248	−16,340
North Fulton	23,351	1,414	Riverdale	17,058	366
Woodstock	21,997	774	Norcross	16,909	39,266
SW Cobb	19,296	2,759	Cumberland	14,916	12,590
North Gwinnett	17,856	816	NE Clayton	11,522	−10,708
Lilburn	16,706	2,412	South Cobb	10,560	−4,295
East Fayette	15,378	1,928	Tri-Cities	10,368	−17,881
Sandy Springs	15,212	6,154	Airport	7,509	−3,724
West Fayette	15,072	1,379	SE Atlanta	6,623	−9,302
East Central Cherokee	12,704	400	Sandy Springs	6,154	15,212
Cumberland	12,590	14,916	NE Cobb	5,875	49,253
North Henry	10,594	813	Central Gwinnett	5,702	53,604
South Rockdale	9,571	501	Marietta	4,583	3,604
South Clayton	8,772	2,948	Roswell	4,358	32,689
South Henry	8,425	−329	NW DeKalb	4,265	−1,514

Source: Atlanta Regional Commission, *1997 Population and Housing.*

superdistricts with the largest white increase in the 1980s, only one (Norcross) is among the 12 superdistricts that gained the most blacks. Conversely, the areas that had the largest black population gains in the 1980s were mainly in DeKalb (Southeast, Northeast, South, and Southwest). These areas had almost no white gain, and in fact most of them show white population losses. Overall, black and white population growth in superdistricts in the 1980s were negatively correlated with each other (–0.27), meaning that, in general, where one group was growing in number the other was shrinking or barely increasing. If that trend continued, Atlanta would move toward increased racial residential separation.

That trend toward racial separation was not as strong in the 1990s, and as Table 5.4 shows, in some of the growing superdistricts it has been reversed. Of the 12 superdistricts with the largest white increases in the 1990s, 6 of

Table 5.4. The Twenty Atlanta Superdistricts with the Largest Increases in White and Black Population, 1990 to 1997

	Areas Ranked by Size of White Population Increase			Areas Ranked by Size of Black Population Increase		
Superdistrict	1990–1997 White Population Growth	1990–1997 Black Population Growth		Superdistrict	1990–1997 Black Population Growth	1990–1997 White Population Growth
Central Gwinnett	39,810	5,233		South DeKalb	11,580	1,487
North Fulton	36,211	4,776		SE DeKalb	7,490	5,776
North Gwinnett	33,307	2,559		Chamblee	7,114	–117
NW Cobb	28,676	3,327		Central Gwinnett	5,233	39,810
Woodstock	18,508	994		North Fulton	4,776	36,211
Roswell	15,363	3,154		SW Atlanta	4,755	433
NE Cobb	14,751	2,839		NW Cobb	3,327	28,676
Snellville	12,590	1,449		Roswell	3,154	15,363
South Henry	12,505	3,022		South Clayton	3,083	11,522
West Fayette	11,779	1,703		South Henry	3,022	12,505
South Clayton	11,522	3,083		Sandy Springs	2,894	6,881
SW Cobb	10,833	1,772		Shannon	2,846	1,108
North Henry	10,655	1,046		NE Cobb	2,839	14,751
East Gwinnett	10,079	614		Riverdale	2,812	3,388
East Henry	8,851	621		NE Atlanta	2,588	2,418
Norcross	8,279	1,904		North Gwinnett	2,559	33,307
East Central Cherokee	8,260	957		Buckhead	2,556	4,174
East Douglas	7,494	1,497		Cumberland	2,240	4,506
West Douglas	7,079	630		Marietta	1,978	2,451
Sandy Springs	6,881	2894		Norcross	1,904	8,279

Source: Atlanta Regional Commission, *1997 Population and Housing.*

them also appear among the 12 superdistricts with the largest black population increases. Unlike the 1980s, now both racial groups' populations are growing in the same superdistricts, and the correlation between black and white population change in the 1990s is positive (0.24). This reversal from the 1980s means that blacks and whites are not just moving into the same counties, some are also moving into the same superdistricts within their counties of residence (though some local racial residential separation persists in subareas of superdistricts, as many blacks and whites settle in different census tracts, neighborhoods, and suburban subdivisions). We must also note that the size of the black increases in areas that are popular with whites (e.g., Central Gwinnett, North Fulton, North Gwinnett) is so much smaller than the size of the white population increases that it will actually only reduce racial segregation by a small amount. Although the momentum toward integration is positive, in the form it is currently taking in the most popular, booming suburbs, it will be a very slow, gradual process.

Some parts of metropolitan Atlanta have made small shifts toward racial integration and residential stability. However, given the seriousness of the problems produced by racial residential segregation,[27] one might say that Atlanta ought to be taking large strides in that direction, but in reality we are just taking baby steps toward integration and better housing options. Ideas about what might be done are included in the final section on policy suggestions.

Suburban Sprawl and Income Categories

As we finished writing this chapter, the U.S. Department of Housing and Urban Development released results of its 1995 American Housing Survey. It provides evidence showing that the amount of rental housing that is affordable to the lowest-income-level families is actually shrinking. It also finds that severe shortages of low cost housing for the less affluent is a common problem in suburban and city neighborhoods in Atlanta and other metropolitan areas throughout the country. In this section we use Atlanta Regional Commission data to examine the housing locations of low-income Atlantans.

Residential separation between poor people and those who are not poor is less severe than racial separation in Atlanta and other metropolitan areas. Research suggests that from 1970 to 1990 the degree of segregation experienced by low-income people in Atlanta changed very little,[28] but that research does not take the differing experiences of Atlanta's poor blacks and poor whites into account. The various racial and income groups in Atlanta have not all equally participated in the shift to the suburbs. Middle class whites and blacks have left the city of Atlanta in large numbers, albeit in different directions. The black middle class is highly suburban. Over 70 percent of all black households in metro Atlanta with annual family incomes of $30,000 to $75,000 live outside Atlanta's city limits, mainly in the southern parts of Fulton and DeKalb counties. This is a much higher percentage than in most other major metropolitan areas.[29] The white middle class is distributed mainly in Atlanta's northern suburbs, and most of the poor whites have also left the city and live in northern suburbs. Similarly, Asian and Latin American immigrants, be they affluent or poor, to a large extent are located in suburban areas. In contrast, most (62% in 1990) of metro Atlanta's poor blacks reside in the city of Atlanta, and of the poor blacks who live in the city, most (51% in 1990) are in neighborhoods that have very high poverty rates (40% or more of the households below poverty level).

The contrast between how Atlanta's white poor have been able to leave the old core of the metropolitan area (i.e., city of Atlanta and Fulton and DeKalb counties) and enter the newer suburbs while most of the black poor have been locked into thew old core is striking. Back in 1970, some 70 percent of all the poor whites in what was then a 5-county Atlanta metro area resided in Fulton and DeKalb counties, 36 percent lived within the city limits, and 24 percent lived in Cobb and Gwinnett counties. In 1990, only 40 percent of all the metro area's (now 10 counties) poor whites lived in Fulton and DeKalb counties, 13 percent lived in the city of Atlanta, and 34 percent lived in Cobb and Gwinnett counties. The picture is quite different for poor blacks. Back in 1970, some 94 percent of all poor blacks in metro Atlanta lived in Fulton and DeKalb counties, with 82 percent in the city limits, and only 5 percent in Cobb and Gwinnett counties. In 1990, some 88 percent of the black poor were still in Fulton and DeKalb counties, 62 percent in the city of Atlanta, and just 6 percent of the metro area's poor blacks lived in Cobb and Gwinnett counties.

By using another ARC report's data[30] for 1990 and projections for 2005, we can see what knowledgeable planners expect to happen to residents' income levels in metro counties and superdistricts. For Fulton County, ARC planners foresee income polarization, as 7 out of its 12 superdistricts (NW, NE, SE, and SW Atlanta, Shannon, Tri-Cities, and Sandy Springs) are expected to end up in 2005 with higher percentages of poor (under $20,000) and lower-middle-income ($20,000–$39,000) households than they had in 1990, while Fulton County's other five superdistricts (CBD, Buckhead, Roswell, North and South Fulton) experience the opposite pattern (a rise in their percentage of upper-middle- [$40,000–$59,999] and high- [$60,000 and over] income households and a decline in the portion at the low end). Note that the places in which declining economic prospects are predicted mainly include predominately black areas, though NE Atlanta and Sandy Springs are important exceptions. ARC planners project a similar pattern in Gwinnett County—most superdistricts have a rise in less affluent residents, except North and East Gwinnett, where the percentage of high-income people will go up.

ARC projections for DeKalb and Clayton counties in 2005 anticipate downward spirals in economic level. In both counties all superdistricts are projected to have higher percentages of poor and lower-middle-income people in 2005, and lower percentages of people at the higher income levels (especially the airport area, Atlanta-in-DeKalb, and SW DeKalb). To a lesser degree, ARC sees a similar outcome in Cobb County. Except for SW Cobb, the superdistricts here are also expected to have a relative increase in the percentage of less affluent residents, though the change is not as great as in DeKalb and Clayton counties.

In the remaining metro counties, ARC sees a mix of trends from 1990 to 2005. In Henry County a general rise in residents' income levels is foreseen, especially in the East and South Henry superdistricts. In Fayette County a divergence is expected, with the East superdistrict becoming less affluent while the West grows more affluent. Rockdale County is likely to gain a few more residents at the lower end than at the higher end, and Douglas County is projected to do the same but to a greater degree. Finally, ARC anticipates that by 2005 Cherokee County's percentage of high-income residents will decrease slightly and its percentage of lower-income residents will rise a little.

What important conclusions do these ARC projections imply? One is confirmation of what is already known—continuing shrinkage of the middle class in the old core of the metro area. These projections say that the percentage of metro Atlanta's middle-income households residing in Fulton and DeKalb counties will drop substantially, from 48.4 percent (of the lower-middle-income households) and 40.6 percent (of the upper-middle-income households) in 1990 to 41.1 percent and 33.5 percent, respectively, in 2005. The remaining middle- and high-income households here will be spread more thinly across Fulton and DeKalb counties but will grow more concentrated in northern Fulton County.

An interesting but less well known conclusion from ARC's projections is the expected decline in the percentage of metro Atlanta's low-income households residing in the old core of the metro area. ARC's numbers suggest that the percentage of Atlanta's households having incomes under $20,000 living in Fulton or DeKalb counties will decline from 62.0 percent in 1990 to 53.9 percent in 2005. So just over half of the low-income households will still live in Fulton and DeKalb counties, and almost half will live in areas in the outlying suburban counties, with the largest increases in the percentage of poor expected to be in the Airport area, Marietta, Cumberland, Lilburn, Norcross, and eastern Fayette County. This projected pattern does not support the idea that as suburban sprawl continues all the poor in Atlanta will be "locked in" to the worst parts of the old metropolitan core; but neither does it suggest massive movement by the poor to very promising areas. Instead, its prediction for the near future is that half of the poor will remain in the core, while the rest shift outward to a few suburban residential areas where low-cost housing may be available, most likely in older suburban areas that are now starting to have increasing home and apartment vacancy rates. Data we have reviewed on home prices and apartment rentals in the more popular suburban areas does not auger well for the entry of many low- and moderate-income residents, and if the experience of the past two decades continues, whites will have better chances than blacks.

William J. Wilson's book, *The Truly Disadvantaged* (1987), made researchers and policy makers more concerned about the problems facing people living in neighborhoods with high concentrations of poverty. In Atlanta, as in many cities, blacks face these problems (e.g., high unemployment, violent crime, ineffective schools) much more than do whites. Using the same measure that Wilson did (a "high poverty" area is a census tract in which 40 percent of its residents are below the federal poverty line), we find that despite some change for the better, poor blacks in Atlanta are still very likely to be relegated to areas in which poverty is highly concentrated, whereas poor whites are not. In 1980 there were 33 tracts in the 10-county area in which 40 percent or more of the black residents were poor. These 33 high-poverty tracts had 71,461 black residents (not all of whom were poor), or 14.9 percent of the total metro black population. In 1990, there were 44 high-black-poverty tracts, holding 93,185 blacks or 13.7 percent of the black population. This means that the black poor became a little less concentrated—more poor black areas existed and they were distributed over a wider area, and a slightly smaller portion of the black population was living in those high poverty areas. On the other hand, for whites the problem of highly concentrated poverty is hardly an issue in metro Atlanta. In 1980 there were only three tracts in which 40 percent or more of the white residents were poor, and those tracts included only 1,904 whites. In 1990, there were no tracts in which 40 percent or more of the whites were poor.

Our assessment of what the housing options for low-income people will be is not very positive if the status quo continues. While it is true that as sprawl extends outward a substantial number of poor people will move out of the city of Atlanta and old metropolitan core, with whites having a better chance to do so than blacks. But suburban residential development is uneven and does not provide enough affordable housing throughout the new areas. Instead much of the new housing is high priced, and the poor in the suburbs will probably have to settle in small pockets where the homes and apartments are older and the other amenities and quality of life elements are not as attractive. For the low-income people who either are unable (or do not want) to move away from the city or the old metropolitan core, their housing and other life chances are quite limited and are related to ongoing political and economic developments (e.g., housing initiatives and policies begun by the AHA, the Empowerment Zone, the Atlanta Project, several nonprofit housing organizations, grassroots advocacy groups, the banks and mortgage lenders, and others in the private sector of housing).

Policy Ideas Dealing with Suburban Sprawl

Poor people and members of racial minority groups are subjects that usually do not arise in discussions of Atlanta's sprawl-related problems (e.g., pollution, traffic congestion) and proposed solutions (e.g., cleaner burning gasoline, reductions in road building). Perhaps this is because it is believed that they are not affected by sprawl since they do not live in great numbers in the northern suburbs where these problems are so obvious, or maybe they are not included in these discussions because they are not a main cause of the problem (i.e., poor people drive cars less so they are not a major source of air pollution). Less benign reasons may account for why they are not thought of when talk turns to the problem of sprawl, but this is not the real issue here. What matters, as we have tried to show, is that Atlanta's poor and its racial minorities are affected by suburban sprawl, and their existence and needs should also be factored into our thinking about what will reduce the problems of sprawl. The ideas suggested below focus on policies and actions that deal with sprawl without ignoring racial minorities and the poor.

Growth Controls, Limits, and Incentives

If, in response to Atlanta's air pollution problem, we actually have a large cutback in new road projects, would it be a blessing in disguise that helps rectify the problem of sprawl, or would it only make the situation worse? No one really knows the answer to this yet, and more analysis is needed. On one hand, as Congressman John Lewis (1997) pointed out in announcing his opposition to any new highway projects in Georgia's 5th district, a moratorium on major road construction could stimulate the development of better and more efficient forms of mass transit, which would help reduce air pollution and might cut down on auto traffic through neighborhoods.[31] A better mass transit system would be beneficial to the whole community, especially for the poor and racial minorities if it was designed in a way that brings them greater access to jobs, better housing, and health care. It might also slow the growth of new or existing industrial and commercial developments in the metro counties and encourage those that are built to take a different form, probably along the lines of mixed use developments and the "new urbanism" style advocated by those who favor neighborhoods in which most of one's daily needs can be met without heavy reliance on long distance car trips.[32] This too would be beneficial to racial minorities and the poor, but only if strong efforts to include rather than exclude them as residents and participants are made (e.g., using techniques to achieve stable racial residential integration described by DeMarco and Galster [1993]; requiring that all residential developments include some low-income dwelling units in them or else have a linkage provision requiring some financial provision for subsidy of low-income residences in a nearby area).[33] Furthermore, a temporary cessation of new highways might curtail the tendency of the middle and upper class to move farther away to the outskirts of the metropolitan area, thereby slowing or reversing tax base erosion in counties like Clayton and DeKalb that are projected to have an economic decline. This too would have beneficial consequences for the poor and the racial minorities in metropolitan Atlanta.

On the other hand, it is possible a ban on highway construction would have no positive and several negative consequences for the poor and the racial minorities. For example, a ban on new roads might be more apparent than real (e.g., so many road projects have been grandfathered in that much new road work will continue even after an official ban on new projects is declared), and suburban sprawl with the negative consequences described above would continue. Or as Wayne Shackelford, Commissioner of Georgia's Department of Transportation, contends, a real ban on road building in the current metro counties may not lead to slower but better development in the heart of metro Atlanta but instead may backfire and encourage developers to build new road, residential, and commercial projects in the next tier of counties even farther out.[34] That outcome is likely if the push for or against expanding the Metropolitan Atlanta Rapid Transit Authority (MARTA) or improving mass transit is deadlocked and if developers decide that the 10 ARC metro counties are too "anti-growth" to bother with anymore. The outcome then is stagnation, with worse employment prospects and a wider gulf between Atlanta's poor and affluent, and more separation between whites and blacks.

Since no one can be sure about which of these outcomes is more likely to follow from an air-pollution–induced moratorium on road construction, we should be cautious and not doctrinaire in making a policy suggestion. Our inclination is to view a road moratorium coupled with other policies (e.g., strong growth controls, mixed-use development with linkage to low- and moderate-cost housing, the "new urbanism," and imposition of impact fees covering some of the social costs of developments) as having more potential for improving the situation than for worsening it. Research on the effects of various forms of growth control in other communities shows that they do not really reduce growth very much, but they can produce growth that has more benefits to the public and the less advantaged.[35] For this reason we think stagnation is an unlikely outcome, and we suspect that the metropolitan Atlanta market is currently attractive enough to induce businesses to continue to invest and build here even if more stringent requirements and "strings" were attached in the form of impact and linkage fees that contribute to the costs of pollution control/abatement, low-cost housing subsidy, and school construction.[36]

Dispersing the Poor or Improving Their Neighborhoods?

Back in the 1960s members of the Kerner Commission asked whether it is better to adopt policies that would improve schools, job prospects, housing, safety, and health conditions of the poor in city ghettos or to adopt policies that would enable people to move out of ghettos and into communities with more prosperity, security, and opportunity. They decided that it was not an either/or issue and recommended many policies to accomplish both goals. Over the years some of these have been implemented, often with less than full commitment or competence, and emphasis shifted back and forth between the two alternatives.

We suggest that both policies are indeed necessary. Research on Chicago's Gautreaux Assisted Housing Program provides strong evidence that low-income people have improved living situations and more opportunities when they move to suburban areas.[37] This has led to other "moving to opportunities" programs in Baltimore, Boston, Chicago, Los Angeles, and New York. These programs ought to be studied to learn how to maximize their success. They should also be designed in a way that insures they minimize the problems associated with suburban sprawl. This means that moderate- and low-cost housing ought to be incorporated along with housing in higher price ranges into mixed-use developments laid out in ways that maximize energy efficiency and minimize heavy automobile use (e.g., work, child care, and residence in close proximity to each other). Funding for this may be available through private sources or from agencies like Georgia's Department of Community Affairs, which now offers money to assist developers of low- and moderate-priced housing.

At the same time, it is unrealistic to think that all the inner-city poor can or should be dispersed across the metropolitan area and their current locations turned into offices or luxury apartments for the affluent. Presently, the private sector is not producing much decent quality low- and moderate-priced housing in the inner city. Instead, it is trying to attract upper-income residents (e.g., the fast growth in very expensive loft apartments; the new apartment complex [450 Piedmont] across from the Civic Center, where one-bedrooms rent for $630 to $950 a month and two-bedrooms are $1250 to $1470).

The city does need more middle-class residents, and having a great many of them would somewhat alleviate suburban sprawl. But programs that give private residential developers incentives to build good quality, lower cost housing should be developed also, in both the city and the suburbs. A hopeful sign is that the recent proposal of the "Atlanta Renaissance Program," which has a goal of adding over 50,000 new middle-class residents to the city, also mentions 25,000 units of "affordable" housing within the next 10 years. Another promising development designed to avoid suburban sprawl, announced in May 1998, is the construction of a residential and mixed-use neighborhood around the Lindbergh MARTA station. The efforts of such agencies as the Empowerment Zone, the AHA, the Atlanta Project, the Corporation for Olympic Development in Atlanta, and several neighborhood community development corporations have been criticized widely, but they are important players in deciding on land use and social and economic programs in low-income neighborhoods. They too need to take responsibility for finding ways of working with nonprofit housing organizations (e.g., Charis, Habitat for Humanity) and private-sector housing companies to create better housing, along with more jobs and better health and educational services.

Finally, more attention, publicity, resources, and assistance should be given to the hardworking groups that are trying to develop affordable housing in metropolitan Atlanta. Most are nonprofit groups and are listed in the Community Housing Resource Center's *1997 Survey of Affordable Housing Production*. This year they produced 234 single-family units and about 2,400 multifamily units. Most are located in Fulton and DeKalb counties and are

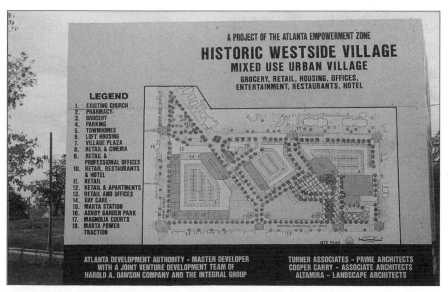

The Historic Westside Village, a planned in-fill development near Clark Atlanta University, is a collection of retail shops, entertainment venues, professional offices, loft housing, a hotel, and a movie theater.

affordable to households with incomes far below the metro area's median. The report given to the Atlanta Housing Forum lists four types of obstacles that must be overcome in order for these nonprofit groups to increase their production of housing for low-income households: (1) financial problems (funds to acquire land; money to rehab or build houses); (2) bureaucratic problems (e.g., dealing with city or county government officials and regulations; meeting bond deadlines); (3) people problems (e.g., reliable, honest contractors; difficulties with appraisers); (4) community problems (e.g., high crime/drugs in area; opposition from neighbors). Policies designed to address these obstacles should be given a high priority by those parties interested in reducing the negative impact of suburban sprawl and uneven development.

Postscript

A revised version of this chapter, based on 1999 data, was presented at the 2000 annual meeting of the Urban Affairs Association in Los Angeles. No major findings or conclusions mentioned here change in a significant way, but anyone interested in the updated version of this chapter can obtain it by contacting the first author.

Notes

1. Quoted in David Goldberg, "Deadline Is Looming for Regional Plan," *Atlanta Journal-Constitution* (December 29, 1996), p. D6.
2. Kenneth T. Jackson, "The Effect of Suburbanization on the Cities," in Philip C. Dolce, ed., *Surburbia: The American Dream and Dilemma.* Garden City, NY: Anchor Books, 1976, p. 90.
3. Ibid., p. 91.
4. National Advisory Commission on Civil Disorders, *Report of the National Advisory Commission on Civil Disorders.* New York: Bantam Books, 1968, p. 1.
5. Bernard Weissbourd, "Segregation, Subsidies, and Megalopolis," in Sylvia Fleis Fava, ed., *Urbanism in World Perspective.* New York: Thomas Crowell, 1964, pp. 540–556.
6. Bert Roughton, "The Right Place, The Right Time," *Atlanta Journal-Constitution,* February 16, 1998, pp. E1, 4; Bert Roughton, "Blood, Money Produce High Drama," *Atlanta Journal-Constitution,* February 16, 1998, p. E5.
7. John R. Logan and Harvey L. Molotch, *Urban Fortunes* (Berkeley: University of California Press, 1987); Joe R. Feagin and Robert Parker, *Building American Cities: The Urban Real Estate Game,* 2d ed. (Englewood Cliffs: Prentice Hall, 1990); Gregory D. Squires, *Capital and Communities in Black and White* (Albany, NY: SUNY Press); Norman Krumholz, "Metropolitan Development and Neighborhood Revitalization," in W.D. Keating, N. Krumholz, and P. Star, eds., *Revitalizing Urban Neighborhoods* (Lawrence: University of Kansas Press, 1997), pp. 211–221.
8. David Goldberg, "Deadline Is Looming for Regional Plan," p. D6; David Goldberg, "ARC's Job: Plot a Course for Better Air Quality," *Atlanta Journal-Consti-*

tution, December 1, 1997, p. E3; David Goldberg, "Area Planners Urge EPD to Lower Air Quality Goal," *Atlanta Journal-Constitution,* February 13, 1998, p. G5; David Goldberg, "Metro Anti-Pollution Plan Falls Short," *Atlanta Journal-Constitution,* February 19, 1998, p. F2.

9. Diane R. Stepp, "Cobb Schools: Plan to Solve Crowding Gets Schrenko OK," *Atlanta Journal-Constitution,* January 28, 1998, p. B1.

10. Diane R. Stepp, "Counties Turn to Borrowing for Schools," *Atlanta Journal-Constitution,* January 12, 1998, p. C1.

11. Stacey Shelton, "Despite ARC Objections, Gwinnett Complex OK'd," *Atlanta Journal-Constitution,* March 25, 1998, p. C1.

12. Mickey H. Gramig, "Service Merchandise Closing Another Setback for S. Fulton," *Atlanta Journal-Constitution,* January 1, 1998, p. D1.

13. Stacey Shelton, "A Complex Situation," *Atlanta Journal-Constitution,* February 9, 1998, p. E1.

14. H.M. Cauley, "Cascade Corridor: Southside Atlanta Neighborhood for the Influential," *Atlanta Journal-Constitution,* January 11, 1988, Homefinder, pp. 8–9.

15. Bill Dedman, "The Color of Money," *Atlanta Journal-Constitution,* May 1–4, 1988.

16. Gregory D. Squires, "Friend or Foe? The Federal Government and Community Reinvestment," in W.D. Keating, N. Krumholz, and P. Star, eds., *Revitalizing Urban Neighborhoods.* Lawrence: University of Kansas Press, 1997, pp. 222–234.

17. Fredrick D. Robinson, "Not Just Rebuilding Buildings, But Rebuilding Lives," *Creative Loafing,* April 25, 1998, pp. 24–25.

18. Gina S. Mangham and Gina Snyder, "Public Housing for Not-So-Poor," *Atlanta Journal-Constitution,* March 29, 1998.

19. Frederick D. Robinson, "Not Just Rebuilding Buildings, But Rebuilding Lives."

20. Research Atlanta, *Atlanta in Black and White: Racial Attitudes and Perspectives.* Atlanta: Research Atlanta, 1995.

21. Susan Harte, "Atlanta Bucks Trend in Housing Activity," *Atlanta Journal-Constitution,* February 4, 1997, p. E1.

22. Atlanta Regional Commission, *1997 Population and Housing.* Atlanta: Atlanta Regional Commission, 1997, pp. 2–3.

23. Data from the 1970 census found so much growth that in 1973 the Census Bureau designated Atlanta as a 15-county metropolitan area. Based on results from the 1980 census the number grew from 15 to 18, and after the 1990 census (in 1992) metro Atlanta was redefined as 20 counties (Barrow, Bartow, Carroll, Cherokee, Clayton, Cobb, Coweta, DeKalb, Douglas, Fayette, Forsyth, Fulton, Gwinnett, Henry, Newton, Paulding, Pickens, Rockdale, Spalding, and Walton). ARC uses different criteria to decide which and how many counties are in metro Atlanta, but it too has enlarged the area. In 1973 Douglas and Rockdale were added. ARC boundaries for metro Atlanta remained the same until 1989, when Henry was added, and in the early 1990s it became 10 counties with the addition of Fayette (1991) and Cherokee (1993).

24. U.S. Department of Housing and Urban Development, *U.S. Housing Market Conditions: Regional Activity, Southeast/Caribbean.* Washington, DC: Department of Housing and Urban Development, February 1998.

25. We are using ARC data and, unfortunately, ARC lists whites as an individual category but groups blacks and all other racial groups together in one category rather than separately. To make it less cumbersome, in the text of this chapter we will refer to "blacks," but readers should realize that the ARC data really refers to "blacks and others."

26. J. John Palen, *The Suburbs*. New York: McGraw-Hill, 1995, p. 118.

27. Douglas S. Massey and Nancy A. Denton, *American Apartheid*. Cambridge: Harvard University Press, 1993.

28. Alan J. Abramson, Mitchell S. Tobin, and Mathew R. VanderGoot, "The Changing Geography of Metropolitan Opportunity: The Segregation of the Poor in U.S. Metropolitan Areas," *Housing Policy Debate* 6 (1995), pp. 45–72.

29. Robert M. Adelman, "A Multivariate Analysis of Urban Poverty: Contrasting Race, Region, and Metropolitan Areas." M.A. thesis, Department of Sociology, Georgia State University, 1997.

30. Atlanta Regional Commission, *Atlanta Region Outlook*. Atlanta: Atlanta Regional Commission, 1997, Table A4.

31. John Lewis, "We Must Move Beyond Asphalt," *Atlanta Journal-Constitution*, November 10, 1997.

32. David Goldberg, "New Urbanism Ideals Take a Stand on Where We Live," *Atlanta Journal-Constitution*, March 2, 1998, p. E3.

33. D.L. DeMarco and George Galster, "Prointegrative Policy: Theory and Practice," *Journal of Urban Affairs* 15 (1993), pp. 141–160.

34. David Goldberg, "Deadline Looming for Regional Plan."

35. Kee Warner and Harvey Molotch, "Power to Build: How Development Persists Despite Local Controls," *Urban Affairs Review* 30 (1995), pp. 378–406.

36. The 1990 Georgia Development Impact Fee Act ought to be examined closely by planners or activists concerned about the costs of urban sprawl. This law limits the use of impact fees on developers to just seven basic categories of capital improvements (water supply, wastewater, roads, stormwater, parks, public safety, and libraries). Other costly growth-related capital expenses such as schools, government offices, courthouses, health facilities, and solid waste facilities, as well as all maintenance and operating costs, cannot be paid for by imposing an impact fee or exaction on developers according to the current law (Georgia Department of Community Affairs). A change in state law is needed, and the Impact Fees for Education Coalition advocates one (Rick Badie, "Growth's Downside: Jampacked Schools," *Atlanta Journal-Constitution*, December 24, 1997, p. E2).

37. James Rosenbaum, "Changing the Geography of Opportunity by Expanding Residential Choice: Lessons from the Gautreaux Program," *Housing Policy Debate* 6 (1995), pp. 231–269.

CHAPTER 6

Widening Educational Gap

Russell W. Irvine

Starting around the mid-1960s, the relationship between central cities and their suburban communities began to change. At that time, most cities experienced changes in the development patterns between themselves and their outer fringes. Previous outward growth had been characterized by the expansion of the healthy urbanized core. However, by the 1970s it became clearly evident that the new outward growth was increasingly characterized as "subtractive" from the older urbanized areas. Cities were losing large segments of their population while taking on additional social service responsibilities in the midst of a stagnant or a shrinking tax base. Suburban areas had an expansion of their population and assumed different, if not lesser, social service responsibilities in the midst of expanding financial resources with a growing tax base. As a consequence, in the past 30 years most American cities suffered from what could be defined as urban sprawl.

"Urban sprawl" is a generic term used to describe what is in fact a two-part process. On the one hand, there is sprawling low-density growth at the suburban fringe, on the other hand, there is the concurrent disinvestment and abandonment of older/urbanized communities.[1] There are factors that stimulate sprawl, such as the desire of many for low-density residential choices, access to and availability of adequate infrastructures, and quality of education. Sprawl is often supported by public subsidies for roads, sewers, water lines, mortgages, and tax breaks. The conditions within Metropolitan Atlanta not only match this definition of urban sprawl but also have additional features of the problem, which gives Atlanta and its outer fringes a degree of uniqueness. In the late 1960s, local county governments made decisions as to where a mass transit system (MARTA) would be located. Federally funded highway construction, in the same time period, combined with local political considerations, dictated much of the physical direction that Atlanta sprawl took. Atlanta's sprawl was further affected by the practices of major lending institutions, which collectively determined eligibility for home mortgages or other forms of venture capital needed for business formation. Whether intentional or not, metropolitan planning and coordinating agencies like the Atlanta Regional Commission (ARC) may have exacerbated the problem of urban sprawl.[2]

Corresponding with the dramatic transformation of American cities, like Atlanta, were major social policy initiatives relating to the poor. President Lyndon B. Johnson, in the mid-1960s, launched the War on Poverty and, in so doing, expanded the role of government in providing services to the poor and other disadvantaged Americans. Before these initiatives commenced, around 1964, few people thought much about the poor or the obligation the federal government might have in the elimination of poverty. Michael Harrington[3] argued that the poor in America, before the 1960s, were invisible. Johnson's insistence in ending poverty forced a number of issues to the forefront of public policy discussion. Of immediate concern was the need to give greater specificity in establishing the exact relationship of education to ameliorating poverty and, conversely, how poverty affects the amount and quality of education one receives.

From 1964 to the present, there has been a fierce debate about the nature of poverty itself, apart from sources of its elimination. The questions included: What is poverty? Who are the poor? How extensive is poverty in America? William O'Hare estimated that there were nearly 40 million Americans who lived in poverty in 1994. Of U.S. residents, 14.5 percent were poor.[4] However, there is considerable variation in the rate of poverty between the states. The states in the South and Southwest, in general, have the highest poverty rates.

States that have a large share of people at risk of being poor (minority and immigrant populations) have higher poverty rates. Poverty rates vary according to the following population characteristics: location, education, family status, race/ethnicity, and age. Twenty-one percent of individuals residing in central cities live in poverty; 32 percent of individuals with less than a high school diploma are poor; 39 percent of individuals living in female-headed families are poor; 31 percent of both African Americans and Hispanics, compared to 9 percent of whites, are poor; and finally, 22 percent of children under 18 live in poverty.[5]

One's location, level of education, family status, race/ethnicity, and age are all strong predictors of high poverty rates. This is particularly the case if an individual possesses two or more of the characteristics. For example, nearly two-thirds of black children living in a female-headed household were poor in 1994.[6] What, then, are the corollaries of urban sprawl, as it relates to educational outcomes for those who by choice or circumstance live in the urban core?

The Problem

The shift in the urban to suburban relationship significantly affected the quality of life issues between these two widening social settings. One dimension of the quality of life is the quality of education offered children in urban schools versus quality of education offered children in suburban schools. An inquiry that purports to explore, to any depth, the link of the quality of education received by children within these different settings is daunting. This present work does not purport to make such a claim; however, the hope is to lightly probe some of the issues that might have broader implications for a future investigation.

Notwithstanding the unevenness of the school terrain, which varies between urban and suburban areas in terms of resources and personnel, schools will continue to play a critical role in determining life outcome chances. Decisions made by elementary school personnel relative to how pupils are sorted by ability, decisions made by secondary personnel relative to curricular tracks, or decisions made by students to remain in school are pivotal junctions that have consequences relating to obtaining and holding decent employment throughout one's adult life.[7]

Underlying Conditions

Atlanta, not unlike other comparable cities, exhibits contradictory sides. Atlanta's chamber of commerce and other booster organizations speak proudly of Atlanta as "a city too busy to hate." Members of its black constituency, in turn, principally through black-oriented publications such as *Jet* and *Ebony,* speak equally pridefully of Atlanta as the "Black Mecca." Indeed, from many vantage points, Atlanta is the jewel of the South, with a booming economy and a glistening skyline that proclaim its arrival as an international center of business, commerce, and culture.

There is another less attractive side to Atlanta, however. This side is the one neither whites nor blacks are proud of. Both blacks and whites seem reticent to address the soft underbelly issues of Atlanta. This hesitancy may be predicated on the fact that in the views of blacks and whites alike some social problems are intractable. The less attractive side of Atlanta suffers social maladies that breed drugs, crime, human misery, and wrecked lives. The disturbing stories in Atlanta's recent past go to the heart of some of these problems. For example, the missing and murdered children saga some 15 years ago held Atlanta in near hysteria.

Before the Atlanta community could recover from this two-year reign of terror that claimed the lives of nearly 30 black boys, Atlanta was rocked, a few years later, with the stunning findings in a series published by the *Atlanta Journal-Constitution* called the "Color of Money."[8] The report documented that whites received five times as many home loans from Atlanta banks and savings and loans as blacks of the same income.

In 1988, two educational researchers, Gary Orfield and Carole Ashkinaze, began their inquiry into the quality of education in metro Atlanta. It was one of the first broad-based studies of Metropolitan Atlanta, documenting the widening disparities between the black urban poor and the affluence of white suburbia. Their findings, part of the Metropolitan Opportunity Project, were published in 1991 in the book, *The Closing Door: Conservative Policy and Black Opportunity.*[9] Orfield's central argument was that, although Atlanta during the 1970s and 1980s experienced a boom in its overall economic growth, blacks, though occupying key institutional positions in the city, such as mayor and school superintendent, continued to experience a widening gap in economic well-being when compared to whites of the sprawling suburban areas.

As the 1990s dawned, notwithstanding an emerging black middle class, spurred by local affirmative action initiatives, another segment of blacks were, relatively speaking, worse off economically. While Orfield and Ashkinaze described the phenomena of the Atlanta experience over the past two decades, blacks in other cities such as Detroit, Cleveland, Houston, Dallas, New York, Philadelphia, Los Angeles, and Chicago were experiencing parallel stagnation in their economic and employment opportunities.

The Atlanta experience was, indeed, a part of the national black experience. A new term, the "underclass," was coined to give language to this phenomenon. William Julius Wilson, a Harvard University professor, captured succinctly the dynamics and paradox of this experience in his seminal work, *The Truly Disadvantaged: The Inner City, the Underclass and Public Policy.* Wilson's central thesis centers on the combined effects of the transformation of the American economy during the 1970s and 1980s with concomitant changes wrought in the composition of urban communities.[10] Middle-class families left the cities. Many cities became inhabited largely by the poor and working-class families.

Economically stable black families, even during down turns in the local economy, helped shore-up basic institutions such as churches, schools, stores, and recreational facilities. Their presence, additionally, helped provide mainstream role models that fostered and buttressed the notion that education is a meaningful pursuit, family stability is expected over single-parenthood, and work is preferable to welfare.

The steady out-migration of stable middle class and working families from central cities, Wilson argues, exponentially accelerated the experience of social isolation. More importantly, the job network system that undergirded the process of securing jobs diminished.[11] The lack of access to "legitimate" jobs paved the way for the emergence of what James Blackwell called the subterranean economy.[12] In former times, such a structure was made up of individuals engaged in organized vices such as prostitution, gambling, and racketeering. More recently, this economy has consisted of gang-related activities, primarily the trafficking of drugs.

The pernicious nature of the development of urban America, from 1970 to the present, is characterized as the *concentration effects*—that is, "social transformation of the inner city [that] has resulted in a disproportionate concentration of the most disadvantaged segments of the urban black population" in geographically specific pockets of inner-city communities.[13] There exists in such communities, a high incidence of crime, joblessness, out-of-wedlock births, female-headed families, and welfare dependency. Wilson utilizes census data from Chicago to illustrate his point of the dramatic increase in poverty areas. Data from Atlanta parallels not only that of Chicago but of the other comparable cities throughout the country.

Demographic Profile of Minority Populations

Too often in America, and most especially in the South, group diversity is viewed in terms of blacks and white. The Atlanta community is culturally rich and extremely diverse. Starting in the mid-1970s extending to the mid-1990s, Atlanta, ethnically, took on cosmopolitan features normally regarded as characteristic of many cities of the North. Atlanta, during this period, saw an influx of ethnically diverse populations willing to call metro Atlanta their home. These groups were attracted to the Atlanta area for a variety of reasons. Many such groups were forced here as refugees, owing to difficult political and economic conditions in their home countries. Others settled in Atlanta for the business, employment, and educational opportunities offered in the region.

Approximately 20 distinct ethnic groups reside in greater metropolitan Atlanta. These groups include: Indian-Americans; Korean-Americans; Ethiopian- or Eritrean-Americans; Lao-Hmong-Americans; Chinese-American; Nigerian-Americans; South Americans consisting of immigrants from Argentina, Bolivia, Brazil, Chile, Colombia, Ecuador, Paraguay, Peru, Uruguay, and Venezuela; Japanese-Americans; Cuban-Americans; Somalia-Americans; Afghan-Americans; Caribbean-Americans; Vietnamese-Americans; Mexican-Americans; Cambodian-Americans; and Puerto Rican-Americans. Over 200,000 former refugees and immigrants live in the Metro Atlanta community.

There are no common themes or circumstances that tie these diverse populations together. According to data provided in 1994 by Regional Ethnic Community Profiles, these groups reside in each of the 10 metro counties except in Cherokee, Douglas, Henry, and Rockdale counties. Data collected by the State Department of Education show that every ethnic group is represented in their student body population. Though this chapter acknowledges Atlanta's rich ethnic heritage, the focus, because of space restraints, will be on three major population groups—whites, blacks, and Hispanics. However, Table 6.1 displays school enrollment data for all ethnic groups.

Blacks moving into DeKalb and Clayton counties are not as economically affluent as blacks moving from these counties into other metropolitan counties. In the past five years, there has been an explosion of new housing development, especially in DeKalb County. Much of this development has been south of I-20, starting from Columbia Drive at I-20, then going south for about one mile. New subdivisions such as Columbia Crossing, Springside Villas, Cascade Manor, and Newberry Downs provide expanded home ownership opportunities for local residents.

The greatest concentration of new home construction is off of River Road. Within the span of 10 miles, from Flakes Mills Road on the east to Bouldercrest Road on the west, the following new subdivisions have been added within less than five years: Soapstone Ridge; Conley Downs; River Park; River Ridge Estates; Riverview Chase; Riverside Estates; Cameron Hills; River Lake Estates; Broad River Point; Misty Lake; River Mill; and Riverside Station.

Three factors appear to make construction of new homes a viable venture. The first is the inducement for developers. Land in these counties is relatively cheap. Lots in south DeKalb average about $20,000 to $30,000 compared to lots selling in Gwinnett, Cobb, or North Fulton counties for $100,000 or more. The second factor, which makes home construction attractive for both builders and potential buyers, is the relative ease of access to an interstate highway. The location and ease of access to I-20 makes owning a home in this location even more attractive. The third factor involves redlining by bank and other lending institutions.[14]

The response of elected officials on the Atlanta City Council, the Fulton County Commission, and the Georgia State Legislature and by members of the U.S. congressional banking commission led by Congressman John Lewis was a move to strengthen the Community Reinvestment Act. This act makes banks affirmatively obligated to lend money to all parts of their communities. Banks and mortgage companies immediately announced plans to lend upward of $65 million to black mortgagees. Shortly after the lending practices had been exposed, developers rushed to accommodate the anticipated demand for new housing.

According to ACORN, a Washington-based community group, Atlanta

Table 6.1. Public School Enrollment, 1996–1997

District	White	Black	Hispanic	Asian	Indian	Multiracial	Total
Atlanta	3,795 (6.3%)	54,027 (90.1%)	1,137 (1.9%)	785 (1.3%)	27 (0.0%)	164 (0.3%)	59,935
Cherokee	20,892 (94.9%)	501 (2.3%)	444 (2.0%)	142 (0.6%)	33 (0.1%)	6 (0.0%)	22,018
Clayton	16,536 (40.3%)	20,621 (50.2%)	1,308 (3.2%)	1,848 (4.5%)	60 (0.1%)	710 (1.7%)	41,083
Cobb	63,657 (74.5%)	15,445 (18.1%)	2,707 (4.1%)	2,450 (2.9%)	142 (0.5%)	1,028 (1.2%)	85,429
DeKalb	13,240 (15.0)	65,903 (74.7%)	3,618 (1.0%)	3,474 (3.9%)	110 (0.1%)	1,900 (2.2%)	88,245
Douglas	12,881 (81.5%)	2,530 (16.0%)	155 (1.3%)	101 (0.6%)	74 (0.5%)	71 (0.4%)	15,812
Fayette	14,828 (85.3%)	1,820 (10.5%)	230 (3.5%)	387 (2.2%)	25 (0.1%)	93 (0.5%)	17,383
Fulton	29,672 (50.3%)	24,311 (41.2%)	2,046 (4.7%)	2,126 (3.6%)	42 (0.1%)	816 (1.4%)	59,013
Gwinnett	68,492 (77.3%)	9,148 (10.3%)	4,136 (1.3%)	5,937 (6.7%)	98 (0.1%)	785 (0.9%)	88,596
Henry	14,460 (83.9%)	2,311 (13.4%)	226 (1.3%)	174 (1.0%)	3 (0.0%)	53 (0.3%)	17,227
Rockdale	10,279 (80.3%)	1,954 (15.3%)	270 (2.1%)	194 (1.5%)	44 (1.5%)	60 (0.5%)	12,801
Total	268,732 (53.0%)	198,571 (39.1%)	16,277 (3.2%)	17,618 (3.5%)	658 (0.1%)	5,686 (1.1%)	507,542

Source: Ga Public Education 1996–1997 Report Cards. Georgia Department of Education.

exceeds the national growth rate for home mortgages to blacks and Latinos.[15] From 1995 to 1997, loans from commercial lenders to Atlanta minorities grew faster than loans to whites. ACORN's study found slower growth rates for blacks and Latinos nationally. The rate of government-subsidized lending, which targets low-income borrowers, was higher for minorities in Atlanta: 30.3 percent for blacks and 57.7 percent for Latinos. The ACORN study differs from the Community Reinvestment Act reporting in that the ACORN one is broader because it includes more lenders.[16]

Most of the purchasers of homes in Atlanta's housing divisions, early in the 1990s, were first-time homeowners. The cost of these homes was relatively modest, most starting at $60,000 to $70,000. However, even at these modest prices, purchase of such houses usually still required that both parents work. One critical implication relating to the ease and availability of these new home developments is the impact they have on property value of older homes in these areas. Often the newer homes are located within blocks or across the street from homes twice the value of the new structures.

There is only anecdotal evidence as to what appears to be taking place in the south end of DeKalb County, which has far-ranging implications for education and in other respects. The older, first-generation black, DeKalb County residents are being replaced by both an economically poorer and less well-educated population of younger blacks. Stable middle-class families moving out of the urban areas appear to be replicated in certain suburban areas of metro Atlanta, most notably in DeKalb County. It is less clear as to whether a similar occurrence is happening in Clayton County. More systematic evidence has to be gathered to determine with accuracy what if any sociological changes are in fact occurring in regard to the shift in social class within these two counties.

These demographic shifts have not only impacted these school systems but have taxed the counties' resources in a more general way. The most immediate impact on the school system is the overcrowding of the schools in these areas. The DeKalb County Board of Education has authorized the construction of 10 new school buildings, all south of I-20.

The new residents are still relatively poor. Consider data related to the percentage of students eligible for free or reduced lunch programs. What this school data seems to indicate is that while blacks are, indeed, moving from the central city, their suburbanization movement places greater financial demands on the counties to which they are moving. As Table 6.2 indicates, the Atlanta Public School System, from 1994 to 1997, experienced an actual decrease in the percentage of students eligible for free or reduced lunch. The decrease over this three-year period was 5 percent. The opposite was true in the case of students in school systems of Clayton and DeKalb counties. In each case, there was an increase in the percentage of children needing assis-

Table 6.2. Percentage of Students Eligible for Free
or Reduced Lunch

	1994–95	1995–96	1996–97
Atlanta	76.6	79.9	71.6
Clayton County	43.2	45.8	47.9
DeKalb County	49.0	51.3	54.1

Source: Ga Public Education 1994–1995, 1995–1996, 1996–1997
Report Cards. Georgia Department of Education.

tance. The increase in Clayton County was 4.7 percent and in DeKalb
County the increase was 5.1 percent. Even more of an impact can be
observed in the number of children receiving Aid to Families with Dependent Children (AFDC) benefits, which is funding drawn from county
resources. Table 6.3 presents this data from all 10 of the metro counties and
shows trends over time.

Cherokee, Fayette, Gwinnett, Henry, and Rockdale counties all experienced a significant decrease in the numbers of children receiving AFDC benefits over the 25-year period from 1970 to 1995. The most dramatic increase
in the number of children receiving AFDC benefits was in Clayton and
DeKalb counties, again the counties with the largest increase in percentage
of blacks. This pattern is indicative of the population shift from the city of
Atlanta to suburbs east and south of the city, but also there is a concomitant
shift in poverty. Within Clayton County, from 1970 to 1995, there was a 4.8-fold increase in the ratio of children receiving AFDC benefits. In DeKalb

Table 6.3. Children Receiving AFDC Benefits
(per 10,000 Residents)

Area	1970	1980	1990	1995
Atlanta MSA	257	227	216	291
Cherokee	125	92	64	79
Clayton	71	101	151	341
Cobb	75	65	58	117
DeKalb	99	122	182	371
Douglas	118	141	96	184
Fayette	209	30	22	48
Fulton	473	527	533	679
Gwinnett	119	38	31	67
Henry	186	235	117	120
Rockdale	275	124	124	135

Source: "Atlanta Region Outlook," Atlanta Regional Commission
(October 1997).

County, over the same time period, there was a 3.7-fold increase in the number of children receiving AFDC benefits. Individuals receiving AFDC provide another measure of children living in poverty. Impoverished children are more likely to receive fewer educational opportunities and lack access to health care and are at higher risk for substance abuse and crime. Families living in poverty are at risk on a number of dimensions. Mothers are at risk in delivering low-weight babies, juveniles stand a high risk of being committed to state custody, and children from such families are likely not to complete high school.

To combat poverty in the metro area, The Atlanta Project (TAP) began a welfare-to-work initiative. TAP is a liaison between businesses that need workers, and the Department of Family and Children Services (DFACS), which is responsible for preparing welfare recipients for work with the assistance of state education programs. In 1997, TAP referred 1,278 people from welfare offices to participate in businesses, however, only 154 were hired. The reason cited for the low numbers hired is that the recipients left on metro-area welfare roles are those that are hardest to place in jobs because they lack work experience, have few skills, or have substance abuse problems.

In an effort to overhaul welfare and put people to work, some metro-area chambers of commerce encourage their members to provide job opportunities and training programs. However, many of the program's employers feel it is DFACS's responsibility to equip welfare recipients with job skills. In response to President Clinton's directive for government bodies to participate in the welfare-to-work effort, the Atlanta based Centers for Disease Control and Prevention (CDC) has taken on the responsibility of training workers rather than waiting for DFACS to do so. CDC established a special orientation and training program for its welfare hires and created a remedial on-site English program. In order to guarantee the success of the worker, each one is assigned a mentor. With these measures, as well as training programs at DFACS and the Department of Technical and Adult Education, the 12 percent hiring rate in the TAP program is expected to improve.[17]

Data found in Table 6.4 profiles the dropout rate for the 10-county region. The educational benefits believed to be available in the suburban school districts are, at least for blacks, nullified by their very act of suburbanization. The dropout rate, in overall terms, increased over the seven-year period, 1990 to 1996. Cherokee County, during the seven years, had a one-third reduction in its dropout rate. Cobb and Rockdale counties each had a modest decrease in their respective dropout rates. Fayette, Fulton, Gwinnett, and Henry counties each increased their dropout rate by 1.5 times. Douglas County's dropout rate over the same period was 1.6 times. However, the DeKalb County School dropout rate increased by a factor of 3.28 and Clayton increased its dropout rate by a factor of 2.97.

Table 6.4. School Dropout Rates

Area	1990	1991	1992	1993	1994	1995	1996
Atlanta MSA	4.4	4.6	4.1	4.7	4.7	6.6	6.7
Cherokee	6.4	8.8	5.4	7.0	9.4	12.2	2.0
Clayton	4.6	4.0	53.7	8.7	5.5	9.8	13.7
Cobb	4.3	5.1	3.5	2.9	5.8	3.8	4.2
DeKalb	2.5	2.9	3.1	3.4	5.0	6.3	8.2
Douglas	5.5	6.0	6.3	5.5	6.4	7.2	9.0
Fayette	3.6	4.0	2.7	2.7	7.1	4.4	5.7
Fulton	3.8	2.8	2.7	4.7	6.1	4.6	6.0
Gwinnett	2.9	4.0	3.5	2.8	1.3	4.3	4.4
Henry	5.8	6.7	5.8	7.2	5.9	8.2	9.2
Rockdale	5.5	6.6	3.8	4.4	9.2	12.1	5.0

Source: "Atlanta Region Outlook," Atlanta Regional Commission (October 1997), p. 32.

A 1999 report from Market Street Services, funded by the Georgia Department of Industry, Trade, and Tourism, indicates that the biggest threat to the Atlanta region's economic health is the steady rate of high school dropouts. Most of these dropouts end up working in low-wage jobs that provide services to skilled workers who migrate to Atlanta. The U.S. Department of Education dropout rate figures show a fluctuating dropout rate in the region as opposed to a steady downward trend, which is ideal. According to the ARC director Harry West, "this is the most important issue facing our region. The Atlanta region has never produced its workers and has always had to import them." Regional planners are scheduled to obtain the proposed strategies, resulting from Market Street Services' review, in order to better train labor within the region.[18]

Another reason people choose to move to the suburbs is to avoid crime and remove their children from the influence of other children prone to delinquency. Statistics compiled by the juvenile court systems of both Clayton and DeKalb counties are not particularly encouraging along those lines. Clayton County Juvenile Court aggregates data from six categories of juvenile offenses. Data are reported on three racial groups: whites, blacks and Asians. Combining white male and female offenses for 1992, their total offenses are 2,165. For black males and females in 1992, their offenses totaled 1,113. Five years later, in 1997, the offenses for whites totaled 2,420. For black male and female offenses the total was 2,754. For whites, over the five-year period, there was a 1.1 percent increase in their juvenile crime rate. For blacks, the reported juvenile crime rate was 2.4 times more in 1997 than it was in 1992.

Caution should be given to summarily drawing a conclusion based on this data. Factors such as bias on the part of the police and differential rates of apprehension might account for some of the variance in this data. Juvenile crime statistics mirrored the adult crime statistics in Clayton County. This would suggest an overall increase in crime regardless of population group.

There is, in general, a positive relationship between per capita income and all the measures of academic achievement as measured by Scholastic Aptitude Test (SAT) scores, Hope Scholarship eligibility, and percentage of students who attend college within the state of Georgia (see Table 6.5). This is, however, an anomaly in regard to income reported for the city of Atlanta school performance. Both the city of Atlanta and Fulton County share overlapping geographical boundaries and each, coincidentally, has the same per capita income, $34,056.

There is a less direct relationship between Atlanta's high per capita income and school performance data. Atlanta, because it is the economic hub of the metro area, has the distinction of having a significant number of high-income earners sending fewer of their children to the Atlanta public schools or, alternatively, few of these high-income earners have children of school age.

Moreover, the high per capita income within Atlanta is at variance with the fact that 71.6 percent of students in Atlanta public schools (APS) receive free or reduced lunch. In short, there cannot be a reliable conclusion about

Table 6.5. The Rank of Per Capita Income, Achievement, Hope Scholarship, and College Attendance by County

System	Income	Achievement	Scholarship (%)	College (%)
Atlanta	$34,056	869	47.5	19.9
Fulton	$34,056	1029	71.7	41.2
Cobb	$27,044	1049	71.7	46.8
DeKalb	$25,881	945	60.8	37.8
Fayette	$25,602	1055	68.8	55.4
Gwinnett	$25,142	1040	80.8	53.8
Cherokee	$21,745	1003	72.9	31.6
Rockdale	$21,656	1021	66.2	52.8
Douglas	$19,701	984	57.9	28.4
Henry	$19,326	1001	53.8	46.8
Clayton	$18,862	947	57.1	42.5
Georgia	$21,726	976	57.9	38.8

Source: Ga Public Education 1996–1997 Report Cards. Georgia Department of Education. Achievement was defined as scores on the Scholastic Assessment Test (SAT); scholarships are given to students eligible to receive Hope Scholarship funds; and college attendance is limited to students who attended a college or university within Georgia as of the school year ending 1997. These percentages do not reflect the number of students who may be attending colleges or universities outside of Georgia, nor do they reflect college attendance a year or more after students may have completed high school.

academic performance and income for the APS, other than to say that the system's high rate of poverty and low test scores are consistent with studies that have documented this relationship.

Of the Atlanta metropolitan counties, Clayton County is the poorest, with a per capita income of $18,862. Yet Clayton County outcompetes DeKalb County in the percentage of its students who enroll in Georgia colleges and universities. On the SAT, Fayette County students scored highest (1055) in the metro counties, while the city of Atlanta students scored lowest (869) of the metro schools. That represents a disparity of 188 SAT scores between students within the APS and students within the Fayette County public system. Fayette County ranks first in SAT scores, first in the number of its students who go to a college or university in Georgia, and 50th in the number of students eligible for the Hope Scholarship funds. The criteria for a Hope Scholarship are based on those students whose core curriculum at their respective schools reflect four units of English, three units of math, three units of science, three units of social studies, and two units of a foreign language.

Of the numbers of students eligible to receive Hope Scholarships, Gwinnett County public school students have the highest representation of eligible students. The Cherokee County school system is next highest in percentage of its students eligible to receive Hope Scholarship funds. Nearly 73 percent of students in this county are eligible for such funds.

A comparative study of DeKalb and Clayton counties reveals the following: DeKalb on a per capita income basis ranks third of the metro counties, eighth in number of students entering colleges or universities in the state of Georgia, seventh in number of students eligible for Hope Scholarships, and tenth on the SAT scores of its students. As noted above, Clayton ranks as the lowest in per capita income, sixth in students sent to colleges and universities in the state of Georgia, ninth in number of students eligible for Hope Scholarships, and ninth on SAT scores of its students.

Blacks in every category where education performance is required, such as in a college preparatory curriculum, are underrepresented, based on their percentage of the state school population (Table 6.6). However, they are overrepresented, based on their percentage of the state school population, in categories where educational performance signals a lack of preparedness, such as those awarded general diplomas, those academically retained, or those who fail to pass minimal graduation requirements and are therefore awarded certificates of performance.

The elementary, middle school, and high school experiences are the crucial educational foundations for life. Taken collectively, they determine most of one's critical life outcome chances. The decision to terminate one's formal education at the high school level, as opposed to continuing on to college, means literally forgoing over half a million dollars in earnings over a life-

Table 6.6. Black Percentage Representation

	1994–95	1995–96	1996–97
In state	37.3	37.5	37.5
College prep	24.9	25.6	27.9
General diploma	45.8	47.3	45.7
Cert. of performance	66.7	64.0	64.1
Retained	52.8	53.5	53.7

Source: Ga Public Education 1994–95,1995–96, 1996–97 Report Cards. Georgia Department of Education.

time. A high school dropout can expect over a lifetime to earn $608,810. A high school graduate over a lifetime can expect to earn $820,000. An individual holding a bachelor's degree can expect to earn $1,420,850. The expected annual income for an individual with "some high school" in 1995 was $25,268. A high school graduate, in 1995, could expect to earn $32,708 annually. The figure for a four-year college degree in 1995 was $52,949. The curricular track assigned by the ninth year in school provides a trajectory, all other things being equal, as to how and under what circumstances these persons will spend the rest of their lives.

Blacks are represented in all 10 of metro Atlanta county schools. In the school year 1994–95, only Rockdale County had a higher percentage of blacks in college preparatory programs than their percentage in the county school population. In other words, in percentage terms more blacks were enrolled in college programs than would be expected based on the percentage in the county. The nature of the school track students are placed in has long-term financial and personal benefits.

The nature of Atlanta's economy is expected to place the greatest demand on individuals with advanced or college degrees. The local economy, between now and the year 2020, will demand more college-educated people. There is currently, in this region, a vast oversupply of unskilled or semi-skilled workers. College graduates make up the majority of executive, administrative, and managerial positions. Unemployment will almost exclusively be a problem for those with a high school diploma or less.[19]

Barriers to Academic Achievement

No two groups share identical values or value orientations, whether pertaining to educational, social, political, or economic issues. The collective life history and the daily press of life account for the variety in values and outlook that groups hold. Traditionally, most groups new to American life place inordinate stress on the importance of hard work and expect high academic achievement for their children. Success in school helps secure the future success of their children.

Common to virtually all of the new immigrants, who have chosen to settle in metro Atlanta, is the importance of family cohesiveness, personal achievement, and economic stability (Ethnic Regional Community Profiles). All view education as essential for their children and make deep sacrifices to ensure the success of their children. The children, for their part, attempt to perform well in school as a means of demonstrating respect for their families and the confidence placed in them.

It is beyond the scope of this study to provide a group-by-group analysis of academic performance for each ethnic population within the greater Atlanta community. Further analysis is not offered because neither state nor local school system data provide for a five-group classification scheme. Students are classified as White, Black, Hispanic, Asian, or Native American. There is an "Other" category but, for the purpose of this chapter, it will not be used here. It is to be expected that the two largest minority populations in metro Atlanta are African Americans and Hispanics. The following is an attempt to understand the underlying issues related to school performance. African Americans will be discussed first, followed by a discussion of the issues pertinent to Hispanics.

By the mid-1980s, within many urban schools, a new development relating to a lower achievement orientation was taking root. Some astute educational researchers felt they had uncovered the applicable explanatory model that purported to account for this phenomenon. The lack of academic effort put forth by many blacks was due to the fact that these individuals secretly felt that the rumor of black intellectual inferiority had a merited foundation. Putting forth intellectual exertion and failing would, in their minds, confirm and therefore validate the rumor of inferiority. Avoiding academic and intellectual activity, such as underperforming in school and in other intellectual pursuits, is a form of adaptive behavior.

The more compelling explanation, the one advanced by Signithia Fordham and John Ogbu, has greater appeal.[20] The work of these authors looks at an occupational ecological perspective to determine what factors impede or enhance academic performance of various minority populations within a larger majority culture. When presenting the Fordham–Ogbu research or the earlier work of Ogbu research to my university classes, primarily teachers in the metro Atlanta area, there is near universal and intuitive agreement that what he is saying is what they observe in their day-to-day interaction with minority students. What follows draws on the research Fordham and Ogbu conducted in the public schools of Washington, D.C. It appears, however, to capture much of the local Atlanta experience.

Fordham and Ogbu note that the near universal feature of minority status is one of a lower level of achievement compared to achievement among members of the majority. The authors see the need to differentiate between minority groups with the view toward accounting for differences in their values regarding education. Minority groups are categorized as: autonomous minorities, immigrant minorities, and caste-like minorities. Autonomous and immigrant minorities share in common the expectation for improvement of their economic, political, and social status. Both autonomous and immigrant minorities voluntarily immigrated to America. This immigration was, in the main, predicated on the expectation of an improved life. Academic achievement patterns, among the children of voluntary immigrants, appear to be reflected in the general eagerness and optimism with which they confront the learning environment.

Intellectual exertion, which means doing well in school for caste-like minorities, is more problematic. Caste-like minorities, as Ogbu explains, did not choose to participate in this society. Subordinate or caste-like minorities were involuntarily incorporated into American society by slavery or conquest. Native Americans, Hispanic Americans, Native Hawaiians, and African Americans are examples of pariah or caste-like groups. Accordingly, African Americans have in common with Mexican Americans this feature in their history. Both groups were subjected to domination and share the experience of having been segregated.

How then is group membership related to high or low school performance? Ogbu asserts that groups in America participate at different levels in the occupational hierarchy. There exists an ecological structure wherein groups are assigned or allowed to participate in their "appropriate" niche. African Americans have historically experienced, and continue in large part to experience, constraints on how high in the occupational structure they are permitted to ascend. In a word, they face a job ceiling. The job ceiling grew out of a history of racial segregation both in the workplace and in schools. For members in the lower rungs of the socioeconomic ladder among African Americans, the job ceiling is particularly poignant in that it has given rise to disillusionment about the value of schooling. For such individuals situated at this level, it dampens the enthusiasm they might otherwise have toward schooling and intellectual effort, since many view these expenditures of effort as ultimately pointless.

In the provocative book, *The Declining Significance of Race,* William J. Wilson attempted to observe the changing nature of the social class structure among blacks during the decades of the 1960s and 1970s.[21] Through the intervention of government-led affirmative action mandates and the simultaneous shift in the nature of the American economy, some blacks were, by the mid-1970s, in a more occupationally advantageous entry-level position than whites. Blacks were able to take advantage of the changing racial climate and the improved opportunity structure, as no other generation before, and experienced, nominally, some facets of the American dream.

The black community, over the past 30 years or so, has become both more economically and more socially differentiated. One unintended consequence of this has been more social isolation of one segment of the black population and more economic differentiation between them. The latter segment of blacks are what Wilson termed "the truly disadvantaged." These are individuals trapped in the iron-grip of poverty.

At this point, it is useful to combine features of Wilson's macroeconomic or structural variables with Ogbu's sociocultural variables. As Ogbu notes, there develops within groups or subgroups orientations, qualities, competencies, and behaviors fostered by the system of status. A concomitant feature of the differentiation among blacks over the past 30 years has been the bifurcation of distinct status cultures. On the one hand, the more affluent blacks see the opportunity structure as permeable and open. Their values are mainstream, approximating those of the dominant culture. There is, on the other hand, a segment loosely described as "underclass" whose status culture is defined in terms of its oppositional character.

There is an oppositional social identity and an oppositional cultural frame of reference. The formation of these oppositional constructs helps the minority population. In this instance, blacks establish boundaries between themselves and the dominant white society. Since a segment of blacks share common values with the dominant society, black oppositional behavior among the urban underclass is simultaneously a reputation of not only whites but also of that segment of blacks who appear to be "acting white."

School achievement and academic performance are spheres of intellectual activity in which oppositional behavior operates. This area is viewed as the prerogative of whites. The use of standard speech, studying hard, reading books, attending lectures, and listening to European classical music are things white people do. Any black who either enjoys or engages in these activities is accused of selling out or "acting white." There is some empirical evidence, particularly in the area of language.

University of Pennsylvania Professor William Labov, in a meeting of the American Association for the Advancement of Science, notes, "It's not unusual to see language diverge where people are isolated by geography, but what we're seeing in the inner-cities is a symptom of cultural isolation."[22] Labov points out that all language is learned subconsciously at an early age, however the continued distinctive language patterns, with particular emphases, are a conscious effort by people to identify with their peers. This is often the case where children coming from homes where standard English is spoken will give stress to black vernacular as a mechanism of group identity.

The barriers to achievement differ from group to group as well as variations within groups. In using the term Hispanic, I am restricting myself to those students that are of Mexican origin or descent. Ogbu argues that since Mexican Americans share a caste-like status like that of African Americans, many Mexican Americans and Native Americans believe the public schools are agents of assimilation into the Anglo cultural frame of reference. Mexican Americans, he further argues, view efforts of assimilation as detrimental to the integrity of their language, identity, and culture.

Outside this context, studies of Mexican American children, in regard to their academic performance, fall into roughly three broad categories of explanation: (1) those differences in social and economic background that may influence educational attainment of all adolescents regardless of ethnic background; (2) those that stress factors such as English-language ability, school segregation, cultural differences, and ethnic discrimination; and (3) those that emphasize the relevance of migration during childhood.[23]

In a study comparing the academic performance of white and Mexican origin adolescents, John R. Warren found that social background factors play a large role in determining the relative educational success of adolescents from different ethnic origins.[24] The occupation and level of education of household heads, income, family composition, and size were found to have major consequences for educational success. Paths to equality of educational outcomes rest in equalizing social and economic circumstances among different ethnic groups.

Conclusion

This chapter has emphasized several points. The first concern was to specify the nature of the relationship of the urban to suburban settings. Historically, urban communities have fed into suburban communities with individuals seeking low-density housing, an escape from crime and other urban problems, and a search for better education for their children. The first-generation blacks in the suburban communities replicated the experience of the dominant culture in seeking these ends.

It would appear, for some African Americans, the quest for life in the suburbs has essentially been a reproduction of many of the features of the urban environment they sought to escape. In the late 1990s, the increased poverty rate, higher incidence of crime and violence, and lower academic performance in suburban schools confronted blacks seeking a better way of life for themselves and their children. Fairly inexpensive housing and other accommodations in Dekalb and Clayton counties have attracted many blacks to these counties. However, economic development and employment opportunities are lowest in these two counties. This requires longer commute times for residents employed in the areas of business and employment growth.

The real issue facing minority populations is access to quality educational opportunities within city of Atlanta schools and throughout schools in the metro Atlanta area. These populations are reaping the educational benefits that the larger culture is accorded routinely. Blacks and other minorities are consistently overrepresented in low achievement categories, such as in high retention rates, and in general, high school diploma tracks. There is clearly a need to continue to stress high expectations for achievement among minority student populations. What follows are specific recommendations to achieve these objectives.

Policy Recommendations

The problems confronting metro Atlanta in finding opportunities to enhance life outcomes for its poor and minority community are national in scope. Many of the initiatives proposed to correct some of these problems are drawn from programs and proposals identified in other cities throughout America. The first several recommendations are specific to the problems in the metro Atlanta area. The latter recommendations are broader and meant to encompass issues that have national ramifications. On balance, the quality of education within the metropolitan counties is good, particularly when examining the issue of quality in other metropolitan areas. The quality of education within the city of Atlanta is another matter. However, compared to cities such as Milwaukee, Detroit, Washington, D.C., Baltimore, and Chicago, Atlanta public schools, while in need of improvement, are not faced with the level of difficulties experienced in some of these cities' schools.

State Resources

Schools should work to assure equity in the distribution of state resources. Data presented in Table 6.5 indicate the disparity in the rate of students in the city of Atlanta and in the counties who are eligible to receive Hope Scholarship funds. Gwinnett County has the highest percentage of its students eligible to receive these funds. The APS ranks lowest with only 47.5 percent of its students eligible for these funds. The state average is 57.9 percent. The APS should commit, at least in the short run, to bring its student eligibility level to the average of the state. Mindful that such an objective might lead to grade inflation, it is proposed that enrichment or support programs be put in place to assure that grades accurately reflect an increased level of scholastic performance. Such awards are, on an annual basis, worth in excess of $1,600 per student. Two hundred additional students from APS receiving Hope Scholarships would mean the annual awarding of $320,000, or $1,280,000 over a four-year college period.

Educational Benefits

Schools should seek to distribute educational benefits as equitably as possible. As a percentage of the state's school population, blacks represent 37.5 percent of the state's students. Yet statewide they are enrolled in 27.9 percent of the college preparatory programs, receive 45.7 percent of the general diplomas, and participate or are awarded 64.1 percent of the state's certificates of performance. As a marketing and employment credential, certificates of performance are virtually worthless. School districts should seek to dramatically reduce or eliminate this category of high school graduation.

Business Community Involvement

Schools should work with the business community. While there are inherent problems in the mixture of the public sphere with the private sphere, as a matter of economic reality, the coalition of businesses and schools should be encouraged. Businesses have a vested interest in the quality of workers schools produce, and schools, particularly in poor neighborhoods, could benefit from the resources businesses possess that could enhance schools.

Student Achievement Levels

Schools should set high expectations for all students. In El Paso, one of America's poorest school districts, the majority of students pass the state achievement test.[25] Following El Paso's lead, educators, parents, and interested community members should work together to specify what students should learn and clearly and consistently communicate these expectations to children.

Teacher Qualification

Schools should make recruitment of quality teachers a priority. Often students with the most urgent needs are assigned teachers who are the least prepared to meet them. Some states, such as North Carolina, have a teacher recruit program called "teaching fellows," which offers a $20,000 scholarship for high-achieving students who agree to teach in the public school for four years. These scholarships are open to all prospective teachers, regardless of race. Of late, it has been the practice to match students with teachers of the same race. No hard evidence has yet been put forth that better learning will result from this arrangement. It is concluded, therefore, that students do not so much need teachers "that look like them" as they need "good" teachers.

Academic Climate

Schools should encourage a culture of learning. Many states and local school districts have moved aggressively to reconstitute poorly performing schools. States have taken over the day-to-day operation of certain schools. In different degrees of supervision, the schools of Baltimore, Washington, D.C., Cleveland, and Chicago, among others, have closed or reconstituted certain schools because of an abysmal academic climate. What such schools foster is a climate of nonachievement, where failure may be the norm. If Ogbu's thesis is correct and if minority populations wish to succeed economically and occupationally, the fear of "acting white" must be reversed.

Student Safety and Welfare

Schools should provide a safe and secure learning environment. Where conditions warrant, school districts should aggressively make repairs on old school structures. When new construction is under consideration, districts should build schools that anticipate growing enrollment. School districts should also anticipate the demands for new technology in the schools of the future. School personnel and those committed to the welfare of children must believe that all children can achieve, and if first they believe, we think they can.

Notes

1. Richard Moe, "Communities at Risk: The Consequences of Sprawl," *Planning and Zoning News* (January 1994), pp. 12–14.
2. David Goldberg, "Deadline is Looming for a Regional Metro Plan," *Atlanta Journal-Constitution,* December 29, 1996, p. D6.
3. Michael Harrington, *The Other America: Poverty in the United States.* Baltimore: Penguin Press, 1962.
4. William P. O'Hare, "A New Look at Poverty in America," *Population Bulletin* 51, no. 5 (September 1996), p. 5.
5. Ibid., p. 7.
6. Ibid., pp. 7–8.
7. Talcott Parsons, "The School Class as a Social System: Some of Its Functions in American Society," *Harvard Educational Review* 29, no. 4 (Fall 1959), pp. 297–318; Ray C. Rist, "Student Social Class and Teacher Expectations: The Self-Fulfilling Prophecy in Ghetto Education," *Harvard Educational Review* 40, no. 3 (August 1970), pp. 411–451.
8. Bill Dedman, "The Color of Money," *Atlanta Journal-Constitution,* May 1–4, 1988.
9. Gary Orfield and Carol Ashkinaze, *The Closing Door: Conservative Policy and Black Opportunity.* Chicago: University of Chicago Press and The Metropolitan Opportunity Project, 1991.
10. William Julius Wilson, *The Truly Disadvantaged: The Inner City, the Underclass and Public Policy.* Chicago: University of Chicago, 1990, p. 48.
11. William Julius Wilson, *When Work Disappears: The World of the New Urban Poor.* New York: Alfred A Knopf, 1996.
12. James E. Blackwell, *The Black Community: Diversity and Unity.* New York: Harper & Row, 1975, p. 91.

13. William Julius Wilson, *The Truly Disadvantaged*, p. 58; William Julius Wilson, *When Work Disappears*.
14. Bill Dedman, "The Color of Money," *Atlanta Journal-Constitution*, May 1–4, 1988.
15. ACORN, *Giving No Credit Where Credit is Due: An Analysis of Home Purchase Mortgage Lending in Thirty-five Cities, 1995–1997*. Executive Summary. Washington, DC: ACORN (November 1998), p. 2.
16. Rob Chambers, "Atlanta Exceeds U.S. in Minority Lending, Study Says," *Atlanta Journal-Constitution*, August 10, 1998, p. E1.
17. Christy Oglesby, "Welfare-to-Work Initiative Falling Short," *Atlanta Journal-Constitution*, March 1, 1998, p. G1.
18. Kimberly Byrd, "Region Supplies Too Few of Its Skilled Workers," *Atlanta Journal-Constitution*, August 26, 1999, p. J1.
19. "College Degree Pays Big Dividends," *Atlanta Journal-Constitution*, September 4, 1997, p. G3.
20. Signithia Fordham and John Ogbu, "Black Students' School Success: Coping with the Burden of Acting White," *Urban Review* 18, no. 3 (1986), pp. 176–206.
21. William Julius Wilson, *The Declining Significance of Race*. Chicago: University of Chicago Press, 1978.
22. Sinithia Fordham and John Ogbu, "Black Students' School Success."
23. Mike Toner, "White-Black Vernacular Gap Widening," *Atlanta Journal-Constitution*, February 15, 1998, p. A6.
24. John R. Warren, "Educational Inequality among White and Mexican American-Origin Adolescents in the American Southwest: 1990," *Sociology of Education* 69 (April 1996), pp. 142–158.
25. Ibid., p. 143.

CHAPTER 7

Urban Sprawl and Legal Reform

William W. Buzbee

This chapter examines the legal frameworks within which sprawl-related decisions occur and suggests reforms that may deter sprawl, or at least address its associated harms.[1] Well-established legal presumptions and traditional roles of federal, state, and local government make difficult any significant new attempts to alleviate and prevent harms associated with urban sprawl's cross-jurisdictional effects and roots. Sprawl and current legal frameworks are mismatched. Local governments traditionally make land use choices, yet sprawl arises out of dynamics, causes and effects that tend, at a minimum, to be regional. Any shift away from state and local governments' primacy in regulating land use, however, would be a major change in allocations of governmental responsibilities. Nevertheless, an increased federal role is constitutionally permissible, politically likely, and desirable. If federal reforms to deter sprawl or address its ills are enacted, monetary incentives in the form of conditional federal spending are preferable to regulatory coercion or substantial federal intervention in land use decision making.

Federalism and Local Primacy over Sprawl Policy

This section examines sprawl policy in light of the divisions of authority among federal, state, and local governments. This examination of the federalism framework reveals that the federal role can be expanded further, but authority over the most significant land use and transportation decisions affecting sprawl have traditionally been the domain of state and local governments and for pragmatic reasons will likely remain principally in those fora.

The Traditional Dominant Local Role in Land Use Decision Making

Local governments have long been in charge of land use and zoning activity, though state governments occasionally intervene.[2] Given the polycentric nature of land use decision making, where many affected people and interests are likely to want a say in how land is developed, local and county governments are often the only level of government that knows of, or has the capacity to discover, the preferences of local constituencies. State, county, and local governments often appear to favor powerful economic interests or their own agencies over the interests of dispersed citizens, but there have also been instances of state and local government opposition to developer or industry proposals.

Even when the federal government enacts laws and regulations impinging on local and state land use primacy, local and state governments retain a substantial role. For example, the effectiveness of federal environmental legislation such as the Clean Air Act and the two most recent amendments to federal transportation law depends upon planning activity that is sensitive to local politics and priorities.[3] Under such federal legislation, state and local governments are offered the chief planning role, especially regarding land use. This role is conditional, based on either the receipt of federal dollars or on state or local officials displacing federal officials who would otherwise implement and enforce federal programs. The federal government cannot bear the burden of taking over local planning activity but is dependent on state and local cooperation and planning due to the huge administrative responsibilities and local knowledge needed for local and state land use planning.[4] Land use planning is likely to remain primarily the domain of state and local governments even if federal goals and incentives seek to shape those local decisions.

The Absence of Regional Political Units

One of the most intractable problems for efforts to address sprawl and its harms is the absence of political units coextensive with the geographic reach of major metropolitan areas. Local governments are usually the chief land use policymakers, but sprawling metropolitan regions typically encompass many local jurisdictions, none of which has authority to address such regional issues. In some cities, such as New York, a single mayor and city council wield most governmental clout and govern a jurisdiction that is smaller than the entire sprawling metropolitan area but nevertheless encompasses millions of residents and several counties making up five boroughs. In contrast, in many of America's more recently expanding cities, such as Atlanta, no single mayor is the chief executive for more than a tiny segment of the metropolitan area. Many areas in sprawling metropolitan regions are

not even incorporated and thus can only look to county or state governments for necessary services or political action.

The mismatch between regional development and numerous independent municipal or county governments means that no single government
unit has an incentive to take the lead and suggest measures to address
sprawl's harms. Similarly, no local government has authority to impose any
regionwide sprawl policies. Outlying municipalities and counties will often
oppose anti-sprawl policies due to their interest in securing ongoing residential and business expansion.[5] Central urban cities usually have a major
stake in reducing sprawling development trends, but they lack authority over
outlying areas and are often in positions of fiscal weakness due to the movement of capital and increased social welfare expenditures.[6]

One partial solution for rapidly sprawling cities seeking to address
broader regional problems is the step New York took approximately one
hundred years ago: combine independent local jurisdictions. Such an event,
however, is unlikely. Metropolitan government campaigns in most cities
have been defeated and are viewed as lacking in political viability.[7] For an
expanded city to be incorporated and a single mayor or city council to
assume chief governing roles would require the unlikely action of numerous
local officials surrendering power and perhaps their jobs. It is difficult to see
how such consolidation and coordination would come about in the absence
of a period of heightened citizen political involvement sufficient to persuade
the state government to modify the authority granted to local governments.

Authorities and Regional Problems

Even if metropolitan areas lack a unitary legal and political identity, and
municipalities or counties often wield the most significant political clout in
sprawling jurisdictions, state departments, special districts, authorities, and
public corporations can be authorized to address regional problems such as
sprawl. In many states, state departments, particularly transportation
departments, make many of the decisions that spur sprawling patterns of
development. The mission vision of these agencies, coupled with powerful
entrenched interests supporting these agencies' roles, can lead largely self-
sufficient and insulated state agencies directly or indirectly to cause substantial harm.[8]

Three common methods of addressing an intractable problem for which
no single governmental unit can take action are for state or local governments to create separately chartered authorities, public corporations, or special districts.[9] These entities are usually created to address a particular type
of problem or issue. These newly created entities seldom require explicit
weakening of preexisting departments' or governmental units' power but can
be given authority to sidestep or trump these other units' areas of authority.

Such authorities, public corporations, and special districts offer a potential means to address regional problems, but they have one substantial drawback. Such quasi-governmental entities are subject to few democratic constraints, tending to be led by appointed officials and sometimes having their own separate budgetary allocations or revenue sources.[10] Much as a state department can act with little heed for citizen priorities, authorities, public corporations, special districts, and commissions are vulnerable to entrenched bureaucracies, special interest capture, and insensitivity to citizen needs and desires. These types of regional entities thus create a means to address sprawl's ills but are largely insulated from democratic accountability.[11] Legal and political constraints on their actions are few.

The lack of democratic accountability of these regional entities causes a further harm. Sprawl and numerous other issues facing growing metropolitan areas need both regional units of government and alert citizens participating in governance at the regional level. If states create special regional entities that are not democratically elected and are only indirectly, if at all, accountable to citizen concerns, then little political deliberation focused on regional issues is likely to occur. In the words of Professor Richard Briffault, one confronts a "chicken and egg" problem in seeking to create effective regional units or arms of government.[12] Without such regional entities, political activity based on perceptions of a community of interest is unlikely to focus on regional issues. Without citizen clamor for effective regional governance, little incentive exists for local governments, preexisting state departments, or the state legislature or executive to overcome established interests and inertia to support creation of a new form of government. If local governments or states establish appointed and largely unaccountable regional entities, citizen stakes and involvement in the policies of these regional entities will predictably be far less than if these entities had to solicit and maintain public approval. Democratically unaccountable regional entities hence may offer a means to overcome the common lack of any effective regional units of government, but they are at best an imperfect solution.

The Traditionally Limited Federal Role in Land Use Decisions

Despite over 30 years of federal environmental activity and leadership, land use decisions and processes have remained quintessentially the province of local governments. Recent decisions by the U.S. Supreme Court make unlikely any substantial expansion of federal authority to displace state and local land use decision making. These cases, however, preserve the option of a greater federal role in addressing ills associated with urban sprawl. This section starts by reviewing constitutional limitations on federal authority, particularly over land use decision making. It then turns to examine areas in which conditional federal spending has influenced state and local land use decision making. This section concludes that an expanded federal role is constitutional, likely, and potentially a partial solution to address sprawl.

Constitutional Constraints on a Federal Sprawl Role

Although under our Constitution the federal government is a government of limited authority, most federal expansions of authority since the New Deal have been justified and upheld under the authority granted by the Constitution's Commerce Clause.[13] Although approximately 50 years of Supreme Court decisions upheld expansions of federal legislative and regulatory authority under the Commerce Clause, the Court in 1995 signaled an unwillingness to rubberstamp such expansions. In *United States v. Lopez*,[14] the Court struck down the Gun-Free Zones Act of 1990 as beyond federal authority.[15] Urban sprawl, however, tends to be driven by national real estate markets and financing institutions that do business in numerous states. Sprawl's effects are also often regional, especially in sprawling multistate metropolitan areas such as New York, Philadelphia, Seattle, and Portland. The federal government could intervene more forcefully to address sprawl's ills without running afoul of constitutional limitations on its Commerce Clause authority. *Lopez* thus may be of limited significance in itself, but taken in conjunction with numerous other recent cases involving issues of federalism and "takings," any expansion of federal authority that excessively impinges on areas of traditional state and local activity may be vulnerable to constitutional attack.[16]

New York v. United States[17] is a case of particular importance to federal efforts to encourage state actions to deter sprawl or address its harms. In *New York*, the Supreme Court stated that the federal government could not simply order or "commandeer" state governments to take desired actions. Instead, due to implicit constraints on federal authority found in the Tenth Amendment, federal ends can be encouraged only by offering states the option of displacing direct federal enforcement of federal laws and regulations (assuming the area of regulation is justifiable under the Commerce Clause or other independent grants of federal authority), or by offering financial incentives to states in the form of conditional grants where the desired end and the grant subject are related.[18] So long as the conditions attached to federal dollars are related to the purpose of the funded regulatory scheme, and there is no federal "coercion," conditional federal spending will pass constitutional muster.[19] More recently, in *Printz v. United States*, the Court extended *New York* by concluding that the federal government cannot commandeer state bureaucratic processes to further federal goals or implement federal programs, even where that burden is only a small administrative obligation.[20]

The Court's 1999 trio of divided federalism decisions, particularly *Alden v. Maine,* less directly bears on the federal government's authority to create incentives for states to further federally defined ends but again reveals the Rehnquist Court's active revisiting of the contours of state and federal authority.[21] They also make clear the limited menu of regulatory strategies that remain on a firm constitutional footing. Based on the Eleventh Amendment and preconstitutional conceptions of sovereign immunity, the Court broadened the scope of state immunity from private causes of action for damages based on federal law, even if brought in state courts.[22] The Court, however, once again cited *South Dakota v. Dole*'s blessing of conditional federal spending as a means to enlist states in pursuit of federal ends, indicating that states can voluntarily elect to participate in federal programs: "Nor, subject to constitutional limitations, does the federal government lack the authority or means to seek the States' voluntary consent to private suits."[23] The Court in *College Savings Bank* similarly reaffirmed the federal government's ability to use its spending power to secure state "agreement . . . to actions" that "Congress could not require them to take."[24] These cases will change the dynamics of federal–state negotiations about the obligations accompanying receipt of federal dollars, requiring explicit state waivers of sovereign immunity if states or arms of the state are to be vulnerable to suits in federal or state court for failure to abide by federal laws, regulations, or particular conditions linked to conditional federal dollars.[25] It appears, however, that citizen suits against states for injunctive or declaratory relief seeking to compel state officials to take action in compliance with previous state commitments remain available under *Ex Parte Young*.[26] States deciding to assume regulatory responsibilities due to receipt of conditional federal dollars or due to a choice to displace federal regulators can likely still be held to such commitments in either state or federal courts despite these recent modifications of the bounds of federal and state authority.[27]

This recent wave of federalism cases affirms that the authority of the federal government is limited. They signal to sprawl reformers that major new areas of federal intervention will be scrutinized and possibly frustrated by federal courts, particularly if they rely heavily on judicial enforcement by citizens against states as states.[28] Although the Supreme Court for a short time embraced Professor Wechsler's much cited theory that allocations of authority between the federal government and the states would adequately be "safeguarded" and maintained by the political process without judicial intervention, the Supreme Court has clearly reentered the arena of federalism.[29] Nevertheless, as developed in greater detail below, these cases also reaffirm the federal government's important ability to offer conditional federal dollars to encourage modified state and local government behavior.

Despite the limited role the federal government has historically played in

land use decision making, a combination of federal, state, and local intervention is likely. From both the political–economic theoretical perspective
and an empirical perspective, all entities and individuals confronting benefits, harms, and opportunities associated with sprawl can look to all levels of
government to play roles in advancing sprawl or anti-sprawl goals. Each
sprawl partisan, including private entities and all affected government officials, sees an array of harms and benefits in status quo arrangements and also
sees an array of opportunities and risks in proposed new initiatives.

Anti-sprawl advocates are particularly likely to seek federal intervention
due to the perception, confirmed in numerous empirical and theoretical
political science analyses, that local governments generally will be more
focused on growth goals than will federal and possibly state officials. As concluded by Paul Peterson, policies with the goal or effect of redistributing
wealth, as would many anti-sprawl reforms, will generally be avoided by
local governments, but are more likely to be enacted by central governments.[30] As one moves from local, to state, to federal fora, one can anticipate
relatively greater interest in policies with the goal or effect of redistributing
wealth. Hence, rational anti-sprawl reformers will seek reforms from federal
officials, and to a lesser extent state officials, rather than expend substantial
resources in seeking anti-sprawl measures from local officials. Local officials
are least likely to be amenable to enactment of such initiatives and typically
lack authority over the multiplicity of jurisdictions affected by sprawl.

Conditional Federal Dollars as Anti-Sprawl Incentives

One of the traditional methods for the federal government to encourage
state or local actions consistent with a federal goal is to provide conditional
federal funding for certain state or local activities. Given the substantial
undercutting by the Supreme Court of other federal strategies to enlist states
in furthering federally defined ends, conditional federal spending has
become a particularly significant regulatory strategy. *New York v. United
States* and the 1999 *Alden* trio of state immunity decisions reaffirmed the
constitutional validity of such uses of federal dollars.

The basic concept of conditional federal spending is that state or local
governments receive or seek federal funding for activities consistent with a
desired federal end.[31] Alternatively, state or local actions inconsistent with
federal goals can lead to the potential loss of otherwise available federal dollars or other forms of subsidy such as insurance. Such dollars seek to entice
state or local activity but do not force state or local participation or compliance. When a variety of targeted grants or subsidies are available or vulnerable to loss, states and local governments can seek the particular array of
programmatic supports that best meet a jurisdiction's interests.

Conditional federal spending influences federal, state, and local activities in several ways. All conditional federal funding or related preclusion of federal subsidy laws requires federal officials to review state or local activities and use of dollars. This routine oversight in itself creates incentives for state and local officials to consider repercussions of their actions that might otherwise be neglected. The mere existence of oversight deters sloppy work and also reduces the risk of corrupt or patronage-driven development projects. Furthermore, manipulating the federal financial spigot directly increases the odds that particular federal goals will be considered. Such regulatory programs put federal officials in the position of potentially reviewing state, local, or private sector activity and thus impinge on state and local autonomy and the market's operations. They do not, however, preclude state or local governments from deciding to proceed with a project if they are willing to live with the reaction of the federal government. In addition, despite the presence of federal financial incentives, state and local governments remain the primary decisionmakers regarding land use, as they have been for many decades. All conditional federal spending schemes leave state and local governments with greater locally sensitive discretion than would be the case with direct federal intervention.

The federal role in influencing sprawling development patterns has to date been most substantial in its significant underwriting of state and local transportation projects, although its tax policies, particularly deductibility of home mortgage interest, have also influenced urban form.[32] In addition, apart from the political opportunities for credit and patronage that highway spending offers, many safety, health, and environmentally oriented laws use the coercive clout of highway funding cutoffs, often referred to as "crossover" or "crosscutting" sanctions, to enlist state and local governments in working to achieve goals first articulated in the federal legislature.[33] While such transportation funding is often provided to states or local governments based on criteria that require no project-specific commitment to fulfill particular obligations, this funding is nevertheless loosely conditioned in the sense that recipients must use the dollars for the designated purpose. Recipients must also follow procedural requirements, such as providing opportunities for public participation. Additional targeted uses of federal dollars should be considered to alleviate ills associated with sprawl. As shown in the next section, similar conditional uses of federal dollars have been effective, although certainly imperfect, in encouraging states to further federal goals that impinge on traditional local and state primacy over land use decision making.

Conditional Federal Spending Regulatory Precedents

A detailed analysis of regulatory precedents is beyond the scope of this chapter, but a handful of regulatory precedents offer a useful model for sprawl reformers. Several recent laws that use conditional federal spending to influence state and local land use patterns provide a model for efforts to structure an effective federal role to address sprawl's impacts. This section primarily focuses upon the structures and efficacy of the Coastal Zone Management Act (CZMA),[34] the Intermodal Surface Transportation Efficiency Act (ISTEA) and its successor, the Transportation Equity Act for the 21st Century (TEA-21),[35] brownfields grants, and earlier transportation laws requiring avoidance of harms to environmental amenities and historic sites. This section also briefly discusses a few additional regulatory precedents.

The CZMA seeks to protect coastal areas by offering federal grant dollars to states that, in a manner consistent with broadly worded federal statutory and regulatory guidelines, create plans to protect those areas.[36] Under the CZMA, states have substantial flexibility in the coastal protection measures they adopt.[37] States creating coastal plans are granted authority to ensure that federal projects in that state are consistent with the state plan. Most coastal and Great Lakes states have prepared plans to comply with the CZMA. A related statute, the Coastal Barrier Resources Act (CBRA) similarly seeks to protect coastal areas through federal financial incentives.[38] CBRA, however, does not provide federal dollars for particular state actions but prohibits federal subsidies or insurance for new development in undeveloped coastal barrier islands.[39] Both CZMA and CBRA provide programmatic, predictable incentives to direct development in ways avoiding environmental harms, yet without requiring any federal displacement of local choices.[40] States using federal CZMA dollars have varied coastal protection strategies.[41] Critics assail this inconsistent protection of coastal zones in various states and question if the law adequately ensures the protection of irreplaceable coastal resources.[42] Others praise the flexibility CZMA provides to states.[43]

The ISTEA statute, recently reauthorized and amended in TEA-21, provides federal funding for transportation projects undertaken at the state and local level. Only in the last decade has the federal government allowed and even required state and local governments to consider using federal transportation dollars for projects other than roads. ISTEA and TEA-21 no longer are as biased in favor of highway expansion as was much earlier federal transportation funding, but it is far from clear that these more flexible laws will result in fewer highway expenditures. TEA-21 is only a small break from the traditional spending focus on new highways; TEA-21 provides the overwhelming majority of its funding for yet more highway construction, with many of those dollars guaranteed to states.[44] Nevertheless, ISTEA and its successor, TEA-21, encourage consideration of environmentally sensitive choices, dovetailing their provisions with Clean Air Act sections encouraging transportation development projects that would either improve air quality or at least prevent additional deterioration in air quality.[45] Apart from gross violations of federal laws like the Clean Air Act, however, the planning processes encouraged under these newer federal transportation laws do not preclude the same conjunction of patronage politics and established political and economic interests from emerging at the end of planning processes with yet more highway construction using federal dollars.

The main strategy in ISTEA and TEA-21 to avoid patronage-driven transportation decisions is in their provisions mandating a more open and participatory planning process as a condition for receipt of federal dollars.[46] ISTEA and TEA-21 supporters hope that this combination of more flexible federal dollars and a more participatory mode of decision making will lead to transportation dollars being used in ways that will create less environmental destruction and greater public benefits.[47] As with the CZMA, however, federal oversight and possible financial coercion remain the primary means for encouraging a more open and at least potentially environmentally sensitive transportation planning process at the state and local level.

Federal transportation laws have for decades prohibited federal approval or funding of any projects that would destroy park spaces or historic sites. Like coastal zone and barrier laws, this preclusion of federal funding for environmentally harmful projects has been instrumental in some high visibility battles stopping major highway projects that would otherwise have destroyed parklands.[48]

A different type of federal spending incentive exists in the current federal brownfields initiative.[49] The EPA offers $200,000 grants to developers and local or state governments seeking to redevelop brownfields sites. This initiative lacks explicit legislative authorization but has widespread political support and appears generally consistent with federal hazardous substance laws' goals. The combination of federal seed money and state regulatory schemes offering guidance and approvals to entities voluntarily cleaning up contamination at brownfield sites has led to the rehabilitation and reuse of numerous brownfields sites. Reinvestment in brownfields occurs most often in central urban areas that offer prime real estate locations for residential or commercial use. One important lesson from brownfields redevelopment efforts is that where a market opportunity can be seized (or created), minor federal monetary incentives, in conjunction with cooperative state or local governments, can be effective in modifying land use decisions and encouraging urban center reinvestment.[50]

Direct subsidy programs that seek to encourage farmers through actual cash payments to retain and restore wetlands have similarly met with political and private sector support and success.[51] Federal historic preservation grants and tax incentives constitute another limited but effective spending program that already provides some encouragement for central urban reinvestment. An expanded program generally encouraging reuse of central urban properties would further discourage sprawl.[52]

Most anti-sprawl strategies, if implemented with conditional federal spending encouragement, will ultimately depend on an interested and active public that supports efforts to address sprawl's ills. While citizen support cannot be assumed, conditional federal dollars can at least serve to encourage more open state, regional, and local planning processes. Laws and regulatory schemes that encourage opportunities for broad participation can, by modifying what might otherwise be insulated or uninformed decision making, change officials' assessments of sprawl-related measures. Where such participatory rights are not only encouraged but made a condition precedent to receipt of federal dollars, as under ISTEA and its successor TEA-21, such participatory opportunities are likely to arise.

Even under routine state and local land use and transportation planning, public efforts to influence discretionary state and local decisions remain the heart of any anti-sprawl strategy. Because most major land use and transportation decisions involve discretionary government approvals of projects involving adverse environmental impacts, active participation in environmental impact statement processes that accompany most such decisions provides a key opportunity to gather information and influence government plans.[53] An active public can influence and possibly change a project simply because it is viewed as bad policy. Many projects contributing to sprawl's ills are legal and appear rational to project proponents but are imprudent and costly when viewed from a broader societal perspective. Creative use of Title VI litigation to deter uses of federal dollars that might exacerbate environmental and racial inequities may also succeed in slowing or deterring developments that would lead to more sprawl.[54]

A weakness in many federal programs that seek to achieve their goals through conditional federal spending is their minimal usage of citizen litigation to ensure that these laws are effective and implemented in accordance with their terms at both the state and the federal levels.[55] For example, federal, state, or local government actions inconsistent with legal requirements in coastal laws can likely be pursued under the federal Administrative Procedure Act[56] and analogous state laws. Other persons or entities acting inconsistently with CZMA mandates' goals, or local or state plans, however, are likely vulnerable only to the indirect pressure of federal funding cutoffs or causes of action possibly available under state law. ISTEA and TEA-21 similarly lack the crucial "citizen suit" provision found in most environmental laws.[57] Case law is limited, but courts interpreting ISTEA have allowed suits against federal agencies under the Administrative Procedure Act. It appears, however, that the law did not provide a basis for suits against private entities or state or local agencies acting in violation of ISTEA.[58] TEA-21 even more explicitly limits options for citizens seeking, through litigation, to force private, state, or local compliance with TEA-21's provisions.[59] Mere federal reliance on monetary incentives without substantial opportunities for citizen participation, especially in the form of litigation, leaves these programs vulnerable to failure and unresponsiveness.

While the discussed regulatory schemes continue to provide benefits and constitute a potential model for other sprawl-targeted use of federal conditional dollars, other conditional federal spending programs have met with only limited success in efforts to encourage regional planning and the creation of regional planning organizations. Other federal programs have sought through conditional federal dollars to further particular, more targeted goals such as revitalizing impoverished neighborhoods. These programs have had, at best, limited success in attaining their declared goals.

Thus conditional federal funding is far from a panacea; as with any government program or regulatory technique, failure or limited success is a distinct possibility. Nevertheless, the use of conditional federal dollars, especially when linked to requirements of a more open and participatory planning process, offers several marked advantages over more prescriptive or punitive regulatory strategies to address sprawl's ills. Use of the federal monetary carrot reduces the need for more rigid forms of regulatory intervention or one-size-fits-all provision of federal dollars. Such flexibility is especially important to address a complex institutional problem such as sprawl. Every jurisdiction confronts a different state of development and political and economic climate. As with international environmental regimes, monetary enticements to encourage participation in anti-sprawl initiatives are likely the most effective device to surmount complex institutional frameworks where no unitary entity with coercive authority exists and where different local needs may lead to different levels of interest in such programmatic goals.[60]

Conditional Federal Spending Enactment and Implementation Politics

This chapter's call for increased use of conditional federal spending to encourage state and local governments to consider anti-sprawl incentives is incomplete without a brief analysis of the type of conditional federal spending incentives that are best suited to address sprawl. A wide range of funding strategies fall within the general constitutional category of conditional federal spending. Federal dollars can be offered or provided to state and local governments through general revenue sharing, which only loosely defines required uses; through so-called block grants that broadly specify the purposes of the funds but provide few regulatory requirements for how those ends are to be met; through dollars that are distributed to all states (often through general revenue sharing) but which are vulnerable to loss should recipients fail to meet federal requirements; or through project-specific grants that must be sought through a competitive application process. Many funding strategies fall somewhere in between these general categories or share attributes of each.

In a paradoxical quirk of funding politics, the one type of funding strategy that appears consistently to meet with broad-based federal, state, and local support, regardless of party affiliation, is federal funding that can only be obtained through a project-specific state or local government application, often in a competitive grant setting. Support for such funding strategies is paradoxical because such application-based funding strategies involve federal officials in detailed evaluation of a grant applicant's proposal. Project-specific, application-based funding schemes are thus in many respects the opposite of the popular block grant or revenue sharing strategies often advocated by critics of federal micromanagement. Such funding strategies in fact look a good deal like much-criticized categorical grants, perhaps distinguishable primarily in their less detailed regulatory and reporting requirements.

Application-based funding schemes offer several benefits in their implementation. Programs like the federal brownfields initiative, which requires grant applicants to define and propose a particular project, create a market for creative thinkers interested in working to combat social ills like abandoned brownfields. A state or local government succeeding in obtaining a merit-based grant can claim political credit for bringing additional, elective dollars into the jurisdiction. Federal officials can similarly claim credit for funding a particular tangible project. State and local governments having little actual use for such targeted federal funds are unlikely to seek them, especially if such funds require matching state or local expenditures or applications require substantial investments of time and money. Applicants expending the time and money to seek such funds are likely to have actual programmatic need for the funds. Federal officials providing such funds are also accountable for imprudent goals or ineffective programs, facing scrutiny and criticism if federal funds do little to achieve desired ends.

Application-based federal funding thus appears to have broad-based political support and to provide a high degree of accountability at all levels of government. One accountability risk of such schemes, however, is the unlikelihood that not-for-profits such as environmental groups or other citizen groups will be able to scrutinize and participate in local or state efforts to obtain or decide how to spend project funding. Local businesses and industry may have proportionately greater influence where regulatory schemes rely substantially on state and local applications for project-specific funding rather than on more narrowly targeted funding criteria secured in fewer but higher stakes federal legislative or regulatory battles.

This chapter therefore suggests that conditional federal funds should seek to target desired sprawl-related ends in application-based programs, much as a few sections of the TEA-21 law seek to encourage innovative means to facilitate reverse-commutes and development of alternative modes of transportation. Eligibility for such dollars should include requirements that recipient jurisdictions provide substantial opportunities for public participation in choosing uses for such funds. Historic preservation laws, brownfields initiatives, and wetland-protecting subsidies have been similarly structured and have met with political support and greater apparent programmatic success than less targeted grant schemes or mandate-based regulatory regimes. Regulatory schemes relying on crossover and crosscutting sanctions may also be effective, but their political unpopularity makes them of questionable utility for anyone advocating increased federal support for anti-sprawl incentives.

Additional Sprawl Strategies and Reforms

The question that remains is how to convert a general goal, such as reducing sprawl's ills, into tangible programs with discrete and achievable goals. What particular regulatory tools should be considered if a jurisdiction decides to initiate anti-sprawl efforts? The following section offers a brief discussion of several regulatory strategies to address sprawl and its ills. These strategies could independently be embraced by state and local governments, or they might appropriately be encouraged by federal legislation providing incentives for such strategies through the conditional federal spending regulatory carrot. None of these strategies alone will prevent sprawl, nor is any combination of these strategies likely to fully achieve such an end. These strategies would, however, act as disincentives to sprawl, might alleviate some of the ills associated with sprawl, and, at a minimum, would reduce ways in which current legal regimes encourage sprawling patterns of development.

More creative imposition of development fees or taxes could help deter sprawling development, although such fees would have to be substantial to actually redirect real estate development projects. Several states now impose fees on developers of new real estate. Such fees create a mild disincentive to new development but appear to be primarily revenue-raising measures, in some instances financing the purchase of other green spaces. State and local governments should also allow denser, mixed-use new urbanism forms of development.

To deter mothballing of urban center properties by real estate speculators, urban centers seeking development might enact a split rate property tax, taxing land at a higher rate than buildings. While such a tax strategy would discourage real estate mothballing or underutilization of property, it could also cause the undesirable wiping out of small businesses, low-income housing, and neighborhoods that retain a distinctive character. To avoid such harms, a split rate tax strategy might best be targeted to metropolitan center properties that are unused or being used for low-intensity, low-employment uses such as surface parking.

A more nuanced federal transportation funding scheme might also reward states or metropolitan governments, especially multijurisdictional entities, that create land use planning schemes that direct development into the urban center and develop strategies to encourage greater reliance on rail and alternative forms of transit. If federal highway and transportation dollars were adjusted to reward states or local governments imposing a tax or fee on new development on the urban periphery, or on development that involved clearing of green spaces, state and local governments would have increased incentives to enact such measures. Sprawl could also be discouraged through imposition of congestion fees on users of highways. Although toll booths are less common today than 20 years ago, scanning equipment would allow collection of such user fees without adding to traffic tie-ups. Such fees could constitute a regressive tax unless offset with some income-linked rebate system, but they would create a direct disincentive to drive alone on highways. Such fees would also marginally increase the relative attractiveness of areas offering untaxed transportation alternatives.

A related but differently targeted financial incentive scheme would reduce federal transportation dollars to high vehicle mile per capita metropolitan areas, particularly where cars tend to have only one passenger. Under such a scheme, cities that develop mass transit and alternative transportation options (or improve the status of such options), and hence reduce average vehicle miles traveled per capita, would be financially rewarded, while cities dependent on single-passenger, high-mileage trips would be financial losers. Current law provides similar incentives but only to the extent that state and local efforts are inadequate to meet federal Clean Air Act requirements.

A related strategy could require that transportation and sprawl-related projects proceed only after an assessment of costs and benefits associated with those plans. Particularly in areas such as major infrastructure investment, where political patronage and pork-barrel politics are a substantial likelihood, an assessment of overall costs and benefits often reveals the actual lack of societal benefits of major government projects.

Federal, state, or local acquisition of green spaces or creation of zoned urban growth boundaries can also deter sprawl, create substantial benefits, and alleviate negative effects of current sprawling development. The power of all levels of government to acquire land in consensual transactions is unquestioned, plus governments have the ability to acquire land for the public good under the power of eminent domain. Government acquisition of land for green space or for alternative transportation uses is a direct means to combat ills associated with sprawl. Such acquisitions might be of a fee simple interest or of conservation easements limiting future uses of such land. To encourage such acquisitions, federal subsidization for federal, state, or local acquisitions should be expanded from often minor support and funding available under the Land and Water Conservation Fund.

Green space creation and preservation are better achieved by acquisition than through regulatory constraints. Outright acquisitions of significant green spaces can create recreational amenities and help preserve biodiversity. Protected green spaces and parks also often enhance surrounding land values and can reduce the visual blight of unmitigated sprawling business and residential development. Protected green spaces, particularly metropolitan area parks, are able to support a variety of recreational activities and can also act as a focal point for more vital social, political, and market activity. Municipal parks that are well maintained often act as a magnet, attracting more concentrated forms of mixed-use development. Furthermore, such parks also provide an amenity often missing from the sprawl landscape—a public commons.

No-build or no-growth areas imposed by regulatory restrictions, however, pose a mixed package of benefits and risks. Oregon's highly touted urban growth boundaries have contributed to that state's economic vitality and the city of Portland's economic boom, but where low density or no-build rings of land are placed at a substantial distance from the urban center, they appear to lead to accelerated growth and building on previously green spaces inside the growth boundary. Such urban growth (or containment) strategies can also raise equity concerns due to suddenly enhanced values of land inside an urban growth boundary, while usually rural or agricultural properties outside of the boundary experience an immediate loss in land value due to reduced potential for real estate development. To avoid such inequities, any jurisdiction enacting an urban growth strategy should include a combination of either compensation or tax benefits to real estate owners outside of urban growth boundaries. Government acquisition of land for parks, in contrast, is generally viewed in a more positive light than policies suddenly constraining land uses but without any accompanying payment or other use of monetary incentives.

Nevertheless, provided states leave landowners with profitable uses for their lands, states still have substantial latitude to limit types of land uses, especially where those uses of land can be linked to externalized harms. Direct government intervention in land use patterns by land acquisition or regulation is a major and intrusive form of government intervention, but the experience of Portland, Oregon, shows that even if such a strategy leads to fewer environmental benefits than anticipated, it may reduce overall harms associated with rapid urban sprawl and contribute to enhanced metropolitan vitality and higher property values. The dynamism of real estate and recreational, social, and political activities in and near the large parks in America's older cities offers another potential vision for urban form that should be encouraged in this country's younger, sprawling metropolitan areas.

Conclusion: The Uphill Battle for Anti-Sprawl Law and Politics

Given sprawl's complex roots and the mismatch of legal frameworks, jurisdictional boundaries and sprawl's dynamics, proposals to address sprawl's ills face an uphill battle. Sprawl is not solely the result of unintended harms or side effects, like the environmental destruction of a water body or air resource due to industrial pollution. Sprawling development patterns directly constitute harms while they also generate benefits. The effects of sprawl flow from private and government decisions that reflect both a desire for the benefits of sprawling development and responses to government-created incentives for sprawling development patterns. Nevertheless, sprawl may be ripe for the same kind of entrepreneurial politics that led to enactment of many of this nation's environmental laws. Now and into the foreseeable future, many politicians are likely to perceive the changing demographics of the United States and the potentially wide support for efforts to combat the ills of sprawl. In New Jersey, for example, Republican governor Christine Todd Whitman has recently made sprawl and green space initiatives a centerpiece of her administration. Similarly, several decades ago, Oregon Republican governor Tom McCall supported and enforced environmental laws and supported efforts to contain urban sprawl with urban growth boundaries. In 1998 and 1999, Georgia Democratic governor Roy Barnes seized on sprawl as one of his early initiatives. At the federal level, in 1998 and 1999, vice president and presidential hopeful Al Gore made sprawl reform a major campaign talking point.

Such a conjunction of constituency support for anti-sprawl measures and politicians perceiving political advantage in leading anti-sprawl initiatives is essential both for enactment of sprawl reform policies and for the success of post-enactment implementation efforts. All localities within a metropolitan region have incentives to shirk and let others provide essential amenities and policies to address sprawl's harms, but they nevertheless share an interest in ensuring that the metropolitan region offers decent housing, jobs, and attractive recreational opportunities. A combination of these emerging issues and shared interests of diverse constituencies in anti-sprawl measures may give rise to contexts suitable for successful anti-sprawl politics.

The law, however, is likely only to be of limited help in actual implementation of sprawl reforms. In contrast to federal environmental laws that have had unexpected success and teeth due to deadlines for particular private and government actions and authorization of citizen lawsuits for violations of those mandates, most sprawl reforms will succeed or fail in political arenas. Sprawl reforms do not lend themselves to the same kind of discrete goals and statutory mandates that can compel government action and reduce the risk of interest group derailing of regulatory initiatives. Given the decentralized nature of land use and transportation planning, sprawl reforms are unlikely to contain firm goals and mandates that can be enforced in the courts. Any new federal legislative initiatives encouraging state and local anti-sprawl efforts will require substantial public participation at the state and local implementation stage.

Instead of securing anti-sprawl implementation through the assistance of courts, the far less certain fora of state and local legislative and regulatory politics are likely to be the site of efforts to implement sprawl-reducing measures. Citizen participation and advocacy in these state and local fora may be allowed or even invited, but given the complexity and fragmented nature of decisions in these tribunals, effective advocacy by dispersed citizen or not-for-profit groups will be difficult. If democratically unaccountable authorities become the main venue for review of regional decisions influencing sprawl, the public's voice is particularly at risk of going unheard.

If a culture of professionalism prevails, and senior state or regional officials have publicly committed to enact anti-sprawl measures, one still might see substantive and effective measures to address sprawl's ills. The institutional complexity and skewed political and economic incentives that have contributed to existing sprawling urban forms may occasionally be overcome by conditional federal spending incentives and political entrepreneurs embracing anti-sprawl policies. Sustained and effective anti-sprawl measures, however, are likely to remain a rarity.

Notes

1. The author thanks Robert Bullard and Glenn Johnson of the Environmental Justice Resource Center at Clark Atlanta University and the Turner Foundation for their support for the research from which this chapter is drawn. Portions of this chapter are drawn from a more extended discussion of sprawl and legal frameworks in William W. Buzbee, "Urban Sprawl, Federalism, and the Problem of Institutional Complexity," published in *Fordham Law Review* 68 (1999), p. 57. That article contains much more extensive citation to the many legal, political, urban policy, and economic resources addressing issues discussed in this chapter. The author thanks Lisa Chang for her suggestions and support. Additional thanks go to Frank Alexander, Vicki Been, Richard Briffault, Richard Foglesong, Robert Schapiro, and research assistants Gordon Hamrick, Michelle Van Wiggeren, and Alan Chan.
2. Daniel R. Mandelker, *Land Use Law* 1–2, 3d ed., Charlottesville, VA: Michie, 1993 (noting that all states authorize local governments to use comprehensive planning as a guide for land use controls).
3. See Clean Air Act, 42 U.S.C. § 7410 (1994) (State Implementation Plan provisions); Transportation Equity Act for the 21st Century, Pub. L. No. 105-178, § 1203, 112 Stat. 107, 107-79 (1998) (to be codified at 23 U.S.C. 134[a]) (setting

forth requirements for metropolitan transportation planning process); id. §
1204, 112 Stat. 180-84 (to be codified at 23 U.S.C. 135[a]) (setting forth
requirement for statewide transportation planning).

4. John P. Dwyer, "The Practice of Federalism Under the Clean Air Act," *Maryland Law Review* 54 (1995), pp. 1183, 1217–1218, 1223–1225.

5. Urban policy critic William Whyte noted this tension between urban governments and exurban or suburban counties 40 years ago. See William H. Whyte, Jr., "Introduction" to *The Exploding Metropolis* (New York: Simon & Schuster), note 4, p. 13 (discussing "anti-city bias of the rural counties" throughout the United States); see also Richard Briffault, "The Local Government Boundary Problem in Metropolitan Areas," *Stanford Law Review* 48 (1996), pp. 1115, 1133–1141 (discussing consequences of locally bounded regulation).

6. Robert H. Freilich and Bruce G. Peshoff, "The Social Costs of Sprawl," *Urban Law* 29 (1997), pp. 183, 195–198.

7. Richard Briffault, "Local Government Boundary Problem," note 5, pp. 1117–1118.

8. The Georgia Department of Transportation (DOT), for example, is an agency with a culture and history aimed at new highway construction and little interest in transit alternatives. Without a constitutional amendment, DOT could not use gas tax dollars on projects other than roads and bridges. Recent legislation bypasses Georgia's DOT to establish a new regional commission, the Georgia Regional Transportation Authority, that will wield substantial oversight authority over any transportation-related project in the Atlanta metropolitan area. See Georgia Regional Transportation Authority Act, ch. 32, 1999 Ga. Laws 38 (available in Westlaw, GA LEGIS 38); David Firestone, "Georgia Setting Up Tough Anti-sprawl Agency," *New York Times*, March 25, 1999, p. A20.

9. For a general discussion of the uses of authorities, including judicial and scholarly assessments of authorities, see Comment, "An Analysis of Authorities: Traditional and Multicounty," *Michigan Law Review* 71 (1973), pp. 1376, 1377–1378, 1418–1420, 1422–1425, reprinted in Clayton P. Gillette, *Local Government Law* (New York: Foundation Press, 1994), pp. 670–683.

10. Donald Axelrod, *Shadow Government: The Hidden World of Public Authorities—and How They Control Over $1 Trillion of Your Money* (New York: Wiley, 1992), pp. 15–20, 35–62; Robert G. Smith, "The Changing Role of Funding in Authority Policy Implementation," in Jerry Mitchell, ed., *Public Authorities and Public Policy: The Business of Government* (Westport, CT: Greenwood Press, 1992), pp. 83–95 (describing self-financing strategies for authorities and particular authority projects and their financing). Georgia's new Regional Transportation Authority consists of members appointed by the governor. See Georgia Regional Transportation Authority Act, ch. 32, art. 4(a).

11. Clayton P. Gillette, "Fiscal Federalism and the Use of Municipal Bond Proceeds," *New York University Law Review* 58 (1983), pp. 1030, 1065–1066.

12. Richard Briffault, "Local Govern,ent Boundary Problem," note 5, p. 1169.

13. See generally, Richard A. Epstein, "Constitutional Faith and the Commerce Clause," *Notre Dame Law Review* 71 (1996), p. 167 (advocating for a pre-New Deal interpretation of the Commerce Clause); William N. Eskridge Jr. and John

Ferejohn, "The Elastic Commerce Clause: A Political Theory of American Federalism," *Vanderbilt Law Review* 47 (1994), p. 1355 (examining the development of federalism in the context of the Commerce Clause); Herbert Hovenkamp, "Judicial Restraint and Constitutional Federalism: The Supreme Court's *Lopez* and *Seminole Tribe* Decisions," *Columbia Law Review* 96 (1996), p. 2213 (critiquing the *Lopez* and *Seminole Tribe* Commerce Clause decisions of the Supreme Court).

14. 514 U.S. 549 (1995).
15. See id. at 552.
16. John Copeland Nagle, "The Commerce Clause Meets the Delhi Sands Flower-Loving Fly," *Michigan Law Review* 97 (1998), p. 174 (exploring the reach of the Commerce Clause and the *Lopez* case in the context of a constitutional challenge to the reach of the federal endangered species law). A separate development that may also confound anti-sprawl efforts is an increasingly antiregulatory body of "takings" jurisprudence. Recent Supreme Court cases involving claims of regulatory takings have created disincentives for federal or state efforts to modify land uses to reduce environmental harms. Compare *Hadacheck v. Sebastian*, 239 U.S. 394 (1915) with *Dolan v. City of Tigard*, 512 U.S. 374 (1994) and *Lucas v. South Carolina Coastal Council*, 505 U.S. 1003 (1992). These cases indicate that a requirement of compensation under takings claims is a distinct possibility where governments restrict land uses either in the form of direct prohibitions on all economically productive land uses or bargained-for-permits conditioned on a permittee providing some kind of environmental benefit that is inadequately linked in type or in proportion to the anticipated harms of the proposed conduct. A narrow majority of the current Supreme Court views land use regulations to further environmental ends with particular disfavor. A further complicating variable for anti-sprawl efforts is the passage in several states of takings legislation that creates a state law legislative right to compensation for landowners whose land loses substantial value due to use restrictions. See Mark W. Cordes, "Leapfrogging the Constitution: The Rise of State Takings Legislation," *Ecology Law Quarterly* 24 (1997), p. 187. Similar bills have been proposed by several federal legislators, but such bills to date have been defeated. For a discussion of one of the leading federal takings bills, see Sharon Buccino, "Turmoil Over 'Takings': How H.R. 1534 Turns Local Land Use Disputes Into Federal Cases," *Environmental Law Report* 28 (February 1998), p. 10083. For a discussion of how a less compensation-oriented takings jurisprudence would create incentives for a "race to develop," see David A. Dana, "Natural Preservation and the Race to Develop," *University of Pennsylvania Law Review* 143 (1995), p. 655.
17. 505 U.S. 144 (1992).
18. For the Supreme Court's earlier upholding of federal authority to use conditional funding to encourage changed state behavior, see *South Dakota v. Dole*, 483 U.S. 203 (1987).
19. See id. at 210. As stated by Richard Epstein, a strong critic of conditional federal spending, after *Dole* "any constitutional challenges to the conditions attached to federal grants are hopeless under the current law." Richard A. Epstein, *Bargaining With the State*. Princeton: Princeton University Press, 1993, p. 157.

20. *Printz v. United States,* 521 U.S. 898 (1997). For a critique of *New York* and *Printz,* see Roderick M. Hills, Jr., "The Political Economy of Cooperative Federalism: Why State Autonomy Makes Sense and "Dual Sovereignty" Doesn't," *Michigan Law Review* 96 (1998), pp. 813, 824.

21. *Alden v. Maine,* No. 98-436, 1999 WL 412617 (June 23, 1999); see *Florida Prepaid Postsecondary Educ. Expense Bd. v. College Savings Bank,* No. 98-531, 1999 WL 412723 (June 23, 1999); *College Savings Bank v. Florida Prepaid Postsecondary Educ. Expense Bd.,* No. 98-149, 1999 WL 412639 (June 23, 1999).

22. *Alden* thus closed the door on the option seemingly left open in *Seminole Tribe v. Florida,* 517 U.S. 44 (1996), for federal statutory rights to be enforced against states in state courts, even though *Seminole* concluded that "Congress lacks power under Article I to abrogate the States' sovereign immunity from suits commenced or prosecuted in the federal courts." *Alden,* 1991 WL 412617, at *5 (citing and characterizing *Seminole*).

23. *Alden,* 1991 WL 412617, at *31 (citing with a cf. signal *South Dakota v. Dole,* 483 U.S. 203 [1987]).

24. *College Savings Bank,* 1991 WL 412639, at *12.

25. For discussion of ways states can waive and federal actions that will not suffice to create a waiver, see *Alden v. Maine,* No. 98-436, 1999 WL 412617, at *32–34 (June 23, 1999); for discussion of reasons states will still be subject to suits for declaratory and injunctive relief, see id. at *26–27.

26. 209 U.S. 123 (1908) (discussed approvingly, with explanation for why *Young* remains sound law, in *Alden,* 1999 WL 412617, at *26–27).

27. Much as the 1999 trio of federalism cases reaffirm the validity of state waivers of sovereign immunity in connection with receipt of conditional federal dollars, states will be held to waive federalism objections when they choose to displace the federal regulator. See *Hodel v. Virginia Surface Mining & Reclamation Ass'n,* 452 U.S. 264, 288 (1981) (cited approvingly in *New York v. United States,* 505 U.S. 144, 167 (1992)). Even if this waiver logic were held to be modified in light of the 1999 federalism decisions, *Ex Parte Young* still provides for injunctive or declaratory relief against state officials. Federal enforcement against states also remains an option. See *Alden,* 1991 WL 412617, at *26–27.

28. See *Alden,* 1999 WL 412617, at *32 ("[The] second important limit to the principle of sovereign immunity is that it bars suits against States but not lesser entities. The immunity does not extend to suits prosecuted against a municipal corporation or other governmental entity which is not an arm of the state." [citations omitted]).

29. See Herbert Wechsler, "The Political Safeguards of Federalism: The Role of States in the Composition and Selection of the National Government," *Columbia Law Review* 54 (1954), p. 543. For a critique of Wechsler's theory, see William T. Mayton, "'The Fate of Lesser Voices': *Calhoun v. Wechsler* on Federalism," *Wake Forest Law Review* 32 (1997), p. 1083. Wechsler's theory was embraced by a majority of the Court in *Garcia v. San Antonio Metropolitan Transit Authority,* 469 U.S. 528, 551 n.11 (1985). While the cases discussed above do not directly overrule *Garcia,* they reflect a markedly different judicial approach in their active redrawing of the lines of federal and state authority despite Congress hav-

ing drawn different lines in statutes at issue. See Geoffrey Moulton, "The Quixotic Search for a Judicially Enforceable Federalism," *Minnesota Law Review* 83 (1999), pp. 849, 850, 886.

30. See Paul Peterson, *City Limits*. Chicago: University of Chicago Press, 1981, pp. 69–70 (discussing reasons central governments are more likely to enact redistributional policies than are local governments), pp. 90–91 (arguing that larger constituencies influence central governments and will support policies providing "broader and more diffuse" benefits, while local governments will be more influenced by dominant economic interests), pp. 116–123 (observing lack of group politics at local level that might give voice to diffuse citizen concerns), pp. 170–171 (explaining reasons local governments are unlikely to embrace pollution control measures without preceding central government commands due to fear of disadvantaging local business); see also Mark Schneider, *The Competitive City: The Political Economy of Suburbia*. Pittsburgh: University of Pittsburgh Press, 1989 (exploring political and economic incentives of suburban governments, with a particular focus on implications of competition among local governments).

31. See Lynn A. Baker, "Conditional Federal Spending After *Lopez*," *Columbia Law Review* 95 (1995), pp. 1911, 1918; Jerry L. Mashaw and Dylan S. Calsyn, "Block Grants, Entitlements and Federalism: A Conceptual Map of Contested Terrain," *Yale Law and Policy Review* 14 (Symposium Issue 1996), pp. 297, 299 (discussing block grant and entitlement regulatory schemes and stating that such federal grants "each have more varied structures and more heterogeneous purposes than the current debate suggests").

32. See Arthur C. Nelson et al., *Growth Management Principles and Practices*. Chicago: Planners Press/American Planning Association, 1995, pp. 2–3; Paul Peterson, *City Limits*, note 30, pp. 144–146 (discussing federal policies facilitating use of the automobile); id. at chap. 11 (discussing tax policies acting to promote home ownership and suburban development). For a classic exposition of Americans' frequent strong desire for suburban living and related government policies, see Kenneth T. Jackson, *Crabgrass Frontier: The Suburbanization of the United States*. New York: Oxford University Press, 1985.

33. See Advisory Commission on Intergovernmental Relations ("ACIR"), *Regulatory Federalism: Policy, Process, Impact and Reform*. Washington, DC: ACIR, 1984, pp. 8–9 (describing "crosscutting" sanctions as "across the board" requirements attached to federal dollars, while "crossover" sanctions "threaten the termination or reduction of aid provided under one or more specified programs unless the requirements of another program are satisfied"); Julie Roin, "Reconceptualizing Unfunded Mandates and Other Regulations," *Northwestern University Law Review* 93 (1999), pp. 351 and 375 and note 90 (discussing use of federal highway funds "as a recurring tool of persuasion" under other regulatory programs). The conditional federal spending threat of greatest significance to sprawl is found in the Clean Air Act and linked provisions of transportation laws. Where a jurisdiction is not meeting its Clean Air Act obligations, federal transportation dollars are often subject to a project moratorium. See *Environmental Defense Fund v. Environmental Protection Agency*, 167 F.3d 641, 643 (D.C. Cir. 1999) (striking down EPA regulations and discussing restrictions on use of

federal transportation dollars for projects in areas not conforming to Clean Air Act and planning requirements); see also The Transportation Equity Act for the 21st Century, Pub. L. 105-178 (June 9, 1998) (hereinafter TEA-21). TEA-21 largely reauthorizes, but also in substantial part replaces and amends, The Inter-modal Surface Transportation Efficiency Act of 1991, 49 U.S.C. § 10101 (here-inafter ISTEA). For a complete version of TEA-21, plus the accompanying House Conference Report 105-550, see 1998 U.S.C.C.A.N. (112 Stat.) 107. As of the time of drafting and submission of this chapter, no fully conformed version of TEA-21 that combines previous law and amending or new language is yet codified in the United States Code. Numerous TEA-21 provisions link state and local transportation activities to entitlements of federal transportation funding. See, e.g., TEA-21 §§ 1110, 1203, 1204, 3004, 3005, 3037.

34. 16 U.S.C. §§ 1451–1464.
35. Pub. L. 105-178 (June 9, 1998).
36. See The Center for Urban and Regional Studies (University of North Carolina at Chapel Hill), *Evaluation of the National Coastal Zone Management Program.* Chapel Hill: University of North Carolina Press, 1991, pp. iii–vii, 1–31, 53–77 (hereinafter *CZMA Evaluation*) (describing CZMA's provisions and its passage and implementation); see also Bradley Karkkainen, "Biodiversity and Land," *Cornell Law Review* 83 (1997), pp. 1, 81–82 (assessing CZMA as a possible model for enhanced federal efforts to protect biodiversity); J.B. Ruhl, "Biodiver-sity Conservation and the Ever-Expanding Web of Federal Laws Regulating Nonfederal Lands: Time for Something Completely Different?" *University of Colorado Law Review* 66 (1995), pp. 555, 616–620 (same); Martin J. LaLonde, Note, "Allocating the Burden of Proof to Effectuate the Preservation and Feder-alism Goals of the Coastal Zone Management Act," *Michigan Law Review* 92 (1993), pp. 438, 441–446 (describing CZMA and focusing on federal consis-tency provisions' implementation).
37. See *CZMA Evaluation,* supra note 36, pp. 81–166 (reviewing states' varied responses to CZMA incentives).
38. See 16 U.S.C. §§ 3501–3510.
39. Elise Jones, "The Coastal Barrier Resources Act: A Common Cents Approach to Coastal Protection," *Environmental Law* 24 (1991), pp. 1015, 1017.
40. David Salvesen, "Sand Castles: On Topsail Island, Homeowners Discover that Building on Barrier Islands Is Risky Business," *Amicus Jornal* (Winter 1997), pp. 28, 31.
41. See *CZMA Evaluation,* supra note 36, pp. 81–166 (surveying state coastal pro-tection programs).
42. Oliver A. Houck, "Ending the War: A Strategy to Save America's Coastal Zone," *Maryland Law Review* 17 (1988), pp. 358, 359–360.
43. J.B. Ruhl, "Biodiversity Conservation," supra note 36, pp. 616–620. "Swamp-buster" provisions in federal farm bills have similarly provided for losses of fed-eral subsidies should a farmer convert wetlands to crop production. See, e.g., Federal Agriculture Improvement and Reform Act of 1996 § 321(a)(2), 16 U.S.C. § 3821 (Supp. 1999). The efficacy of such provisions is in doubt due to recent shifts in strategies to provide farmers with monetary support; instead of variable price supports, recent legislation relies more on "'market transition

payments'" that are less targeted to particular activities. Without activity-specific subsidies, "swampbuster" provisions lose much of their efficacy. See Bradley Karkkainen, "Biodiversity and Land," note 36, pp. 66–68.

44. U.S. Department of Transportation, *A Summary: Transportation Equity Act for the 21st Century* (Pub. No. FHWA-PL-98-038), pp. 3–7, 44–49.

45. For a sympathetic review of ISTEA's achievement published by a group favoring alternative transportation methods, see Surface Transportation Policy Project, "Green Streets, the 1991 Intermodal Surface Transportation Efficiency Act and the Greening of Transportation Policy in the United States," p. 24. For analysis of the intersection of Clean Air Act programs and federal transportation laws, particularly focusing on transportation planning requirements, see Arnold W. Reitze, Jr., "Transportation-Related Pollution and the Clean Air Act's Conformity Requirements," *Natural Resources and Environment* 13 (1998), p. 406.

46. See 23 C.F.R. § 450.212(c) (ISTEA's implementing regulations).

47. See, e.g., Surface Transportation Policy Project, *A Blueprint for ISTEA Reauthorization: A Common Sense Guide to Transportation Priorities for the 21st Century* (1997), p. 3 (making 25 recommendations to improve and reauthorize ISTEA); Cynthia Burbank and S. Lawrence Paulson, "Congress Battles over Successor to ISTEA," *Public Roads* (July/August 1997), p. 41 (ISTEA "gave states unprecedented flexibility to use federal funds . . . [a]nd it attempted to balance the need for improved transportation with other vital national goals—a cleaner environment").

48. For the most famous case under such transportation law provisions, see *Citizens to Preserve Overton Park, Inc. v. Volpe*, 401 U.S. 402, 411 (1971) (stating that § 4(f) of the Department of Transportation Act of 1966 and another statute with similar language prohibited release of federal highway funds for a new road through a Tennessee park unless there was a federal finding that there was "no feasible and prudent alternative to the use of such land, and . . . [the] program include[d] all possible planning to minimize harm"). Critics question the effectiveness of this provision. See Oliver A. Houck, "Hard Choices: The Analysis of Alternatives Under Section 404 of the Clean Water Act and Similar Environmental Laws," *University of Colorado Law Review* 60 (1989), pp. 773, 821–822.

49. For a discussion of the nature of brownfields and programs to encourage their reuse, see William W. Buzbee, "Brownfields, Environmental Federalism, and Institutional Determinism," *William and Mary Environmental Law and Policy Review* 21 (1997), pp. 1–6.

50. See id. at 12–19; see also William W. Buzbee, "A Roadmap to the Brownfields Transaction-Perspectives and Goals of the Parties," in Michael B. Gerrard, ed., *Brownfields Law and Practice: The Cleanup and Redevelopment of Contaminated Land* (New York: Matthew Bender, 1997), at § 2.03, pp. 107–110, 118–122; Joel B. Eisen, "'Brownfields of Dreams': Challenges and Limits of Voluntary Cleanup Programs and Incentives," *University of Illinois Law Review* 50 (1996), pp. 883, 886; William W. Buzbee, "Remembering Repose: Voluntary Contamination Cleanup Approvals, Incentives, and the Costs of Interminable Liability," *Minnesota Law Review* 80 (1995), pp. 35, 82–96. For a report reviewing how federal agencies have recently sought to coordinate brownfield rehabilitation efforts

and incentives, see United States General Accounting Office, GAO/RCED-99-86, *Report to the Chairman, Committee on Commerce, House of Representatives, Environmental Protection: Agencies Have Made Progress in Implementing the Federal Brownfield Partnership Initiative* (April 1999).

51. See Bradley Karkkainen, "Biodiversity and Land," supra note 36, pp. 68–70 (discussing Conservation Reserve Program, 16 U.S.C. § 3831(b) (1994), and Wetlands Reserve Program, 16 U.S.C. § 3837(a)(e), and accompanying regulations, both of which provide for direct monetary payments to farmers retaining or restoring wetlands). Karkkainen notes that, in contrast to schemes that seek to protect wetlands through regulatory prohibitions, these subsidy programs are "warmly regard[ed]" by farmers subject to their provisions. Karkkainen, supra note 36, p. 70.

52. Rachel L. Schowalter, "Reuse, Restore, Recycle: Historic Preservation as an Alternative to Sprawl," *Environmental Law Report* 29 (1999), pp. 10418, 10424.

53. For assessments of the value of the environmental impact analysis process, particularly in the context of the National Environmental Policy Act, 42 U.S.C. §§ 4321–4370 (1994 & Supp. 1999), see Michael C. Blumm, "The National Environmental Policy Act at Twenty: A Preface," *Environmental Law* 20 (1990), pp. 447, 451; Michael Herz, "Parallel Universes: NEPA Lessons for the New Property," *Columbia Law Review* 93 (1993), pp. 1668, 1669–1670; William H. Rodgers, Jr., "NEPA at Twenty: Mimicry and Recruitment in Environmental Law," *Environmental Law* 20 (1990), pp. 485, 487.

54. See, e.g., Luke W. Cole, "Civil Rights, Environmental Justice and the EPA: The Brief History of Administrative Complaints Under Title VI of the Civil Rights Act of 1964," *Journal of Environmental Law and Litigation* 9 (1994), pp. 309, 311–314 (describing the use of Title VI in battling environmental racism); Steven A. Light and Kathryn R.L. Rand, "Is Title VI a Magic Bullet? Environmental Racism in the Context of Political-Economic Processes and Imperatives," *Michigan Journal of Race and Law* 2 (1996), pp. 1, 5–6 (discussing the benefits of Title VI litigation to minimize limitations and maximize benefits); Bradford C. Mank, "Is There a Private Cause of Action Under EPA's Title VI Regulations? The Need to Empower Environmental Justice Plaintiffs," *Columbia Journal of Environmental Law* 24 (1999), pp. 1, 5 (explaining how a private right of action will serve the purposes of Title VI).

55. For an analysis of why private enforcement may be necessary to implement anti-sprawl control laws, see James Poradek, "Putting the Use Back in Metropolitan Land-Use Planning: Private Enforcement of Urban Sprawl Control Laws," *Minnesota Law Review* 81 (1997), pp. 1343, 1366–1374.

56. 5 U.S.C. §§ 551–706.

57. These provisions empower aggrieved citizens to sue polluters, government officials, or agencies that are breaking the law. Such citizen suit provisions have been essential to prod reluctant agencies or correct illegal agency activity.

58. See *Sierra Club v. Pena,* 915 F. Supp. 1381, 1381 (N.D. Ohio 1996), *aff'd sub nom, Sierra Club v. Slater,* 120 F.3d 623, 624 (6th Cir. 1997); *Town of Secaucus v. United States Dep't of Trans.,* 889 F. Supp. 779, 786–790 (D.N.J. 1995).

59. See TEA-21 at § 1203(f)(2) (to be codified at 23 U.S.C. §§ 134(f)) and

1204(c)(2) (to be codified at 23 U.S.C. Sec. 135[c]). Both provisions, pertaining, respectively, to metropolitan and state transportation planning, state that failures to consider planning factors required by the statute "shall not be reviewable by any court under this title, subchapter II of chapter 5 of Title 5, or chapter 7 of title 5 in any matter affecting" such plans or planning process. Brownfields funding seldom provides opportunities for citizen litigation, although brownfields rehabilitation efforts could implicate provisions in the federal Comprehensive Environmental Response, Compensation and Liability Act (CERCLA), 42 U.S.C. § 9601, or the Resource Conservation and Recovery Act (RCRA) 42 U.S.C. § 6901, both of which do contain citizen suit provisions and other provisions providing for citizen recourse to the courts. See e.g., 42 U.S.C. § 9613 (providing for challenges to CERCLA regulations); id. § 9659 (providing for CERCLA citizen suits); id. § 6972 (providing for RCRA citizen suits); id. § 6976 (providing for challenges to RCRA regulations).

60. See Jonathan Baert Wiener, "Global Environmental Regulation: Instrument Choice in Legal Context," *Yale Law Journal* 108 (1999), pp. 677, 714–726.

CHAPTER 8

Energy Use and the Environment

Dennis Creech and Natalie Brown

Nationwide, cities are grappling with unrestrained urban growth. This problem is especially relevant in Atlanta. Not only does Georgia rank as the fastest growing state east of the Rockies, Atlanta has achieved the designation as the fastest growing metropolitan area in world history.[1] Much of the growth in Atlanta has occurred in low-density, energy-intensive patterns, commonly referred to as sprawl. Rather than build in the existing urban area, sprawl development builds on the outer fringe of the suburbs where the initial land cost may be the lowest, but where infrastructure costs are often higher.

According to one study in Florida, the average cost to provide infrastructure improvements, including installing and maintaining roads, water, gas and electric utilities, sewer facilities, and telephone lines, to the low-density suburban fringe was at least twice the average cost of providing the same services to higher density areas closer to the city center.[2] While some of the infrastructure costs are paid for by outlying county governments eager for development, many costs are subsidized by state and federal agencies. Spending public funds to subsidize sprawl development reduces the funding available to inner city areas, thus enhancing urban decay and reducing quality of life for inner city residents.

Urban "Heat Island" and Deforestation

Sprawl development encourages the destruction of forests, farmland, and wildlife habitat outside the central city and supports wasteful energy consumption associated with commuting from distant suburban subdivisions.[3] Sprawl also fuels deforestation and loss of green vegetation, and it increases energy consumption. Sprawl-driven deforestation occurs at the rate of 50 acres per day. Every week, 500 acres of green space, forest, and farmland in the Atlanta region are plowed under to make way for new housing subdivisions, strip malls, shopping centers, and highways.[4]

Loss of tree cover and rapid clear-cutting translate into increased energy consumption, higher electric bills, more pollution, and more soil erosion and flooding. Urban "heat islands" are another negative result of Atlanta's urban growth. Heat islands are created when urban areas replace trees and greenspace with dark-colored buildings and roads. The following photos illustrate metropolitan Atlanta's expanding heat island (dark colored areas on the satellite images) that occurred in the 1970s, 1980s, and 1990s.

Data from NASA's Landsat satellite show that from 1988 to 1998 the Atlanta metropolitan area lost about 190,000 acres of tree cover. These dark colors absorb the sun's heat and cause the temperatures to increase in the city's urban center and other areas where greenspace has been replaced. Energy consumption by those living and working in the heat island also rises because of the increased cooling requirements. Those most affected by heat islands are low-income populations living in the city who cannot afford air conditioning.

On a sunny summer day, the Atlanta downtown area, Hartsfield Airport, and the Interstate 75 and 85 connector can become up to 12 degrees hotter than the surrounding countryside.[5] This phenomena is known as the "urban heat island" effect. Modern urban areas usually have dark colored surfaces and less vegetation than the surrounding areas. Under the summer sun, these exposed dark exterior surfaces on buildings and pavement become extremely hot. This surface heating, along with the reduced vegetation in the city's center, warms the summer air over urban areas and creates the summer urban heat island. These temperature differences affect the climate, energy use, and habitability of the city.

The removal of vegetation in cities is a primary cause of the urban heat island effect. Here in Atlanta, rapid, poorly planned development has displaced many trees. These trees have been replaced with dark-colored roads and buildings that do not reflect the heat. In fact, the natural landscape declined 60 percent between 1972 and 1993.[6] Landsat satellite images taken in 1997 showed Atlanta to have an average canopy coverage[7] of just 27 percent for the metro area.

Urban heat islands affect the quality of the air. The elevated temperatures in urban heat islands increase emission of carbon dioxide and other pollutants and accelerate the formation of smog and ozone. For every 1-degree increase in temperature above 72 degrees Fahrenheit, the possibility of smog increases by 6 percent.[8] A recent study even suggests that Atlanta may be causing some of its own weather problems. The authors of this study believe

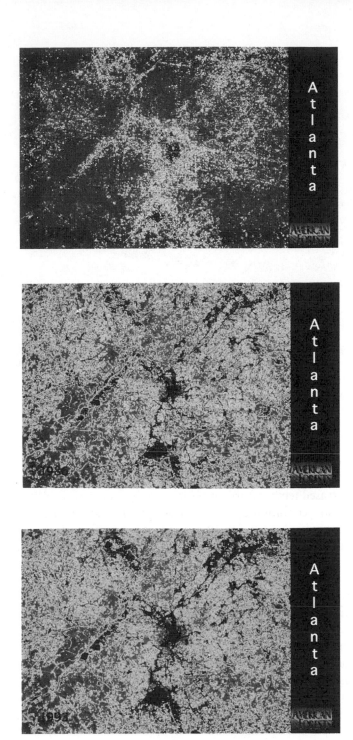

These satellite images show that since 1973 the Atlanta region has lost over 341,000 acres of tree cover and an average of 50 acres per day since 1987 (courtesy of American Forests).

Massive sprawl development is stripping metro Atlanta of its tree cover and is consuming land faster than the population is growing (courtesy of the *Atlanta Journal-Constitution*).

"the heat island's elevated temperatures appear to be causing a low pressure area that produces air movement into the city center, trapping hot air and pollution."[9]

The increased temperatures also increase the use of air conditioners. The additional air conditioning use caused by this urban air temperature increase is responsible for 5 to 10 percent of urban peak electrical demand, at a direct cost of several billion dollars annually.[10] This demand can strain the resources of local utility companies, which in turn can cause brown-outs and force utilities to mobilize old, inefficient power-generating equipment.[11] Forest and ecosystem studies indicate that current ambient ozone levels also cause noticeable foliar damage in many plants and trees. Increased tree damage means decreased canopy cover, which in turn results in higher downtown temperatures.

Most of the Atlanta region's low-income population lives in the city where the heat island effects are most significant. This sector of the region's population contributes the least to the factors that create the heat island effect, but it is negatively affected the most. The negative effects can be seen in terms of exposure to poor air quality and in increased utility costs resulting from the increased need for air conditioning, that is, if the homes have air conditioning available.

Still, the entire Atlanta region suffers from the negative consequences of sprawl. In the summer months, people living and working downtown feel the oppressive temperatures of the urban heat island effect, no longer cooled by the forests and farmlands that once surrounded the urban core. And all of us are exposed to the health hazards that result from air pollution created by cars and power plants as they work to satiate our travel and energy demands.

Housing and Energy Consumption

Energy consumption is greatly affected by population and economic growth. The use of electricity and petroleum is already pervasive in our daily lives, and demographic and economic trends occurring in the Atlanta region are increasing the region's demand for energy. While the single most important factor in increased energy demand is increased population, middle- and upper-income suburban neighborhood development trends of fewer people per household and large homes on large lots that are spread out in isolated subdivisions fuel an even higher growth in total electrical and petroleum demand.[12]

In 1998, metro Atlanta ranked first in the country for the total number of housing permits that were issued in the first quarter of the year. With 13,276 permits, the rate was up 28 percent from the first quarter of 1997.[13] Two housing-related trends in Atlanta are primarily responsible for the fact that the residential sector consumes 37 percent of the electricity and 31 percent of the natural gas consumed in Georgia.[14] The first trend is that larger homes and higher rates of residential construction due to affluence lead to increased energy demand for heating, cooling, and lighting.

Home energy consumption also increases because of the prevalent use of home electronics and appliances, such as personal computers, televisions, microwave ovens, dishwashers, and clothes dryers. Even though home appliances are becoming more energy efficient, the demand for energy is expected to continue to grow in the coming decades. The average residential electricity consumption in the United States increased by 22 percent between 1972 and 1993.[15]

The second trend is the opposite of the first. Low-income families must often live in substandard housing with inefficient appliances and heating and cooling systems. Because of their poor quality construction, these homes are also responsible for large amounts of energy consumption. Although there are large income disparities between the suburbs in the north and south of the region, some of the highest differences are still found within the city of Atlanta. In 1989, the average income of white residents in the city was $61,691, while the average for African American households was only $22,322.[16] These disparities reflect the housing availability and quality.

Urban economists believe wealthy white residents choose to live in the city because of the proximity to certain urban amenities, but low-income white and minority populations remain concentrated within central cities "because of racial discrimination in the suburban housing market and the need to live in older, less expensive housing that cities offer in abundance in comparison to suburban areas."[17] Whereas Atlanta has only 12 percent of the region's population, 65 percent of the public housing is located in the city.[18]

Most middle- and upper-income household budgets are affected little by increases in energy consumption and utility rates. For the most part, increases in average household income have kept up with increases in consumption and energy rates. This is not the case for low-income households. As a share of expenditures for households in different income levels, low-income households spend 30 percent or more of their income for home energy, while people in higher income brackets may spend 5 percent or less. This makes home energy expenditures one of the largest expenses for a low-income household. Considering that 27.3 percent of Atlanta's population lives in poverty, this is a pressing local issue.[19]

The overwhelming majority of Atlanta's new residential construction is occurring in the suburbs and is only accessible by middle- and upper-income residents. Because of this lack of new or quality affordable housing in the city, many poor Atlantans are forced to live in inefficient homes. The energy burden is the percentage of a household's income that is spent on energy bills. Even though today's new homes consume substantially less energy per square foot than they did 25 years ago,[20] the energy burden for low-income families continues to increase.

Low-income households consume fewer resources than any other socio-economic group but use 20 percent more energy per square foot of living space than do middle-income households.[21] In metro Atlanta this is due primarily to the poor quality of the homes, but it is also affected by outdated, inefficient heating and cooling systems. Housing that is not properly insulated and air sealed allows conditioned air to escape, causing the demand for heating and cooling to increase.

Atlanta's metropolitan population has surged past 3 million, and public road mileage has doubled since 1960.[22] The north–south expansion of the metro area that stretched approximately 65 miles just a decade ago now reaches more than 110 miles.[23] This phenomenal growth rate is not projected to subside anytime soon. A recent poll of business and civic leaders ranked Atlanta's increasingly poor air quality as "the one area that most urgently needs to be addressed for metro Atlanta to have healthy, prosperous growth."[24] Third on this list of concerns was traffic. This is not surprising considering the decentralized sprawl pattern of growth.

Because large suburban homes are more spread out and isolated, most people are increasingly dependent on their cars and must travel farther for all their daily activities. Averaging 34 miles per day, metro Atlantans drive more miles per capita than residents of any other city in the United States.[25]

All this driving results in the consumption of tremendous amounts of gasoline and the emission of large quantities of pollutants into the air. Not only is this pollution aesthetically displeasing, it is also harmful to our health. Numerous studies have shown the connection between poor air quality and lung-related illness.[26]

Although Atlanta's rapid growth has provided numerous economic and social benefits to the region, these benefits have been uneven. The sprawl pattern of growth leads to a metropolitan region that is increasingly distant from the traditional city center. Both social and economic benefits that once existed for the residents of the inner city continue their flight to the suburbs.

Most of metro Atlanta's sprawl has occurred in the counties on the north side of the city, in the so-called favored quarter, roughly located in the wedge between I-75 and I-85.[27] This has created problems of economic inequity and decreased environmental quality for the entire metro area. In 1980, the northern suburbs accounted for 44 percent of the 9-county Atlanta Planning Region's population. This share increased to 52 percent by 1990. In contrast, the southern suburbs' share of total population declined from 33 percent to 32 percent over this same 10-year period.[28] The economic imbalance between the north and south sides has increased along with this population change.

A 1995 study by the National Consumer Law Center found that Georgia families receiving Aid to Families with Dependent Children (AFDC) benefits (a monthly cash assistance program for poor families with children under 18 that was replaced in 1996 by Temporary Assistance for Needy Families, or TANF) have the lowest incomes and the highest energy burdens of all segments of the low-income population in the state. In 1992, the energy burden for these families was more than eight times that of middle-income families[29] (see Table 8.1). As the income of Atlanta's northern suburbanites con-

Table 8.1. Home Energy Expenditures

	Georgia (%)	National Average (%)
Low-income home energy expenditure increase from 1988 to 1992	16.21	10.58
AFDC households: Percentage of total income spent for home energy	34.00	25.40
Median income households: Percentage of total income spent for home energy	4.00	3.80

Source: M. Saunders and M. Spade, *Energy and the Poor* (Boston: National Consumer Law Center, 1995).

Table 8.2. Household Energy Burden Energy Price Increase
from 1980 to 1991

	Georgia	National
Energy price increase from 1980 to 1991	78%	63%
1992 Average monthly low-income energy bill	$95.26	$86.38
1992 AFDC monthly benefit for family of 3	$280.00	$378.00

Source: M. Saunders and M. Spade, *Energy and the Poor* (Boston: National Consumer Law Center, 1995).

tinues to increase at a rate much faster than that of the inner city poor, this energy burden disparity will also grow.

Georgia's low-income energy burden is higher than that of most of the nation because Georgia's poor pay more for energy than the national average but receive lower financial benefits than the national average. Georgia's low-income residents' average monthly energy bill is almost $10.00 higher than that of the rest of the nation (see Table 8.2). This difference is not necessarily because of higher utility prices in Georgia but rather is closely related to the poor quality of housing available to low-income residents. Substandard housing increases the cost for both heating and cooling; many of Georgia's low-income families spend more for home energy than families in cooler climates. This disproves the common misconception that warmer climates, such as in Georgia, mean lower home energy cost.

Although the use of air conditioning will increase the annual energy consumption of a household, it can also greatly improve indoor air quality. For those households that do not have, or cannot afford to run, air conditioning, windows must be kept open during the summer months. It has been found that without air conditioning indoor concentrations of ozone can approach 80 percent of outdoor concentrations. Using air conditioning can reduce indoor ozone levels by two-thirds or more.[30] By removing moisture from the air, air conditioning keeps mold and dust mite levels at a minimum, which decreases health risks faced by individuals living in the home.

The Bureau of the Census and the U.S. Department of Housing and Urban Development classify housing units according to whether they have severe or moderate physical problems. These homes are referred to as "physically deficient" housing. In Atlanta, more than 25 percent of poor renters live in deficient housing, and minority populations are even more likely to be affected[31] (see Table 8.3).

More renters than homeowners live in physically deficient housing, and rental units are less likely to be energy efficient. Often the landlord makes the

Table 8.3. Households Living in
Physically Deficient Housing in
Metro Atlanta

Poor renters	25.80%
Poor homeowners	16.90%
All renters	11.70%
All homeowners	3.90%
Poor whites	11.30%
Poor African Americans	35.50%

Source: P. Leonard and E. Lazere, *A Place to Call Home* (Washington, DC: Center on Budget and Policy Priorities, 1992).

majority of the decisions that affect energy consumption in the home, such as efficient windows, appliances, heating and cooling systems, and air sealing, but the renter pays the utility bills. In this situation there is little incentive for a landlord to make a small investment for home energy efficiency improvements. In addition, renters have little incentive or ability to improve a home where they only intend to stay for a short while and where they will not fully receive the payback of efficiency expenditures. Rental units, especially apartments, are not as likely to be targeted for improvements by low-income weatherization programs.

Weatherization and Energy Assistance Programs

Weatherization programs for low-income residences were initiated to promote social equity. Programs were designed to reduce energy consumption and lower energy bills of low-income customers by increasing the energy efficiency of their homes. With the energy burden on the rise for low-income households, this energy conservation purpose is as important as ever.

The majority of the funding for weatherization programs has traditionally been provided by the federal government. Although this is still the primary scenario in Georgia, in recent years some utility companies have begun to invest their resources in weatherization programs. Georgia Power Company, for example, donates approximately $1.7 million per year to the Georgia Environmental Facilities Authority (GEFA) Low-Income Weatherization Program.[32] While some public utility commissions around the country continue to encourage utilities to invest in demand side management (DSM) programs that increase energy efficiency, in Georgia, both electric and gas utility DSM programs have been reduced dramatically.

Utilities that do offer weatherization services continue the practice of promoting social equity among utility customers. Since low-income customers have fewer financial resources as well as fewer energy-using amenities, they are less likely to participate in, or receive the benefits from, most other utility-sponsored programs. It is possible that low-income customers may be subsidizing programs for middle- to upper-income customers via increased energy rates. Low-income customers should therefore make an effort to participate in weatherization and energy assistance programs.

For example, the Georgia Power Company spends a large sum of money each year on its Choice Program to encourage fuel switching among residential customers. Few low-income residents can afford the first cost of a new electric heat pump in order to benefit from the incentive provided by this program. Furthermore, by promoting electric heat, Georgia Power Company encourages greater electric production, which leads to increased air pollutants versus the combustion of natural gas for a comparable furnace.

Additionally, there is a misconception that warm-climate housing does not need to be weatherized. This has led to insufficient weatherization programs in the South. In Georgia and other southern states, weatherization programs have not adopted many cost-effective energy saving measures. Studies show the savings on energy costs from weatherization for southern states is below the national average. This is due in part to the low-quality housing in the South. The Georgia weatherization program also falls below the national average. The performance of the weatherization programs for North Carolina and Virginia, states with similar housing stock and climates, exceeds that of Georgia.

With much of the housing stock physically deficient in Atlanta, weatherizing many low-income residences is especially costly. Nonetheless, appropriate weatherization measures can be cost-effective and can reduce household energy consumption. Affordable housing is an important incentive for "energy savers" regardless of whether they are low-income or upper-income residents.[33] Although lower utility bills more than offset the additional costs of efficiency upgrades, in most instances, the poor cannot afford the initial cost of these improvements.

In the Atlanta area, rather than focus on home weatherization, most energy assistance programs supply funding for the emergency energy needs of low-income and elderly households. These funds are primarily raised by voluntary donations from utility customers. Unfortunately, such programs only offer a temporary fix and do not get at the root of the problem: the availability of energy-efficient, affordable housing in metro Atlanta.

Home energy efficiency is also linked to human health. Homes that have structural problems, leaky ducts, and high moisture levels also tend to be the homes with the most complaints about poor air quality, allergies, and chronic illness. High levels of mold, dust mites, carbon monoxide (CO), and other illness-producing pollutants are often found in substandard housing. The Environmental Protection Agency views indoor air quality as an environmental problem[34] and CO alone causes more poisoning deaths than any other substance.[35] Prevention of indoor air problems can be achieved through many of the same measures used to improve home energy efficiency. Insulation, air sealing, proper ventilation, and proper installation and maintenance of heating equipment are all features that save energy and improve the home's impact on the health of its occupants.

Breathing Unhealthy Air

Because energy consumption and air quality are closely linked, increased energy consumption is a significant negative side effect of our region's boom. The burning of fossil fuels that occurs during most electricity production and the operation of combustion appliances creates air emissions that have harmful effects on human health and the environment. Despite improvements in emissions reductions, electrical generation remains the largest source of air pollution in the United States. Nationally, power plants are responsible for generating 40 percent of carbon dioxide (CO_2), 70 percent of sulfur dioxide (SO_2), 30 percent of nitrogen oxides (NO_x), and 40 percent of fine particulate matter (PM) that is released into the air each year.

Automobiles are the other major source of air pollution. Transportation sources account for 80 percent of carbon monoxide (CO), 45 percent of NO_x, 36 percent of hydrocarbons (HC), 32 percent of CO_2, 19 percent of PM10, and 5 percent of SO_2 emissions nationally.[36] The combination of these air pollutants creates the smog that covers our city on warm summer days.

Ground level ozone is the primary ingredient of smog and is harmful to human health. Ozone causes health problems because it damages lung tissue, reduces lung function, and sensitizes the lungs to other irritants. Scientific evidence indicates that ozone not only affects people with impaired respiratory systems, such as asthmatics, but healthy adults and children as well. Exposure to ozone for six to seven hours, even at relatively low concentrations, has been found to significantly reduce lung function and cause respiratory inflammation in normal, healthy people during periods of moderate exercise. This decreased lung function is often accompanied by chest pain, coughing, nausea, and pulmonary congestion.

Ozone (O_3) is a gas that is formed when hydrocarbons or other volatile organic compounds (VOCs), such as paint thinner, gasoline, and automobile exhaust fumes, evaporate into the atmosphere and react with NO_x pollutants, produced by the combustion of fossil fuels, in the presence of intense sunlight and warm temperatures. Stagnant high pressure weather systems and a lack of wind allow ozone to accumulate in harmful amounts. Because of the weather conditions that facilitate production of ozone, levels typically rise during May through September and are exacerbated by the urban heat island effect.[37]

Tropospheric ozone, commonly known as "ground level" ozone, should not be confused with the protective layer of stratospheric ozone that shields the planet from harmful ultraviolet rays several miles above the earth's surface. The increase in UV-B radiation associated with stratospheric ozone depletion has a substantial impact on human health, including increases in the incidence of and morbidity from eye diseases, skin cancer, and infectious diseases. Although there are some naturally occurring NO_x sources (lightning, volcanoes, etc.), power plants and automobiles are the primary sources. Although the transportation sector does account for 45.8 percent of NO_x emissions in Georgia, electric generating plants are the second-biggest contributor, accounting for 39.3 percent.[38]

In recent years, there has been increasing interest in the impact of poor air quality on human health. Several studies have documented that poor air quality and elevated concentrations of ozone, particulates, carbon monoxide, nitrous oxide, and sulfur dioxide can worsen asthma and other breathing problems. Levels of these pollutants that exceed the Environmental Protection Agency's (EPA) recommended exposure levels have been directly connected to increased respiratory health problems, such as throat irritation, nasal congestion, shortness of breath, chest pain, and lung scarring among people living in the affected areas.[39]

Because it has been determined that exposure to ozone is harmful to human health and the environment, the federal government established standards for ozone in the Clean Air Act. This air quality standard, which is designed to protect human health with an adequate margin of safety, is 0.12 parts per million (ppm), averaged over one hour. Above this concentration, the air is considered unhealthy. Areas with ozone levels greater than the standard are designated as "nonattainment areas." The Atlanta region has been designated a serious nonattainment area for ground level ozone. This designation means that the maximum one-hour daily average of ozone level has and may again reach between 0.16 ppm and 0.18 ppm.[40]

Already lung disease is the third leading cause of death in the United States, and a number of these deaths are caused by poor air quality.[41] Nationally, an estimated 50,000 to 120,000 premature deaths each year are related to exposure to air pollutants. The health costs associated with human exposure to outdoor air pollutants range from $40 to $50 billion annually.[42] In Atlanta, high levels of ozone present one of the most serious air pollution problems. Negative impacts from ozone are most likely to be seen in children, athletes, the elderly, and people with preexisting lung disorders, but anyone exposed to ozone can be adversely affected.

Asthma is a serious breathing disorder that affects a large percentage of the U.S. population. At least 5 percent of the U.S. population, or 14 million people, have asthma.[43] In 1990, national expenditures related to asthma were estimated to total $6.2 billion, and this number was expected to more than double to $14.5 billion by 2000.[44] Each year, about 4,000 people die of asthma.[45] Almost 5 million children in the United States have asthma.[46] Asthma is the most prevalent chronic disease among children.[47] The number of children reported to have asthma, to be hospitalized for asthma, or to die of asthma has increased substantially during the past two decades.[48]

Although asthma can be aggravated by a variety of sources, persons with asthma appear to be especially sensitive to increased levels of ozone. And recent studies indicate that exposure to ozone may in fact cause asthma.[49] Children, because they spend more time outdoors, often engaged in physical activity, generally have different exposure experience to ozone than adults and therefore are especially susceptible to the health risk associated with ozone.

Minority and lower socioeconomic groups are also affected more than the rest of the population. The National Health and Nutrition Examination Survey, done in 1980, found that asthma was most prevalent among males, African Americans, persons living below the poverty level, and persons living in the southern and western sections of the United States.[50] Mortality rates from asthma are higher for males.[51] Mortality rates from asthma are at least 100 percent higher among people of color.[52] The asthma rate among African American children is 26 percent higher than the asthma rate among white children.[53] Hospitalization rates for African Americans, primarily for asthma and pneumonia, are two to three times the rate for whites.[54] Persons with low incomes are less likely to have air conditioners in their homes, increasing their exposure to ozone.

Local studies show that the Atlanta region's poor air quality is impacting our health. It is predicted that over the next 14 years, new cases of respiratory disease will increase dramatically in Atlanta. One study estimated that the total increase in incidence of respiratory disease in the counties of DeKalb, Douglas, Fulton, and Rockdale from poor air quality will increase by 27,118 more cases between 1994 and 2010.[55] Much of this increase can be attributed to the air pollution from automobiles and power plants.

The results of a 1990 Centers for Disease Control and Prevention study in Atlanta suggest that among African American children from low-income families, asthma may be exacerbated following periods of high ozone pollution. This study found that the average number of children's visits for asthma or reactive airway disease was 37 percent higher at the pediatric emergency clinic of Grady Memorial Hospital on the days following elevated ozone levels.[56]

Energy Efficiency

Despite continuing population growth and increasing demand for energy, energy efficiency must take priority over new or increased power generation. Energy efficiency programs are necessary in order to reduce air pollution and improve the quality of life for all Atlanta area residents.

Increasing energy production is not the solution. Most electrical generation is not efficient. Much of the fuel consumed in a fossil fuel power plant is wasted as heat energy. Only 33 percent of fuel energy is converted into electricity, with 67 percent wasted as heat. Additionally, transmission losses account for 7.5 percent of the electricity generated.[57] In Georgia, electrical systems losses (the amount of energy lost during generation, transmission, and distribution of electricity) account for 48.11 percent of total residential energy use.[58] Natural gas production and distribution are much more efficient; combustion of natural gas also produces less air pollution.

Currently in the Atlanta region, there is tremendous potential for energy savings through efficiency. One example is the Department of Energy and Environmental Protection Agency Energy Star Buildings Program. This program helps business and industry plan and implement profitable energy-saving upgrades in their facilities. According to a national survey, as of April 1998, average savings for commercial buildings participating in the Energy Star program were as follows:

- Energy savings: 9.55 kWh per square foot per year
- Energy cost savings: $0.26 per square foot per year
- Percentage of energy reduction: 15 percent per upgrade
- Internal rate of return: 20.5 percent[59]

It has been estimated that commercial office space in metro Atlanta would surpass 100 million square feet by the end of 1998.[60] If all these facilities were to participate in the Energy Star Program, it could result in energy savings of 955 million kWh/year; cost savings of $26 million a year; and more than 1,432 million lbs/year CO_2, 6,589 million g/year SO_2, 2,387 million g/year NO_x pollution avoided through energy saved.[61] If these same reductions were also achieved by the more than 318 million square feet of existing retail space, or by the 4 million square feet of retail space currently under construction, additional energy and dollars would be saved, and the pollution avoided would greatly improve local and regional air quality.[62] Energy efficiency programs would help make energy more equitable, reduce ozone levels, reduce the urban heat island problems, and improve our health.

Improving the energy efficiency of housing in the Atlanta region could play a major role in improving the region's air quality and reducing the energy burden for all families. An important step in reducing the energy burden for all households is to improve existing housing stock and make new housing energy efficient. This is especially pertinent for low-income and affordable housing. Energy-efficiency measures save money, improve human health, reduce pollution, increase building durability, and enhance property values.

Residential conservation programs must focus on demand side management programs that can benefit all income levels. Simple actions such as sealing forced-air ducts can save energy and reduce the need for additional power production.[63] According to Robin Vieira of the Florida Solar Energy Center, other examples of energy saving features for homes include:

- Designing homes that take advantage of natural light and the use of compact fluorescent lighting can greatly reduce energy consumption. Currently, 20 percent of all energy generated in the United States is used for lighting.
- Properly sizing heating and cooling systems. Fifty percent oversizing of a residential air conditioning system causes a 10 percent increase in energy consumption. In Georgia, the majority of cooling systems are oversized.
- Planting trees and shrubs adjacent to homes and buildings will increase shade and lower the outside air temperature, which will dramatically reduce air conditioning requirements.

Habitat for Humanity International has shown that it is possible to make even affordable housing energy efficient. Currently Habitat is working with its local affiliates to make energy-efficient, environmentally friendly construction a priority. Habitat is achieving this by training its affiliates on energy-efficient construction that does not raise the total cost of housing.

Weatherization programs could also play a large role in improving the quality of low-income housing. One Virginia study showed that advanced energy-efficiency improvements used in weatherization programs can result in great savings, even in southern states. Measures like high-density wall insulation and advanced air sealing, previously limited to northern states, have just as great a potential for savings in milder climates. These weatherization techniques would also be expected to reduce cooling loads, which are more significant in the South than in the North.[64]

Community planning is an essential element in energy conservation. A poorly planned sprawling community will not only have higher initial costs, but over the long run it will cost more for infrastructure maintenance and will require much more energy. Citizens, developers, and civic leaders must encourage and legitimize "planned" communities and infill development in place of uncontrolled sprawl.

A plan that encourages infill and higher density development will improve infrastructure efficiency by taking advantage of existing capacity. This type of development saves the community both extension and operating costs.[65] Studies have shown that costs for roads and utilities are approximately 55 percent lower in high-density compared to low-density communities, and high-density communities' total investment costs are approximately 44 percent below low-density sprawl communities' costs.[66]

Compact, better planned communities also require less automobile dependence, thereby reducing auto emissions and improving air quality. Not only do residents drive fewer miles because stores, schools, work, and other activities are closer to home and to each other, in a well-planned, compact, pedestrian-friendly community with sidewalks, many of life's daily activities are within walking distance of each other. Studies show that more than 50 percent of auto trips are less than 3 miles, and therefore many would be walkable or bikeable in a community that has sidewalks that allow for pedestrians.

Public transit systems are also more effective in high-density communities. Where public transit is within walking distance, more people will take advantage of its availability. Planning such as this makes the transit system an integral part of the community, significantly increases ridership, and makes transit a viable option for all the community's residents.[67] Increased ridership also makes public transit more affordable and therefore increases its access to low-income populations. Above all, increased public transit use means decreased dependence on individual automobiles.

Reducing ground level ozone is essential for protecting the health of the region's inhabitants. In February, the Georgia Department of Natural Resources, Environmental Protection Division (EPD) released its long-range plan to attain the federal air quality standards for ground level ozone. This plan relies on a combination of measures, including cleaner-burning gasoline, emissions reductions from power plants and other large industrial facilities, the production of cleaner-burning cars by the automobile industry, requirements for cleaner diesel engines, and the Voluntary Ozone Action Program to reduce NO_x emissions in the region. By reducing NO_x emissions, the EPD hopes to meet the ozone requirements by 2003 or 2005. According to Harold Reheis, director of EPD, "Cleaner fuels and cleaner cars are a step in the right direction to reduce these pollutants; however, we still need to get everyone in Metro Atlanta to drive fewer miles."[68]

Again, energy conservation can play a large role in ozone reduction. By driving fewer miles, we reduce NO_x and VOC emissions from automobiles. By reducing energy consumption in our homes and at work we reduce NO_x emissions and other pollutants from power plants. And because heat is a factor in ozone creation, reducing the urban heat island would also aid in reducing ozone.

Mitigating the Urban Heat Island

Atlantans can shrink the urban heat island through good community planning and innovative construction techniques, as well as decreasing our reliance on automobiles. Urban shade trees and light-colored surfaces can offset or reverse the heat island and save energy.[69] Vegetation and green space need to be an integral part of all community planning in metro Atlanta. Not only do trees increase the shade around buildings and parking lots, but evaporative cooling from plant transpiration can lower air temperatures surrounding vegetation by as much as 9 degrees Fahrenheit.[70] Increasing the tree cover in Atlanta to the recommended level of 40 percent canopy overall (15 percent for central business districts, 25 percent in urban residential neighborhoods and fringe business areas, and 50 percent in the suburbs) would greatly cool the city and improve Atlanta's air quality.[71]

The city of Atlanta has a tree cutting and replanting ordinance that states that permission must be granted for a tree that is more than 18 inches in diameter to be taken down. This ordinance also requires replanting. Unfortunately, this ordinance is often not enforced. According to Edward Macie, urban forestry program manager for the U.S. Department of Agriculture Forest Service's Southern Region, "Today there are more tree ordinances in the Atlanta region than 10 years ago, but they're being enforced with wavering resolve."[72]

Increasing building reflectivity with light colors and decreasing nonreflective surfaces such as asphalt parking lots would also assist in reducing the urban heat island. The Georgia Energy Code was changed to recognize the energy-saving benefits of reflective roofing systems for commercial builders.[73]

Conclusion

According to the California Energy Commission; "[P]eople may not care about energy. But they do care about keeping their houses warm, getting to work, traffic congestion, affordable housing, air and water pollution, and economic development for business. Energy ties all of those individual issues together."[74] Energy consumption patterns of the region's affluent residents that participate in the sprawl way of life lead to increased pollution. Those most affected by this decreased quality of life are the region's low-income residents.

No longer is it the factories that are producing all the pollution. It is average citizens who need to take responsibility for their actions and think about what energy consumption means in their daily lives. The power plants are producing energy to meet customer demands, and cars are creating air pollution because the public is so dependent on them. Sprawl patterns of growth lead to higher energy consumption, which in turn increases pollution emissions from automobiles, electric power plants, and other combustion of fossil fuels. This increase in air pollution is harmful to human health, the local economy, and the environment.

Notes

1. Carolyn Boyd Hatcher, "We Need to Cooperate and Plan to Preserve Our 'City in a Forest,'" *Atlanta Business Chronicle 20 Years of Coverage Anniversary Issue* [Atlanta, GA], June 12, 1998, p. 84. See Robert D. Bullard, Glenn S. Johnson, and Angel O. Torres, "Atlanta: Megasprawl," *Forum*, 14 (Fall 1998), pp. 17–23.

2. Marcy Lamm, "Housing Boom," *Atlanta Business Chronicle* [Atlanta, GA], May 29–June 4, 1998, p. 5B.

3. Charles Seabrook, "Scalping of the Land Makes Atlanta Hot," *Atlanta Journal-Constitution*, February 19, 1999, p. A1.

4. Sierra Club, *The Dark Side of the American Dream: The Costs and Consequences of Suburban Sprawl.* College Park, MD: Sierra Club, 1998, p. 5.

5. Nancy Anne Dawe, "Sprinting toward Sustainability: Tree Planting Programs in Atlanta, GA," *American Forests* 102, no. 2 (Spring 1996), p. 22.

6. Carolyn Boyd Hatcher, "We Need to Cooperate," p. 84. See "We're in It Together," *Atlanta Journal-Constitution*, June 15, 1997, p. F6.

7. Terry Parker, *The Land Use–Air Quality Linkage: How Land Use and Transportation Affect Air Quality.* Sacramento: Air Resources Board, California Environmental Protection Agency, 1997. See "End Pollution Subsidy," *Atlanta Journal-Constitution*, June 10, 1997, p. A26.

8. Christopher Leinberger, "The Favored Quarter," *Atlanta Journal-Constitution*, June 8, 1997, p. G4. See Lucy Soto, "Putting the Brakes On," *Atlanta Journal-Constitution*, December 5, 1995, p. B1.

9. Truman Hartshorn and Keith Ihlanfeldt, *The Dynamics of Change: An Analysis of Growth in Metropolitan Atlanta Over the Past Two Decades.* Atlanta: Research Atlanta, Inc., 1993. The 10-County Planning Region defined by the Atlanta Regional Commission consists of the following counties: Cherokee, Clayton, Cobb, Dekalb, Douglas, Fayette, Fulton, Gwinnett, Henry, and Rockdale.

10. Keith Kozloff, "Power to Choose: Sustainability in the Evolving Electricity Industry," in *Frontiers of Sustainability* (Washington, DC: Island Press, 1997).

11. David Goldberg, "In Search of a Regional Cure," *Atlanta Journal-Constitution*, May 17, 1998, p. D8. See Lucy Soto, "Acting Regionally: Most in Metro Favor Coordinated Growth," *Atlanta Journal-Constitution*, July 6, 1997, p. A11; Julie L. Miller, "Too Much of a Good Thing: Many Question Growth's Price," *Atlanta Journal-Constitution*, July 6, 1997, p. A10.

12. Ellen Keys, *Blueprints for Successful Communities: A Guide to Shaping Livable Places.* Atlanta: The Georgia Conservancy, 1997.

13. George William Sherk, *The Cost of Nonattainment: Atlanta's Ozone Imbroglio.* Atlanta: Research Atlanta, Inc., 1997.

14. Energy Information Administration, Residential Use of Energy in Georgia. Washington, DC: U.S. Department of Energy, 1995.

15. Keith Kozloff, "Power to Choose."

16. Alliance to Save Energy et al., *Energy Innovations: A Prosperous Path to a Clean Environment.* Washington, DC: Author, 1997.

17. Environmental Protection Division, *Georgia's Environment 97.* Atlanta: Department of Natural Resources, 1997.

18. George William Sherk, *The Cost of Nonattainment,* pp. 1–41.
19. National Center for Environmental Health, *Asthma Prevention Program Fact-sheet.* Atlanta: Centers for Disease Control, 1997. See Robert D. Bullard, Glenn S. Johnson, and Angel O. Torres, "Atlanta: Megasprawl," *Forum* 14 (Fall 1999), pp. 17–23.
20. George William Sherk, *The Cost of Nonattainment.*
21. Ibid.
22. National Center for Environmental Health, *Asthma Prevention Program Fact-sheet.*
23. Ibid.
24. Ibid.
25. National Center for Environmental Health, *Air Pollution and Respiratory Health Brochure.* Atlanta: Centers for Disease Control and Prevention, 1994.
26. National Center for Environmental Health, *Asthma Prevention Program Fact-sheet.*
27. Ibid.
28. Mary C. White, Ruth A. Etzel, Wallace D. Wilcox, and Christine Lloyd. "Exacerbations of Childhood Asthma and Ozone Pollution in Atlanta." *Environmental Research* 65 (1994), pp. 56–68.
29. George William Sherk, *The Cost of Nonattainment.*
30. Luke Curtis, "Asthma: New Research on Environmental Inciters," *The Human Ecologist,* no. 70 (Summer 1996), pp. 12–15.
31. George William Sherk, *The Cost of Nonattainment.*
32. Ibid.
33. Ibid.
34. Ibid.
35. Ibid.
36. Mary C. White et al., "Exacerbations of Childhood Asthma."
37. Truman Hartshorn and Keith Ihlanfeldt, *The Dynamics of Change.*
38. Ibid.
39. Mary Beth Walker, *A Population Profile of the City of Atlanta: Trends, Causes, and Options.* Atlanta: Research Atlanta, Inc., 1997.
40. Ibid.
41. Alliance to Save Energy et al., *Energy Innovations.*
42. Jeffrey Schlegel, John McBride, Stephen Thomas, and Paul Berkowitz "Low-Income Weatherization: Past, Present, and Future," in *State of the Art Energy Efficiency: Future Directions.* Washington, DC: American Council for an Energy Efficient Economy, 1991, pp. 161–198.
43. Margot Saunders and Maggie Spade, *Energy and the Poor: The Crisis Continues.* Boston: National Consumer Law Center, 1995.
44. George William Sherk, *The Cost of Nonattainment.*
45. Paul A. Leonard and Edward B. Lazere, *A Place to Call Home: The Low-Income Housing Crisis in 44 Major Metropolitan Areas.* Washington, DC: Center on Budget and Policy Priorities, 1992.
46. Telephone conversation with Cherry Ivy, Georgia Environmental Facilities Authority Low-Income Weatherization Program, June 9, 1998.

47. David Bollier, *How Smart Growth Can Stop Sprawl: A Fledging Citizen Movement Expands.* Washington, DC: Essential Books, 1998, pp. 55–58.

48. United States Environmental Protection Agency, *The Inside Story: A Guide to Indoor Air Quality.* Washington, DC: USEPA, Office of Air and Radiation, September 1993.

49. Scot Finley, "Sick Houses: Using Diagnostic Tools to Improve Indoor Air Quality." *Home Energy* 14, no. 6 (November/December 1997), pp. 15–19.

50. Thomas H. Greiner, "The Case of the CO Leak: Solving the Mysteries of Carbon Monoxide Exposures," *Home Energy* 14, no. 6 (November/December 1997), pp. 21–28.

51. Craig Noble, "The State of Atlanta's Urban Forest," *TreeViews* 3, no. 1 (Winter 1998), p. 4.

52. Ibid.

53. Canopy coverage is a measurement of how much of an area is covered by the leaves in the crown of its trees. See Gary Moll, "America's Urban Forests: Growing Concerns," *American Forests* 103, no. 3 (Autumn 1997), pp. 15–18.

54. Gary Moll and Cory Berish, "Atlanta's Changing Environment," *American Forests* 102, no. 2, (Spring 1996), pp. 26–29.

55. Ibid.

56. Arthur H. Rosenfeld, H. Akbari, S. Bretz, B.L. Fishman, D.M. Kurn, D. Sailor, and H. Taha et al., "Mitigation of Urban Heat Islands: Materials, Utility Programs, Updates," *Energy and Buildings* 22 (1995), pp. 225–265.

57. Gary Moll and Cory Berish, "Atlanta's Changing Environment," *American Forests* 102, no. 2 (Spring 1996), pp. 26–29.

58. Robin K. Vieira and Phillip W. Fairey IV, *Affordable Living Facts: Reasons for Sustainable Land Redevelopment.* Cape Canaveral: Florida Solar Energy Center, 1991.

59. Energy Information Administration, *Electrical Generation and Environmental Externalities: Case Studies.* Washington, DC: U.S. Department of Energy, 1995.

60. Telephone conversation with Danny Orlando, EPA Region 4 Energy Star Program.

61. Jamison Research Inc., "The Metropolitan Atlanta Office Market," in *First Quarter 1998 Update.* Atlanta: Jamison Research Inc., 1998.

62. These numbers were calculated using the EPA Regional Emission Factors for pollution avoided by kWh saved. For Region 4, the emissions factors are: CO_2:1.5; SO_2:6.9; NO_x:2.5.

63. Jamison Research Inc. "The Metropolitan Atlanta Industrial Market" and "The Metropolitan Atlanta Retail Market" in *First Quarter 1998 Overview.* Atlanta: Jamison Research Inc., 1998.

64. Robin K. Vieira and Phillip W. Fairey IV, *Affordable Living Facts.*

65. Kathy Greely, John Randolph, and Bill Hill, "A Warm Wind Blows South: Virginia's Weatherization Evaluation," *Home Energy* 9, no. 1 (January/February 1992), pp. 15–21.

66. California Energy Commission, *Memo to the Euclid Steering Committee Regarding Energy Implications of Alternative Neighborhood Plans* (October 8, 1996). See David Goldberg, "Building a Sense of Community," *Atlanta Journal-Constitu-*

tion, April 28, 1997, p. E1; Don Melvin, "Acworth Looks Back for its Future," *Atlanta Journal-Constitution,* April 21, 1997, p. E1.

67. Real Estate Research Corporation, *The Cost of Sprawl, Executive Summary.* Washington, DC: Council on Environmental Quality et al., 1974.

68. Ellen Keys, *Blueprints for Successful Communities: A Guide to Shaping Livable Places.* Atlanta: The Georgia Conservancy, 1997. See Robert D. Bullard, Glenn S. Johnson, and Angel O. Torres, "Atlanta: Megasprawl," *Forum* 14 (Fall 1999), pp. 17–23; "Road Policy at Deadend," *Atlanta Journal-Constitution,* June 13, 1997; "Building Stronger Community around Transit," in *City Routes, City Rights: Building Livable Neighborhoods and Environmental Justice by Fixing Transportation* (Boston: Conservation Law Foundation, 1998), pp. 60–66.

69. Environmental Protection Division, "EPD Announces Ozone Control Plan," *Georgia Environmental Protection,* Public Notice, February 19, 1998.

70. Arthur H. Rosenfeld et al., "Mitigation of Urban Heat Islands."

71. Robin K. Vieira and Phillip W. Fairey IV, *Affordable Living Facts.*

72. Gary Moll, "America's Urban Forests."

73. Nancy Anne Dawe, "Sprinting toward Sustainability."

74. Gerry Gray, "It's Cool in Florida and Georgia," *American Forests* 103, no. 3 (Autumn 1997), p. 10.

CHAPTER 9

Conclusion: Facing the Challenges Ahead

Robert D. Bullard

Sprawl critics have now amassed allies from inner-city residents, suburban homeowners, rural farmers, academics, activists, and even some business leaders. Why all the fuss about sprawl? Sprawl is not new. However, the undesirable by-products of sprawl development can be readily seen and felt by suburban, central city, and rural residents.[1] Sprawl is costly and the bill is being paid by ordinary citizens.[2] Not only are Atlanta area residents paying for sprawl with their hard-earned dollars, but they are also paying with their health. Sprawl cannot be blamed for all of the social ills in metro Atlanta. However, some clear side effects can be linked to the sprawl development pattern: urban infrastructure decline, core city abandonment, uneven development, racial polarization, social isolation, public education disparities, car dependency, air pollution, public health and safety risks, threat to farmland and wildlife habitat, and diminished quality of life.[3]

The effects of sprawl-driven development can now be readily seen in "living color" on pretty maps, charts, and graphs with the advent of user-friendly geographic information system (GIS) analysis. Good color maps are worth a thousand words. Sprawl can easily be seen with the naked eye as one attempts to get from point A to point B on Atlanta's gridlocked freeways. Freeway congestion tells the story. Sprawl can be reined in with "smart growth."[4]

Building roads to everywhere is the problem—not the solution. One does not have to be a traffic engineer to know that the region's traffic has gotten substantially worse over the past four or five years. Atlanta's regional transportation policies are implicated in land-use patterns, unhealthy air, and sprawl.[5] On average, people in the region drive more than anyone else on the face of the planet. Getting people out of their cars and into some form of coordinated and linked public transit may well be the key to solving a major part of the region's sprawl puzzle.

Generally, major transportation investments in the region support low-density sprawl that generates increased vehicle emission and air pollution. The federal Environmental Protection Agency (EPA) designated the region a nontattainment area for ground level ozone. Given the heavy dependence on the automobile in the region and the limited role of the Metropolitan Atlanta Rapid Transit Authority (MARTA) in the region (MARTA lines only extend into Fulton and DeKalb counties), it is doubtful that emission-control technologies adopted under the 1990 Clean Air Act Amendments (CAAA) are adequate to ensure that transportation fairly contributes to attainment of healthful air quality in the region. The region has to get off the automobile-dependent treadmill if it expects to improve air quality.

It is not difficult for passengers flying into Atlanta's Hartsfield International Airport—one of the busiest airports in the country—to make a quick comparison with the smog-choked skies of Los Angeles. Sprawl is rapidly turning Atlanta into the "New Los Angeles." Poor air quality translates into increased public health risks. Although air pollution is not thought to cause asthma and related respiratory illnesses, it is a major trigger. Asthma has reached epidemic proportions in major metropolitan areas, including Atlanta. The most vulnerable population is low-income African American children. Asthma is the number one reason for childhood hospitalization in Atlanta.[6]

Recently, poor air quality caused several corporations and their workers to take a second look at the region as their future home. Some companies are not willing to subject their employees to the congestion. Like other major urban areas, the Atlanta region will need to face up to the fact that a regional approach is needed to meet the challenges ahead. Many of these challenges cut across city and county jurisdictions. Sprawl has unintended consequences that are not randomly distributed. Sprawl development in the suburbs and rural areas creates disinvestment incentives, depresses property values, and stagnates business opportunities in older inner-city areas where African Americans and other people of color are concentrated.

The Atlanta metropolitan area continues to be racially separate and unequal. Sprawl-driven development fuels this pattern.[7] Some government policies—education, housing, transportation, environment, and lending—have actually exacerbated sprawl-related problems. For example, widening inequalities in public school education, employment, and economic development have enormous social and financial costs for the entire region. Racial barriers still deprive a large segment of the population, especially African Americans, of major investments through home ownership and business development.[8] On the other hand, federal mortgage subsidies facilitated middle-income homeowners' flight out of the central city and near suburbs and into outlying areas while many central city neighborhoods were starving for investment capital.

Generally, state actors have done a miserable job protecting low-income, working-class, and people of color communities from pollution assaults, industrial encroachment, and environmental degradation.[9] In their quest for quality neighborhoods, residents often find themselves competing for desirable neighborhood amenities (i.e., good schools, police and fire protection, quality health care, parks, open space, and recreational facilities, etc.) and resisting outputs that are viewed as having negative consequences (i.e., landfills, incinerators, sewage treatment facilities, polluting industries, chemical plants, etc.).

The middle class–dominated environmental movement built an impressive political base for environmental reform and regulatory relief. Few environmentalists, however, realized the sociological implications of the NIMBY (not in my backyard) phenomenon. Given the political climate of the times, hazardous-waste facilities, garbage dumps, and polluting industries were likely to end up in somebody's backyard. But whose? More often than not, these LULUs end up in poor, powerless communities of color rather than in affluent suburbs. This pattern has proven to be the rule, even though the benefits derived from industrial production are directly related to affluence.

An Agenda for the New Millennium

Communities are not sitting back waiting for government or business to come up with the "silver-bullet" solution. Some communities are taking action on their own.[10] Whether central city, suburban, or rural, it will take a coordinated effort among the divergent interests to fix the Atlanta region's sprawl problem. A long-term commitment is needed to address the legacy of neglect and procedural, geographic, social, and intergenerational inequities that are exacerbated by sprawl. A major challenge facing the region is to create meaningful forms of collaboration among the regional actors.

Social Equity

Broad Coalitions and Alliances

The sprawl issue has the potential for bringing together diverse community-based organizations, homeowners associations, civic clubs, academic institutions, activists, and government to form broad coalitions and alliances. The seamy side of sprawl may serve as a unifying theme to groups whose history has been characterized more as conflict than as cooperation. Working together, neighborhood groups from Atlanta, the suburbs, and surrounding rural areas can band together to arrest sprawl.

Proactive Race Relations Strategy

Race still matters in the United States. The Atlanta metropolitan region is no exception. Improving race relations needs to be an explicit priority in the region. Racial polarization is impeding community and economic development within Atlanta. Attracting middle-income residents, addressing regional transportation, creating a 24-hour downtown, and in general maximizing the city and the region's potential will require examining racial issues and resolving related conflict. Dismantling racial barriers would go a long way toward boosting financial incentives and reinvestment in central city neighborhoods.

Outreach to Atlanta's Urban Core Stakeholders

It makes little sense to have only white men in suits talking to each other about solving the Atlanta region's air pollution, transportation, sprawl, and overall quality of life problems. One need only turn on the television or read the local newspaper to see this one-race scenario play itself out. African Americans and other people of color organizations and institutions are not invisible. They have much to contribute if only given the opportunity.

Plans to Narrow Public Education Gap

Education is an investment in the future and public schools remain an integral part of our nation's future. All public schools are not created equal. Disparities exist within the Atlanta public schools and county schools as well as between central city and suburban schools. Innovative approaches need to be taken to equalize inherent funding inequities resulting from an outdated taxing system. A number of strategies are proposed that include working to assure equitable distribution of state resources; working with the business community, setting high expectations for all students; making recruitment of quality teachers a top priority; encouraging a culture of learning; providing a safe and secure learning environment; and adopting a philosophy that all children can learn. In addition, increased funding, better accountability, improved opportunities for adult learning and continuing education, better planning, master teacher recruitment, innovation, and improved technology are all means to providing quality education in the region.

Housing and Community Development

In-Fill Development

In-fill development should be encouraged in place of uncontrolled sprawl. In-fill and higher density development will improve infrastructure efficiency by taking advantage of existing capacity; save costs for roads and utilities; require less automobile dependence; reduce auto emissions; improve air quality; locate residents closer to stores, schools, work, and other activities; and provide access to pedestrian-friendly communities with sidewalks.

Urban Home Ownership Initiatives

Home ownership can act as a major stabilizing force in urban core neighborhoods. Infusion of capital through home loans offers new hope to once-decaying urban neighborhoods. Neighborhood revitalization initiatives should be undertaken that minimize "gentrification" pressures and displacement of incumbent residents.

Regional Fair Housing Initiatives

Discrimination is still a major barrier to open housing in the region. Discrimination costs. A targeted regional fair housing strategy could maximize housing, employment, and educational opportunity options for low-income persons and people of color in the region. Private fair housing efforts, such as the Atlanta Metro Fair Housing Program, should be expanded and coordinated with state fair housing initiatives. An annual county fair housing "Report Card" could be issued to each county as one tool for evaluating and reporting progress toward open housing in the region.

Anti-insurance Redlining

Special initiatives are needed to eliminate the "discrimination tax" that is levied on residents of metropolitan Atlanta who live in mostly black neighborhoods. Similar efforts are also needed to protect small and minority businesses from this illegal "tax."

Energy-Efficient Housing

Improving energy efficiency in housing is a money saver and could play a major role in improving the region's air quality. Reduction in energy consumption benefits all households. It is especially pertinent for low-income residents since efficiency measures save money, improve human health, reduce air pollution, increase building durability, and enhance property values.

Environmental Reform

Vegetation and Green Space

The region's timberlands and forests are severely threatened by deforestation. Too many trees are flattened to make way for strip centers, outlet malls, and subdivisions. Trees need to be an integral part of all community planning since they increase the shade around buildings and parking lots and lower air temperatures in their immediate surroundings.

Urban Brownfields Redevelopment

Current land use decision making favors development in the suburbs or "greenfields" rather than inner city areas. Some policies even foster abandonment and infrastructure decline. Alternatively, existing policies, such as criteria for funding water/sewer infrastructure could be modified to favor existing, rather than new development. In addition, "brownfields," or abandoned or underutilized property or buildings, need to be reclaimed and brought back into production. Residents in neighborhoods with brownfields sites must be an integral part of the redevelopment process.

Transportation and Land-Use Planning

Promote Transit-Oriented Development

Transit stations can become more than a place where commuters pass through on their way to somewhere else. Planners can shape land uses and development that are amenable to walking, bicycling, and transit use. One measure to combat sprawl is transit-oriented development that promotes more dense, mixed land uses combined with location efficient mortgages. The idea is that money saved from lower transportation costs effectively increases one's disposable income and could be used to qualify a greater number of lower- and middle-income households for home mortgages. The spillover effect is increased home ownership in inner-city neighborhoods.

Streets for Walking, Bicycles, and Transit

As a rule, sprawl development is not pedestrian, bicycle, or transit friendly. Infrastructure enhancements and service improvements are needed to get people out of their homes and cars. Walking and biking are two major travel modes that produce zero pollution. In addition, sidewalks, bike lanes, and jogging paths all encourage physical activity, enhance public health, and promote social interaction and a sense of "community."

Gas Tax Reform

Georgia's has the lowest gasoline tax in the country (i.e., 7.5 cents per gallon). The state limits the use of the gas tax to roads and bridges. It is recommended that the state constitution be changed to allow for Georgia's gas tax to be used for alternative transportation modes.

Equity Analysis and Transportation Planning

In compliance with Title VI of the Civil Rights Act, President Clinton's Executive Order on Environmental Justice, and the U.S. Department of Transportation's (USDOT) Order on Environmental Justice, USDOT should require planning agencies to conduct regular analysis of transportation decision making, policies, investments, and impacts to determine whether decisions have been made in an equitable fashion. It should also enforce the disclosure of geographic distribution of investments. These types of analysis should be an integral part of Transportation Improvement Programs, Major Investment Studies, Regional Transportation Plans, and State Implementation Plans. They should be used as evaluation criteria for the Atlanta Regional Commission (ARC) certification and the approval of state plans.

Air Quality

USDOT should enforce air quality conformity requirements at all stages of the transportation planning process. It should also encourage the spending of Congestion Mitigation and Air Quality (CMAQ) investments to benefit low-income communities and communities of color, especially if these areas exhibit disproportionately high levels of criteria pollutants. USDOT should work closely with EPA and the Centers for Disease Control and Prevention to monitor air quality levels in the region.

Public Health and Safety

USDOT should encourage the National Highway Traffic Safety Administration and other agencies to focus on neighborhood safety issues, particularly pedestrian safety. It should also ensure that a reasonable amount of transportation safety funds are spent on pedestrian-related projects.

Investment in Low-Income Communities and Communities of Color

USDOT should encourage investment of transportation funds in low-income communities and communities of color to support job creation and economic development.

Improving Access to Jobs

Improving low-income residents mobility, particularly for those making the transition from welfare to work, may be the difference between employment and unemployment. Public transportation improvements go hand-in-hand with expanding job opportunities. The region should create Transportation Pilot Programs to improve transportation efficiency, reduce the impacts of transportation on the environment, reduce the need for infrastructure investment, provide efficient access, examine development patterns and involve the community in such efforts. Some of these pilot projects will need to be based in low-income communities and communities of color and focus on environmental justice and transportation equity.

The regional transportation planning process needs to include a thorough and comprehensive assessment of current and future travel needs. This assessment should incorporate transportation options such as transit, walking, and bicycling based on the location and demographics of forecasted population and employment trends. The assessment will also need to quantify the various infrastructure changes that may be needed, such as miles of new roads, sidewalks, and bicycle lanes; public transit and van pool service expansion; congestion pricing; and parking management.

Uniform Local Public Involvement Processes

The ARC should quickly move to formally create a citizen advisory group to provide reaction, guidance, recommendations, and outreach to the public on current and future issues related to transportation, air quality, and growth in the region. The group should have formal membership that is representative of the population, user, and interest groups in the region.

Title VI and Environmental Justice

ARC should demonstrate that its transportation improvement program complies with Title VI of the Civil Rights Act of 1964, which assures that transportation investments promote greater equity in access to opportunities in the Atlanta region. The assessment will also need to address equity, environmental justice, and adequacy and appropriateness of current data, computer modeling capabilities, the process for assessing needs and developing projects, and the use of performance measures. The region's congestion-relieving strategies will also need to meet Title VI and environmental justice requirements.

The existing environmental, housing, health, transportation, land use, and employment laws by themselves have not been sufficient to protect all citizens and communities. Laws and regulations are only as good as their enforcement. The city, county, ARC, Georgia DOT, and USDOT need to take bold steps to ensure that no federal funds or tax dollars are being used in a discriminatory manner. Title VI of the Civil Rights Act of 1964 compliance reviews and equity analysis must be analyzed and scrutinized.

Finally, the Atlanta metropolitan area is faced with some major challenges ahead. How it handles these challenges created by sprawl in the next few years may well determine the area's future as a desirable and livable region. Sprawl is not a necessary by-product of urban growth and economic development. Growth can be planned and managed. However, it will take a concerted effort on many fronts to arrest the runaway sprawl pattern that typifies the Atlanta metropolitan region and most major American urban centers. To continue down the current road of sprawl is too costly for everyone.

Notes

1. Charles W. Schmidt, "The Specter of Sprawl," *Environmental Health Perspectives* 106 (June 1998), pp. 274–279

2. F. Kaid Benfield, Matthew D. Raimi, and Donald T.D. Chen, *Once There Were Greenfields: How Urban Sprawl Is Undermining America's Environment, Economy and Social Fabric.* New York: Natural Resources Defense Council and Surface Transportation Policy Project, 1999.

3. Robert D. Bullard, Glenn S. Johnson, and Angel Torres, "Atlanta: Megasprawl," *Forum* (Fall 1999), pp. 17–23.

4. David Bollier, *How Smart Growth Can Stop Sprawl: A Fledgling Citizen Movement Expands.* Washington, DC: Essential Books, 1998.

5. Sierra Club, *The Dark Side of the American Dream: The Cost and Consequences of Suburban Sprawl.* College Park, MD: Sierra Club, 1998, p. 5.

6. Mary C. White, Ruth Etzel, Wallace D. Wilcox, and Christine Lloyd, "Exacerbations of Childhood Asthma and Ozone Pollution in Atlanta," *Environmental Research* 65 (1994), pp. 56–68.

7. Robert D. Bullard and Glenn S. Johnson, eds., *Just Transportation: Dismantling Race and Class Barriers to Mobility* (Gabriola Island, BC: New Society Publishers, 1997); Conservation Law Foundation, *City Routes, City Rights: Building Livable Neighborhoods and Environmental Justice by Fixing Transportation* (Boston: Conservation Law Foundation, 1998).

8. Joe R. Feagin and Melvin P. Sikes, *Living with Racism: The Black Middle-Class Experience* (Boston: Beacon Press, 1994); Robert D. Bullard, J. Eugene Grigsby III, and Charles Lee, eds., *Residential Apartheid: The American Legacy* (Los Angeles: University of California, 1994); Melvin L. Oliver and Thomas M. Shapiro, *Black Wealth/White Wealth: A New Perspective on Racial Inequality* (New York: Routledge, 1995).

9. Robert D. Bullard, "Building Just, Safe, and Healthy Communities," *Tulane Environmental Law Journal* 12 (Spring 1999), pp. 373–404.

10. Eric Mann, *A New Vision for Urban Transportation* (Los Angeles: Labor Community Strategy Center, 1996); Eric Mann, *LA's Lethal Air: New Strategies for Policy, Organizing, and Action* (Los Angeles: Labor Community Strategy Center, 1991).

Acronyms

ADA	Atlanta Development Authority
AFDC	Aid to Families with Dependent Children
AHA	Atlanta Housing Authority
AMC	Atlanta Mortgage Consortium
ANDP	Atlanta Neighborhood Development Partnership, Inc.
APS	Atlanta Public Schools
ARC	Atlanta Regional Commission
CAA	Clean Air Act
CAAA	Clean Air Act Amendments
CBD	Central Business District
CBOs	Community-Based Organizations
CBRA	Coastal Barrier Resources Act
CCT	Cobb Community Transit
CDC	Centers for Disease Control and Prevention
CDCs	Community Development Corporations
CEQ	Council for Environmental Quality
CERCLA	Comprehensive Environmental Response, Compensation, and Liability Act
CMAQ	Congestion Mitigation and Air Quality
CMS	Congestion Management System
CO	Carbon Monoxide
CO_2	Carbon Dioxide

CODA	Corporation for Olympic Development in Atlanta
COPD	Chronic Obstructive Pulmonary Disease
CRA	Community Reinvestment Act
CSOs	Combined Sewer Overflows
CZMA	Coastal Zone Management Act
DFACS	Department of Family and Children Services
DOT	Department of Transportation
DSM	Demand Side Management
EDF	Environmental Defense Fund
EPA	Environmental Protection Agency
EPD	Environmental Protection Division
FFIEC	Federal Financial Institutions Examination Council
FHA	Federal Housing Administration
FHWA	Federal Highway Administration
FTA	Federal Transit Administration
GDOT	Georgia Department of Transportation
GEFA	Georgia Environmental Facilities Authority
GIS	Geographic Information System
GRTA	Georgia Regional Transportation Authority
GTA	Georgians for Transportation Alternatives
HBCUs	Historically Black Colleges and Universities
HC	Hydrocarbons
HMDA	Home Mortgage Disclosure Act
HUD	U.S. Department of Housing and Urban Development
IRTP	Interim Regional Transportation Plan
ISTEA	Intermodal Surface Transportation Efficiency Act
ITIP	Interim Transportation Improvement Program
LULUs	Locally Unwanted Land Uses
MARTA	Metropolitan Atlanta Rapid Transit Authority
MATI	Metro Atlanta Transportation Initiative
MPOs	Metropolitan Planning Organizations
MTA	Metropolitan Transportation Authority
NAACP LDF	NAACP Legal Defense and Education Fund
NAAQS	National Ambient Air Quality Standards
NACA	Neighborhood Assistance Corporation of America
NASA	National Aeronautics and Space Administration
NCDI	National Community Development Initiative
NEPA	National Environmental Policy Act
NIMBY	Not In My Backyard

NO$_x$	Nitrogen Oxides
O$_3$	Ozone
PEP	Project Evaluation Process
PM10	Particulate Matter
PPM	Parts Per Million
PSG	Partnership for a Smog-Free Georgia
RTP	Regional Transportation Plan
SAT	Scholastic Aptitude Test
SIC	Standard Industrial Classification
SIP	State Implementation Plan
SO$_2$	Sulfur Dioxide
SOV	Single Occupant Vehicle
TANF	Temporary Assistance for Needy Families
TAP	The Atlanta Project
TEA-21	Transportation Equity Act for the 21st Century
TIP	Transportation Improvement Program
TMA	Transportation Management Area
TOD	Transit-Oriented Development
TRI	Toxic Release Inventory
UNAC	Union Neighborhood Assistance Corporation
URFA	Urban Residential Finance Authority
USDOT	U.S. Department of Transportation
VMT	Vehicle Miles Traveled
VOCs	Volatile Organic Compounds
WAP	Weatherization Assistance Program
WHEACT	West Harlem Environmental Action

Contributors

NATALIE BROWN is a research fellow at the Southface Energy Institute. Her primary areas of interest are sustainable community development, environmental quality, and public outreach. Prior to joining Southface, Ms. Brown attended Indiana University's School of Public and Environmental Affairs, where she earned her M.P.H. in environmental policy and natural resource management.

ROBERT D. BULLARD is the Ware Professor of Sociology and Director of the Environmental Justice Resource Center at Clark Atlanta University. He is the author of nine books that address urban land use, transportation, housing, economic development, and environmental policy. His book *Dumping in Dixie: Race, Class and Environmental Quality* (Westview Press, 2000 [3d ed.]) is a standard text in the environmental justice field. His most recent new book, co-edited with Glenn S. Johnson, is entitled *Just Transportation: Dismantling Race and Class Barriers to Mobility* (New Society Publishers, 1997) and addresses transportation and civil rights.

WILLIAM W. BUZBEE is an associate professor of law at Emory University. Prior to joining the faculty at Emory, he practiced law in New York with the firm of Patterson, Belknap, Webb & Tyler doing environmental and litigation work. He teaches environmental law, administrative law, property law, and seminars on advanced environmental law issues, urban environmental law, and regulatory reform. Professor Buzbee has published articles on topics in environmental law and administrative law.

JAMES CHAPMAN has been executive director of Georgians for Transportation Alternatives (GTA) since March 1996. Prior to working with GTA, Chapman spent two years as transportation policy analyst for Campaign for a Prosperous Georgia. Chapman has an M.S. in transportation engineering from the Georgia Institute of Technology and a B.S. in mechanical engineering from the University of Rochester, New York. He is an Atlanta Bicycle Campaign board member and a daily bicycle commuter.

DENNIS CREECH is the founder of the Southface Energy Institute, a private nonprofit organization conducting education and research in energy, sustainable technologies, and applied building sciences. He has served as executive director for over 20 years. He is a nationally recognized leader in the fields of energy efficiency and sustainable buildings and serves on the board of directors of the Energy Efficient Building Association.

RUSSELL W. IRVINE is an associate professor in the Department of Educational Policy Studies at Georgia State University. He holds a doctorate degree from Case Western Reserve University and his specialty is sociology of education. His areas of research have been public school desegregation, the Afrocentric movement in education, and post-modernism and post-structuralism and their implications for educational research and analysis.

CHARLES JARET is an associate professor of sociology at Georgia State University and specializes in race/ethnic relations and urban sociology. He has written numerous articles on changing urban structure and economic inequality, homelessness, the importance of ethnic identity among American Indians, whites, blacks, and multiracial individuals, and attitudes toward racial/ethnic humor.

CHAD G. JOHNSON received his B.A. degree from Morehouse College. He is currently the information specialist and Web site developer at the Environmental Justice Resource Center at Clark Atlanta University. His duties include creating, editing, and managing the EJRC Web site content and layout materials.

GLENN S. JOHNSON is a research associate in the Environmental Justice Resource Center and assistant professor in the Department of Sociology at Clark Atlanta University. He coordinates several major research activities including transportation, urban sprawl, public involvement, facility siting, and toxics. He has worked on environmental policy issues for eight years and assisted R. D. Bullard in the research for the book *Dumping in Dixie: Race, Class, and Environmental Quality* (Westview Press, 2000 [3d ed.]). He is the co-editor of a book entitled *Just Transportation: Dismantling Race and Class Barriers to Mobility* (New Society Publishers, 1997).

KURT PHILLIPS is an M.A. student in the Department of Sociology at Georgia State University, with interests in urban affairs and housing. He has many years of experience teaching in DeKalb County public schools and is an avid bicycle rider.

ELIZABETH P. RUDDIMAN is a Ph.D. student in the Department of Sociology at Georgia State University, with interests in urban affairs and race relations. She is employed by the DeKalb County Board of Health, where she is in charge of information and volunteer service.

ANGEL O. TORRES is the Geographical Information Systems/TRI Training Specialist with the Environmental Justice Resource Center and adjunct professor of sociology at Clark Atlanta University. He holds a Master's in City Planning from the Georgia Institute of Technology. He manages the Center's GIS, Landview III, and Toxic Release Inventory (TRI) activities and is primarily responsible for mapping, demographic analysis, environmental analysis, transportation planning, and location/site analysis.

Index